RHS

STEP-BY-STEP
VEG
PATCH

RHS

STEP-BY-STEP
VEG
PATCH

LUCY CHAMBERLAIN

CONTENTS

WHY GROW YOUR OWN FOOD?

Anyone who has ever picked fresh strawberries will know how unlikely it is that the first harvest will reach the kitchen. The urge to eat them there and then beats all but the strongest wills – the taste is incomparable. That's one of the main reasons why I grow my own food. Freshness equates to flavour and has health benefits too; I harvest crops from my veg patch when they are at their best and packed with vitamins. Compare shop-bought broad beans to home-grown and I promise you'll never buy them again. But that's not all, there are so many other reasons to grow your own: to boost your fitness, to improve your environment, or just for the sheer pleasure of it.

FRESH AND HEALTHY

We are all well aware that the route to good health is through eating more fruits and vegetables, but you may not have considered the direct benefits of growing them yourself. Vitamin and antioxidant levels are at their highest when crops are first picked, with the levels falling by half after a week or so. In shops, you can rarely tell how long ago "fresh" produce was picked or how well it has been stored, especially if it is imported or kept in refrigeration. When you have your own wigwam of runner beans, or a big pot of tomatoes on your patio, you can harvest and eat them within hours, or even minutes.

GOOD FOR THE ENVIRONMENT

Our planet is overheating and, like many people, I'm concerned about the impact of food production on the environment, especially in terms of the "food miles" that build up when we import crops over huge distances. When you grow your own, food miles are reduced to zero and the carbon footprint is negligible. It's pretty fundamental that the world's population has to be fed, and by cultivating whatever space you have, you are doing one small thing to reduce the strain on global supplies. You'll also be able to choose to grow your food organically if you wish. Life revolved around the changing seasons during my childhood on a smallholding, and I can assure you there is no better way to discover the seasonal nature of food crops than to grow your own all year round.

GREATER CHOICE

One of my great excitements when I plan my veg patch is picking varieties. In shops, you have a limited choice of types of strawberries, broccoli, or carrots, for example, because commercial growers are motivated by yield, shelf-life and uniformity, and grow vast monocultures of just a few varieties. When you grow your own, there are thousands of different crops and varieties to try with qualities suited to your own tastes. Many have been developed over generations, but there are new types with extraordinary colours and tastes, extra disease-resistance, or engineered to be dwarf crops for small gardens. You may never see 'Yin Yang' French beans, or 'Double Red' sweetcorn in the supermarket, but you can grow them yourself.

GOOD FOR YOU

If like me, you feel a bit confined in a gym, gardening provides a great alternative to exercise. One hour's digging can burn off more than 300 calories, and light pottering, weeding, mulching, watering, and planting involves lifting, stretching, and bending. It's the perfect workout!

Lucy Chamberlain

YOUR GROWING

SPACE

CROPS IN
SMALL SPACES

There's no denying that having less space limits the amount of fruit and vegetables you can grow, but by thinking laterally you can still produce enough to supplement your needs, even if you can't supply everything. Instead of planting vegetables that take up lots of space but are cheap to buy, choose more space-efficient crops, such as climbing beans, that make best use of the room you have. Prioritize what you grow and plant the crops you like to eat – think quality not quantity, and grow varieties that are expensive to buy in the supermarket.

SMALL BUT PERFECTLY FORMED
Small spaces are actually brilliant for growing fruits and vegetables as they are usually enclosed by walls or fences, giving them similar growing conditions to traditional, walled gardens – just on a smaller scale. A south- or west-facing bed offers the perfect environment for chillies, peaches, aubergines, strawberries, herbs – and any other number of crops that revel in the warmth of the sun. In contrast, north- and east-facing aspects are cooler and shadier, ideal for growing tender lettuces and leafy brassica crops.

Most small plots have a full range of aspects, which means they can provide the complete spectrum of growing environments any kitchen gardener would require. In contrast, large plots may be more exposed, lacking shade, shelter from the wind, or a handy water supply. Weed seeds and birds can also be a problem. This limits the crops that can be grown to those that will tolerate everything the elements throw at them.

Small spaces can be highly productive: the trick is to make use of every inch available, including the walls and fences. Position containers wherever there is enough room, and train growth vertically.

(left) **Cordon tomatoes** will thrive on a sunny patio and make a stunning display as they ripen. Their roomy terracotta pots can be cleaned and reused year after year.

(below) **Growing crops** in a small space makes them easier to maintain. Feeding and watering plants in raised beds and pots is less of a chore than it might be on a large plot.

URBAN GARDENS

Small plots are particularly productive in towns and cities, thanks to the "urban heat island" effect. In essence, large buildings provide shelter from the wind and also absorb heat during the day, which is radiated back at night. This action, along with the heat generated by urban life raises the local temperature by a useful few degrees. This allows urban growers to extend their growing season in spring and autumn, and to benefit from higher summer temperatures than rural counterparts. In practice, it means that long-season crops, such as chillies, sweetcorn and winter squashes, give a better harvest. It can even make growing exotic crops more successful, such as figs, okra, loquat, and tomatillo.

LESS SPACE, LESS EFFORT

Having a small plot brings a range of other advantages, besides the crops you can grow. Although larger sites can accommodate more plants, they take a great deal of looking after. The novelty of pushing a wheelbarrow to your allotment or finding slugs in your car boot on the journey home from the plot can wear thin. Small gardens are far less daunting, especially for those new to growing their own produce. You can cultivate areas in bite-sized chunks; there's little risk of being overwhelmed with weeds, and you won't be tethered to a watering can all summer. It's also easier to nip outside when there is a break in bad weather to tend your plants, or sneak out in your pyjamas in the morning to pick fruit for breakfast.

Space for creative thinking

Making the most of a small plot involves being creative with the space you have and the crops you grow – which is part of the fun. Any object that holds sufficient compost and has drainage holes can be used as a planter, so use your imagination. Certain crops grow well planted together, so try different combinations to create schemes that are both colourful and productive.

THE SKY'S THE LIMIT

Space at ground level is the most limiting factor in small plots, as all plants need room to grow. However, a useful way around this is to plant climbing and trailing crops, and to train their growth vertically, leaving space at their base for other crops.

Climbing French and runner beans, cucumbers, trailing squashes, and cordon tomatoes all produce valuable crops from minimal space. They can either be planted to grow against walls or fences, or at the base of free-standing wigwams, which can even be sited in ornamental beds.

SPEEDY CROPS

To make the most of the space you have, choose crops that can either be harvested over a long period, or those that mature quickly and can soon be replanted. One large pot sown with cut-and-come-again salad leaves will keep the average family supplied for well over two months.

Once cut, these rapid growers will yield again within three weeks. "Baby" vegetable varieties of turnip, cauliflower, beetroot, carrot, and cabbage are harvested within a couple of months of sowing. Another way to ensure maturity within minimal time is to start plants off under cover in pots and modules, or to purchase plug plants. The time saved by planting rather than sowing into the final growing positions allows you to squeeze in another crop or two before the growing season ends.

BOUNTIFUL VARIETIES

As well as choosing crops that mature quickly or over a long period, look for varieties that are known to give a large crop. If you only have space for a few plants, it's worth making sure that the ones you plant are as productive as possible. Some varieties have been bred specifically to suit compact gardens, so do some research or seek trusted advice when deciding what to plant.

(above) **Tasty young turnips** can be harvested a few weeks after sowing. Start early and you can enjoy several crops in the same season.

(left) **Containers** can be planted up under cover in spring to give the crop a head start. They can also be moved to a cool space inside during autumn to grow on for a little longer.

(far left) **A wigwam of beans** will crop all summer, but only takes up the same amount of space as three or four potato or cabbage plants.

MAKING THE MOST OF LIMITED SPACE

1 Hanging baskets These offer a space-saving way to grow many different crops, including mixed summer herbs, salad leaves, tumbling tomatoes, and even chillies. They must be kept well watered and fed, and given a bright spot. Hang near the kitchen for easy picking.

2 Trailing crops Plants like squashes, can be trained along the ground, as well as vertically. Use short canes to train the stems along the edges of beds or paths so they are easy to harvest, and to free up space for planting other crops.

3 Quick spring container crops Make use of vacant planters that are not yet filled with summer bedding. Early Swiss chard and radish will be ready to harvest before you begin to plant out tender ornamental flowers in early summer.

4 Handy mini crops Sow quick crops wherever gaps develop in the garden during the year. Many mature in a matter of weeks so can be sown direct to crop before the end of the season. Also sow between your ornamentals.

5 Wall training Use vertical surfaces to support climbing and trailing crops. Many fruits, including apples, crop very well when trained against walls and fences, freeing up useful bed space.

6 Underplanting Take advantage of the bed space beneath taller crops, like sweetcorn, by underplanting. Kept well watered, lettuce will benefit from the light shade, while long squash stems can be trained out towards the sunlight.

GROWING IN
CONTAINERS

Growing crops in pots is second nature to many gardeners. As well as providing extra growing space, it offers many benefits, such as easier weeding and the option to move your crops under cover for protection or to extend their cropping season. It can also give you a wider choice of crops to grow because you are not limited to growing plants that thrive in your particular garden soil: you can use any soil type in a pot. Feeding and frequent watering are vital to crops in pots, so to help conserve moisture, add water-retaining gel to the compost and mulch the surface to prevent evaporation. If you are short of time, an automatic irrigation system could be a good investment.

Mix and match crops in containers of different sizes and colours. Integrate the pots with ornamental plants to add colour and interest to the display while the edible plants are developing.

CHOOSING THE RIGHT CONTAINER

All containers need drainage holes in the base to allow excess water to drain away. The material they are made of will determine how quickly they will dry out: unglazed terracotta pots are extremely porous and will readily lose water through their sides, especially if positioned in a sunny spot. Conversely, thick-walled concrete tubs are very moisture-retentive. Wooden barrels are best lined with plastic to reduce water loss.

Make sure that you match the container to the crop that you plan to grow. For shallow-rooted crops, such as radishes and salad leaves, the choice is virtually limitless. You can use anything from windowboxes to old boots and kettles, and can really have some decorative fun with whatever you choose, as long as you put drainage holes in the bottom of each container. However, bear in mind the smaller the pot, the more frequently it will need watering. Large crops, such as cabbages and potatoes, will need tubs with a minimum depth and diameter of 50cm (20in).

FRUIT IN POTS

It's crucial to pick a container that is deep and wide enough for long-term fruit crops. Opt for a minimum depth of 30cm (12in) and a width that is at least 10cm (4in) larger than the existing pot. Re-pot annually in early to mid-spring when your tree or bush is still young and its growth rate is rapid. As the plant matures, its growth rate slows – check the roots – if they're not yet filling the compost then don't re-pot until the following year. When the container is large enough to make re-potting unnecessary, simply "top-dress" each spring by replacing the top 10cm (4in) of compost. Stand your pot on "feet" in winter to improve drainage.

Quirky containers

Think creatively when choosing where to sow or plant your crops. Experiment with unexploited growing areas and unusual containers, such as these cress-sown egg shells, which would make an amusing family project. Plant breeders are catching onto the trend for small-scale growing by developing productive, yet very compact, varieties, so look out for these.

CONTAINERS TO TRY

With the wide range of container types available, you will easily be able to find one that fits your garden design. Try to make the most of all of your available space – many pots can be fastened onto walls or fences, so can be incorporated into even the smallest space.

1 Hanging baskets Suitable for tumbling crops such as tomatoes and strawberries, hanging baskets look striking and inviting when planted up with a mix of colourful edible and ornamental plants.

2 Terracotta pots Available in a range of sizes and shapes, these pots dry out quickly but look attractive on a patio and support most crops.

3 Windowboxes Ideal for crops with shallow roots such as salad leaves, windowboxes are best sited close to the kitchen for easy access during cooking.

4 Fabric bags The depth of these bags makes them a great choice for potatoes, which can be easily earthed up during growth. They can then be folded up after your crops have been harvested.

5 Wall pouches These attractive, space-saving devices allow you to make the most of an unused vertical surface. They are ideal for herbs or salad leaves, but will need frequent watering.

6 Wall planters These large containers must be securely fastened as they will need to support the weight of relatively large plants. Keep them well watered, and ensure that fruits are supported.

WINDOWSILLS AND INDOORS

Outdoor residential space may be at a premium, especially in urban areas, but those of us with no garden can embrace an ever-evolving concept: the indoor edible plot. Salad leaves, herbs, microleaves, and sprouting seeds are quick and almost effortless to produce. Improvements in artificial lighting and bespoke "growing systems" mean that quality is no longer compromised, and there are even soilless crops that harbour fewer pests and diseases. Window boxes and balcony pots offer space for bulkier crops such as strawberries, dwarf tomatoes, and baby roots.

PROTECTIVE SPACE

The protected environment of an indoor growing space offers many advantages: no gale-force winds buffeting your crops; no periods of drought or torrential rain; no weed seeds blowing in from neighbouring plots; reduced numbers of pests due to lack of access, and of diseases due to lack of soil; plus thermal insulation offering protection from chills. Indoor growing spaces offer a range of crop-growing opportunities.

(above) **Windowsill propagators** make excellent use of this narrow yet well-lit space available in most homes. As well as being ideal for cultivating microleaves and sprouted seeds, they allow anyone on a budget to raise a large quantity of young plants.

LIGHT AND WATER

As long as adequate light, heat, and moisture are available, all manner of crops can be cultivated. Light levels can easily be boosted by LED or fluorescent bulbs (see artificial lighting, left) so that every spare corner can be utilized. Heat levels are easily controlled via your central heating system, but you can also use electric heat mats to provide a targeted boost.

Watering issues come down to a quick daily check. A showerhead makes irrigating trays and pots a cinch, but if you do use a small watering can, fill it, and let the cold water sit for a few hours to raise it to room temperature. Also be mindful that water softening units add sodium, so also use other water sources, such as water from a dehumidifier, a tap, or rainwater collected outside.

Irrigation can also be entirely automated using timers, trickle irrigation tubing, and moisture-sensitive probes. The issue of space can be minimized by growing on trays stacked in shelving units.

Manufacturers now even offer complete growing kits that combine artificial lights, shelving, and water tanks. Models with adjustable height for lighting allow you to grow the widest range of plants, from low-growing microleaves to taller mature herbs.

Windowboxes provide generous conditions for crops such as herbs, lettuce, and salad leaves. Dwarf varieties of tomatoes, baby roots, and perennial herbs will thrive here too. With a little planning and replanting, you can have harvests for most of the year.

GROWING METHODS

While gloomier spots in the home can easily be remedied with artificial lighting, excess heat encourages sappy growth in plants, so provide this with care. As you become more experienced at indoor growing, you will become aware of your best spaces. Bay windows and deep windowsills offer ideal indoor conditions, however be cautious about exposing delicate seedlings to full south- or west-facing summer sun. Reserve these hothouse positions for your dwarf tomatoes or chillies instead.

Large pots or windowboxes are only an option for those who have balconies

(left) **Growing plants on modified shelving** fitted with growlights minimizes the space taken up and maximizes the opportunity for crops. Manufacturers now sell complete stacked growing units, but you might want to build your own to suit your space.

Artificial lighting

Growlights are increasingly available online and in garden centres, either as individual bulbs or as complete "growing systems". Their purpose is to boost light in indoor growing areas that have low or one-sided light and which would otherwise produce leggy, stretched growth in crops. Standard domestic lighting doesn't offer the full spectrum of light to support strong plants, so look for LED or fluorescent bulbs. LED systems are more widely available due to their improved longevity, reduced heat output, and superior energy efficiency.

and wider window ledges, but small pots of herbs will thrive even on a narrow windowsill.

USEFUL EQUIPMENT

Potting tidies or trays are useful; they have deep sides that keep compost contained when you are propagating or pricking out seedlings. Seed trays and modules are ideal for growing salad leaves and microleaves. The latter, along with sprouting seeds, can also be cultivated on shallow trays lined with moist kitchen paper. You will find that a windowsill propagator becomes the cornerstone of your indoor gardening.

GROWING IN
RAISED BEDS

If you have enough space outside, raised beds are excellent for growing fruit, vegetables, and herbs, and can make an attractive addition to the garden. Their raised level allows you to reach your crops easily and comfortably for weeding, maintenance, removing pests such as slugs, and protecting crops with nets. The additional height also helps the soil to warm up rapidly in spring, naturally extending the growing season by a few weeks. Most raised beds are simple to build, and can be constructed from a variety of materials such as wooden sleepers or bricks.

Long-lasting brick-built structures look good and stand the test of time. To give low-growing crops extra shelter from the wind, leave a 20cm (8in) gap at the top when you fill the bed.

THE BENEFITS OF BEDS

Growing in raised beds rather than in the open ground allows you greater control over the growing conditions of your crops. When you create a new bed, or are renovating an old one, you can fill it with fresh, rich soil to provide perfect growing conditions for your crops. In subsequent years it will be easy to improve the soil or adapt it to suit new crops.

It is far easier to control the pH of a contained area of soil, so crops such as brassicas, which require a slightly alkaline environment, can be easily accommodated. The raised height of the bed also makes it easier to weed, dig over, and remove stones, making it ideal for root crops such as carrots that will suffer in stony or compacted soil. Organic matter can be applied as necessary and there is little wastage, unlike on a larger plot, where it may be added to an area that later becomes a path between beds.

The elevated soil level will provide good drainage. In a garden that is often waterlogged, a raised bed provides a space for herbs and other warm-season plants that revel in a well-aerated plot. These beds are also practical for batch sowing of quick-growing crops such as radishes and salad leaves.

BED MANAGEMENT

Among many advantages, raised beds have just a few drawbacks: soil drains more quickly than in a ground-level bed, so they do need watering more often. Ants like free-draining soil, although regular cultivation will stop them establishing, and snails may like to gather on the bed edges – however, this does make these pests easy to find.

Temporary raised beds

An attractive temporary option, although only suitable for crops with shallow root systems, is to surround wide containers or bags with an edging frame, made from a material such as wicker (shown here). These raised beds can be "constructed" in different locations year-on-year, and once you have harvested your crops, can be taken down and packed away to save space.

DIFFERENT MATERIALS AND DESIGNS

It's simple to build your own raised beds and you can be creative when choosing your edging, as long as you pick materials that are sturdy and durable. If your DIY skills are not up to scratch, there are many kits available.

1 DIY kits Ready-prepared kits, are available in a variety of materials, and can be easily assembled for a neat, stylish effect.

2 Wood Invest in some good-quality timber and ensure that it is properly treated to prevent it from rotting. Be creative: decking, for example, makes excellent edging, while chunky pieces of wood give a modern feel.

3 Metal Raised beds made from metal suit a contemporary design. However, keep the soil well watered as it will be vulnerable to temperature changes.

4 Brick Use new or recycled bricks, breeze blocks, or stone for sturdy, long-lasting raised beds. These often suit a cottage garden design and can be used to create informal seating around the growing area.

5 Recycled materials Think creatively, as materials such as used tyres can make a striking design statement. Bear in mind that old railway sleepers, which were once very popular, ooze tar in hot weather, so are used less widely now.

6 Slate pieces Slate tiles are attractive and can be used to create an edging on a shallow bed. They are relatively fragile, though, and will only support limited weight, so be careful not to overfill the bed.

ESSENTIAL
TOOLS AND EQUIPMENT

Gardening involves many practical and strenuous techniques, but choosing the right tools for the job will make the tasks easier and more successful. For example, using secateurs to cut through very thick stems not only hurts your hands, it can also damage the tool itself. Similarly, budget tools and gardening gloves made of poor-quality materials will wear out more quickly and prove to be a false economy. Buy the best you can afford, and also consider good-quality, second-hand tools.

Growing your own need not be expensive, as many key pieces of equipment can be bought cheaply and re-used. Be prepared by stocking up on the essentials at the beginning of the season.

DIGGING

A good spade and fork are essential for digging, along with a hand trowel for excavating smaller holes. Assess your physical strength before buying a fork or spade – the small blade of a border spade, for example, will allow you to lift a lighter weight of soil than a larger, standard model. Handle designs vary from brand to brand, so choose one that feels comfortable. For repetitive tasks such as digging these are important considerations.

WEEDING

A hoe is useful for removing weed seedlings between crops. Use a long-handled model for larger beds, especially if you find bending difficult, and short-handled "onion" hoes for small areas and raised beds. A hand fork is good for removing weeds, especially those with long tap roots.

PROPAGATION

When preparing a seedbed outside, a rake is extremely handy. The fine teeth filter out clods of earth and loosen weeds and stones so that the soil takes on a fine, crumbly texture, perfect for germination. The edge of a hoe can be used to make drills.

Indoor propagation, or sowing into pots, requires a range of containers and seed compost, as well as labels, a pencil, and a dibber. If you invest in a heated propagator, you will be able to raise a wider range of crops.

PRUNING

A good pair of secateurs is essential. Cutting and pruning are repetitive tasks so a well-designed handle grip will be easier on your hands – try out a selection of models before you buy. If your fruit trees need renovation then loppers and a pruning saw are also invaluable for the more sizeable branches. Telescopic loppers with extendable handles are useful if your plants have reached lofty dimensions.

TOOL MAINTENANCE

Keeping tools clean and in good condition helps to preserve their life and prevent the spread of plant diseases. Clean tools such as secateurs with disinfectant after using them and keep them well oiled and tightened up. Apply oil to tools such as spades and forks to prevent rust.

Reducing plastic and upcycling

You can do your best to avoid single-use plastic in the garden by reusing and upcycling. Some garden centres will take back plastic plant pots, but they can be used for seedlings, or be buried in the soil next to plants to funnel water down to the roots. One-use growing bags are easy to replace with large pots used year after year. Plastic bottles can be cut off and upcycled into cloches, and nets from supermarket produce will help support heavy fruits.

THE GARDEN BASICS

It is best to invest in good-quality tools that will last, so make sure you only buy those you really need – a fork is essential on an allotment but may be unnecessary if you are only growing in pots on a patio.

1 Fork Excellent for loosening and working organic matter into the soil, forks are also useful for lifting crops or moving plants.

2 Spade Ideal for digging over large areas of light soil and moving mulches, a spade is essential for a larger plot.

3 Dutch hoe This versatile tool is ideal for killing annual weeds: it severs the roots so that the plants then die. It is also useful for drawing soil up around crops.

4 Rake This tool is crucial in site preparation: use it to remove stones and clods of earth, level the soil, and create a fine tilth for sowing seeds.

5 Dibber Used for making holes for sowing or planting, a dibber is also useful for marking out seed drills.

6 Trowel The ideal size for creating planting holes, a trowel is an essential tool when transplanting your crops.

7 Secateurs This versatile tool can be used for harvesting crops such as peppers and asparagus as well as for pruning back fruiting bushes.

8 Cloche Useful for warming up cold soil to plant early crops or for providing protection from pests, a cloche is an easy way to get your plants off to a good start.

DECIDING
WHAT TO GROW

It's inevitable to have the odd dearth and glut in your harvests but that's what freezers and friends are for. However with a little preparation, you can minimize the peaks and troughs to ensure a steady flow of fresh produce. While it's not crucial to be very organized on a small-scale plot, time spent planning is time well spent. It is a good idea to start thinking about what you would like to grow the previous autumn when seed companies release their catalogues. Each crop entry in this book gives sowing times and weeks to maturity. These will vary according to where you garden but will help you plan your supply of food.

GROW WHAT YOU LIKE
Make a list of the fruit and vegetables you eat and then create two columns: "to buy" and "to grow". Although self-sufficiency is a brilliant concept, few people have enough space to actually achieve it, so select crops carefully to maximize space. Try to be fairly picky at this stage – for example, if you only have space for containers, devoting them to early, melt-in-the-mouth new potatoes is sensible. Planting your pots and sacks with maincrops, which will take far longer to mature, may not be the best use of the space. At the top of your " to grow" list should be crops that are expensive to buy or difficult to obtain, or those that are at their very best eaten fresh. Bulkier crops, or those that are cheap and readily available, should be at the bottom of this list.

CONSIDER YOUR SPACE
Once you've established your "to grow" crops, calculate how much room you'll need to grow them and which month they'll mature. Compare potential gluts and dearths with the space you have available, and it should become apparent if certain crops need to migrate into the "to buy" column instead. Consider how well certain crops store. For example, having a glut of

chillies to dry and store, or broad beans and blueberries to freeze, is actually a godsend, as these crops preserve very well. Winter squashes and garlic are easy to keep in a dry, frost-free shed or garage. In contrast, you may not have space or inclination to store more than a few pumpkins.

STAGGERING YOUR HARVESTS
It is important to consider how soon you'll be able to eat the produce that you grow, and to sow your seed accordingly. Carry out "successional sowings" – sow a pinch of seeds every

few weeks rather than all in one go for crops such as lettuce, rocket, radish, and spring onions to ensure a constant supply throughout the summer. Alternatively, swap seeds and plants with friends to get a range of cultivars that will mature at different rates. A single sowing of a selection of types can provide a steady supply and a variety of flavours and textures. Another option is to sow some seeds under cover, and some outside. Those that are protected will get a head start. To extend the season, consider growing crops that mature over a long period.

STORING SURPLUSES

If you have a glut and can't eat your fresh crops fast enough, then do not despair. There is a wide range of ways to store surplus crops, but knowing which to use is key, as not all fruits and vegetables suit every method.

1 Drying Vegetables such as onions and garlic should be dried thoroughly before storing – lay them out on racks in a dry, frost-free place. Herbs and chillies can also be dried. Consider drying slices of other crops such as apples and plums in the oven on a low heat to be stored and used in a range of recipes.

2 Freezing This is a useful method for storing a wide range of crops. To prevent berries forming a solid lump when you freeze them, lay them out on trays so that none of them are touching. Vegetables will store for longer if they are blanched – quickly immersed in boiling water – before freezing. This is ideal for crops such as asparagus and sprouting broccoli.

3 Preserving Transforming crops into delicious savoury chutneys or relishes and sweet jams and jellies is an ideal way to preserve a wide range of fruits and vegetables, capturing their flavours when they are at their peak.

4 Storing Many fruits and vegetables will keep well if they are kept in a cool, well-ventilated, frost-free place. Wrap apples and pears in waxed paper to help maintain their juiciness. Keep maincrop potatoes in a cool place in thick paper sacks, which prevent light from reaching them.

(above) **Redcurrants** can be eaten fresh, used to make rich jams and jellies, or frozen for later use, so a glut need not mean that the fruits have to go to waste.

(above left) **Salad leaves** can be expensive to buy and are ideal for sowing successionally, as they will be ready in just a few weeks. Sow a variety of types for a constant supply of delicious, mixed leaves.

THE RIGHT SPOT

The microclimates that your garden creates will inevitably suit some crops better than others. For this reason don't rush in, but instead take a little time to identify the different areas within your plot and then match the crops accordingly. Draw a plan and mark on it where the sun can and can't reach, as this is the primary factor to consider when deciding what crops to grow. You will find that your fruit, herbs, and vegetables will thrive, yield more heavily, and will also show greater resilience to pests and diseases if they are planted in the right position.

HOT AND SUNNY

South- and west-facing sites capture the most sunshine, so count yourself lucky if you have a fence or wall with this orientation. Many crops, such as fruits and fruiting vegetables, rely on sunlight to maximize their sugar levels, so make the most of these areas. These high-sugar crops often require a long growing season and benefit from additional shelter.

BRIGHT BUT COOL

Soil and container compost dries more quickly in sunnier positions, which will affect different crops in different ways. Container-grown fruit trees, for example, produce bigger and sweeter harvests when exposed to full sunlight, but will shed fruitlets if they become dry during the crucial spring fruit-setting period. To ensure a good crop, position them in the sun but try to keep the roots cool and well-watered. By contrast, a potted fig will thrive with hot sun on its roots, as do most Mediterranean herbs.

An open, sunny position is ideal for a range of crops, including carrots, radishes, leeks, lettuces, and potatoes, as long as they are thinned out to allow the plants plenty of growing room and are watered regularly and thoroughly.

SHADE AND MOISTURE

North- and east-facing sites receive less sunlight but are equally useful in the vegetable garden, providing a cool environment that is well suited to leaf crops such as cabbages, kale, spinach, and summer salads.

The main advantage of a shadier spot is that it is easier to maintain cool roots, which allows for steady growth and reduces the risk of premature flowering, known as "bolting". Moisture is lost more slowly from the soil, so crops growing here may require watering less frequently. If, however, you find that these cooler pockets are too moist, add plenty of bulky organic matter, such as composted bark, to the soil to improve drainage. Alternatively, grow your crops in raised beds filled with free-draining soil or compost.

RAIN SHADOWS

One final key area requiring careful management is the base of walls and fences, especially the sides that are facing away from the prevailing wind. These areas often suffer from

(top) **Plant leafy crops** such as colourful Swiss chard in partially shaded, north- or east-facing sites. The plants are well suited to these spots as too much sun can scorch their large, lush foliage.

(above) **Wall-trained fruit trees** take up very little growing space, look impressive, and can be very productive. If they are planted in a "rain shadow", make sure that they are not allowed to dry out when they are in flower or fruit.

"rain shadows", places where rainfall cannot reach the soil. If planting here, keep the area well watered during spring and summer, especially if you are growing fruit crops, which are sensitive to even the briefest of dry spells.

COLD AND WIND

Many large, exposed gardens and plots experience regular prolonged freezes and frosts. Sloping sites and valleys in particular are at risk of collecting cold pockets of air, known as "frost pockets" at their lowest points. A wall, fence, or thick evergreen hedge can also collect cold air if the ground slopes above it. In spots like these, choose vegetables that are robust and hardy. If you wish to grow fruit, choose late-flowering varieties to avoid the worst of the cold, or wrap plants with fleece during frosty spells. Cold soils are less damaging if they are dry, so add bulky organic matter to these sites to help plants overwinter.

Some garden sites are also vulnerable to the wind, which has two major actions: buffeting foliage and drying out plants. While Mediterranean herbs would be quite happy in such conditions, leafy spinach or Swiss chard would soon become tattered. Use screens or more robust plants to deflect or filter fast-moving air, or shield plants in large, thick-walled containers.

If a late cold spell is forecast, cover vulnerable plants with fleece to protect them from frost. Cover flowering fruit trees and bushes too, but remove the fleece on warmer days to allow insects to pollinate the blossom.

THE SOIL

Whether you sow your seeds directly in the ground, or sow crops under cover first and then plant them out, preparing your soil in advance is crucial. Start by identifying your soil type and pH so you can decide whether you need to make any improvements, as some crops prefer certain conditions if they are to thrive. If you decide to dig over your plot each year (see box, right), the best time is between mid-autumn and mid-spring. Break up compacted soil, remove any weeds, and work in plenty of organic matter, such as well-rotted garden compost, to improve yields.

UNDERSTANDING SOIL TYPES

The type of soil you have plays an important role in how well your crops grow, as most plants have preferred conditions – such as warm, light, well-drained soil, or perhaps cool and moisture-retentive. The type of soil you have will dictate how you manage it to get the best results, and how easy it is to work with. The first step is to identify your soil and to check it in different parts of the garden.

SAND, SILT, AND CHALK SOILS

Soils that contain a high proportion of sand drain very freely and lose nutrients quickly, although they warm up rapidly in spring. They are light and easy to dig, but need regular watering and feeding throughout the year. Soils rich in silt and chalk particles also drain freely but retain nutrients better, which makes them better suited to growing crops. All three types can be made more moisture- and nutrient-retentive by regularly digging in well-rotted organic matter, such as garden compost, manure, leaf mould, or composted bark chips. This organic matter adds nutrients to the soil and acts like a sponge, helping the soil to absorb moisture and any fertilizers that you apply, while at the same time keeping the soil structure airy and open.

CLAY SOILS

Clay soils have the opposite qualities to sandy types; they are moisture-retentive and fertile, but slow to warm up in spring, and are heavy to dig. They are also sticky when wet, often becoming waterlogged, and may bake into solid lumps during dry summer spells. Moderate clay soils are good for growing most crops, especially if improved by digging in well-rotted organic matter. If the soil contains a lot of clay and drains very poorly, try growing your crops in raised beds.

LOAM SOILS

This type of soil contains an even mix of sand, silt, and clay, and is a real godsend for gardeners and growers. It is ideal for most fruit and vegetable crops and needs very little improvement.

ACID AND ALKALINE SOILS

Even if your soil is fertile, the crops growing may not be able to absorb all the nutrients they need, which leads

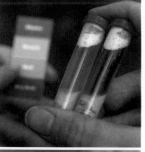

How to test your soil

Soil testing kits are commonly available and are a quick, easy way to find out the pH of your soil (from very acidic (1) to very alkaline (14), with neutral (7) in the middle). Simply shake up a sample of your soil with the testing solution and then judge the colour against the kit's pH chart. Perform the test in several places around your garden, as the pH may vary greatly.

An easy way to check your soil type is to roll some between your fingers. Clay soils have a clinging, sticky texture and can be easily moulded into little balls. Sandy soils are far more crumbly and will not hold together (see image, left). Loamy soils feel silky and mould quite well. Your soil is likely to be a mixture of all three types, but performing this test will help you to tell which one is dominant.

(above) **Digging in well-rotted organic matter** helps to improve the structure of your soil, as well as boosting the nutrient content. Dig in or apply a mulch at least once a year in spring or autumn for long-term benefits.

to deficiencies (see p.248). A common cause is the level of soil acidity, or pH, which can restrict the availability of certain nutrients to plants. While it is possible to alter the pH of your soil to suit the crops you would like to grow, it is a difficult, relentless task that is rarely worth the hard work involved.

Instead, check the pH of your soil (see left) and grow the crops that are best suited to the conditions you have. Brassicas, for example, crop better in alkaline soil, while blueberries must have acid conditions. Alternatively, if you want to grow crops that don't suit your soil pH, plant them in raised beds or containers filled with the right kind of soil or compost for your plants.

(above) **Containers or raised beds** offer the ideal solution to problematic, hard-to-manage soil as they give you the opportunity to start afresh. Fill with a loamy, rich, free-draining soil.

SOIL CULTIVATION

A final consideration is whether to dig the soil over extensively or not. There are two schools of thought, known as the "dig" and "no-dig" approaches. The argument for digging is that it breaks up compacted soil, removes pernicious weeds, incorporates soil improvers, and encourages the deep rooting of crops. A winter dig also exposes pests to predators and cold conditions, and helps to break up heavy clods of earth. Most garden soils will benefit from an initial dig.

However, there is an argument for less disturbance to the soil after the initial dig. The no-dig approach encourages natural fertility to rise and soil structure to stabilize. Weed seeds are not brought to the surface repeatedly, and worms and other beneficial fauna are undisturbed. In spring or autumn, mulches are simply laid on the surface for worms to draw down into the soil.

Ultimately, a combined approach may be best as it is sometimes necessary to dig over compacted areas of soil or deal with perennial weeds that are hard to shift.

For a "no-dig" mulch, lay a thick layer of organic matter such as compost on the soil surface and simply leave it to be broken down.

PLANTING

Raising plants from seed is an inexpensive way of growing many vegetables and herbs, and opens the door to a vast array of home-grown food. If you have limited space, consider which crops should be started under cover and then planted out, which can be grown to maturity indoors, and which can be sown directly outside. Don't waste indoor space on crops such as beetroots that thrive when sown outside. Save it for crops like chillies that benefit from a longer growing season.

INDOOR GROWING

If you plan to grow crops till the point of harvest indoors, then a windowsill propagator is extremely useful (see pp16–17). This will allow you to start off all manner of vegetables with varying germination temperature requirements – for example, chillies require at least 20°C (68°F) to germinate, whereas peas need no additional heat. A small propagator will also allow you to cultivate sprouted seeds and microleaves. Sufficient light is important, so position your young plants in as bright a position as possible, but shield them from strong direct sunlight which could scorch them. Consider buying artificial lighting to help boost multidirectional light.

SOWING UNDER COVER

Sowing seed under cover for outside planting allows you to make an early start and extend your growing season. This is especially useful for long-season plants such as aubergines and peppers, because it gives them sufficient time to mature and set their fruits. Once again, a heated propagator is useful, but avoid sowing seed too early, when lights levels are low, because seedlings will struggle and produce stretched, leggy growth. Early spring is soon enough for most crops. If indoor light levels are a problem, consider buying plug plants for crops that require a longer growing season, particularly if you need just a few plants for a small plot.

POTS, TRAYS, AND COMPOST

Crops that have large seeds, such as runner beans and squashes, can be sown singly in pots. Module trays are ideal for medium-sized seeds such as cabbage and beetroot, while small-seeded lettuces and celery should be sown in seed trays. When the seeds have germinated, transfer or "prick out" the seedlings into pots or modules. Use seed compost as this is finely milled and contains few nutrients.

HARDENING OFF

Young plants grown under cover are delicate. They will not have had exposure to changeable weather or to outside temperatures and so will need to be acclimatized to outdoor conditions before they are planted out. This process is described as "hardening off". Begin by placing crops in a shady, sheltered spot outside during the day and bringing them back indoors at night. This will make the plants more

(above) **Tender plants such as cucumbers** should be started off under cover as their seeds require a minimum temperature of 20°C (68°F) to germinate successfully.

(right) **Growing microgreens in a propagator** offers the earliest crops as long as they are given plenty of light. Harvest them when seedlings develop their first pair of leaves.

robust and adapt them gradually to colder temperatures. Do this for about seven to ten days, depending on the hardiness of your crop. If you are pricking out or planting on into another container or raised bed, water it well and then leave it in a warm spot overnight before you transplant. The aim is to prevent the compost from becoming too cold, as this can cause a transplant shock.

DIRECT SOWING

If given sufficient protection, hardy crops can be sown directly into the ground, which can be useful if you do not have the indoor space to dedicate to a propagation area. Some crops, such as calabrese resent root disturbance, and like most root crops thrive if sown direct. Ensure that you prepare the soil thoroughly in advance and warm the soil using a cloche or cold frame if the weather is cold.

PLANT BUYING OPTIONS

If you don't have the space or time to grow plants from seed there is a range of other options for you to choose from. Plants are available to buy at varying stages of growth and will provide a faster and easier alternative to growing from seed. Bear in mind however, that the number of varieties available is not as great as it is for seeds, and that the process is invariably more expensive.

1 Plug plants Available from garden centres or via mail order, plug plants are crops that are purchased when they are mature enough to plant out. They offer a faster and easier, but more expensive, alternative to growing crops from seed and are ideal if you have a small space and only want a few plants.

2 Tray packs If you are looking for plants to fill a whole row or want to buy in bulk, trays of plants will be more cost-effective than buying individual plants. Buy them while they are still relatively young.

3 Pot-grown plants Crops can also be purchased at a more advanced stage of growth, grown on in individual pots. This method is relatively expensive but it is a good way to buy crops that need a long growing season, such as chillies, peppers, and sweetcorn.

4 Bare-root Plants such as brassica seedlings (shown) are sown in seed beds and then dug up and sold "bare-root". Fruit trees and bushes are also available from autumn to spring. All bare-root plants should be planted straight away.

EARLY START

When growing crops in a limited space you want your plot to be as productive as possible. While you can't make the plot itself any bigger, you can at least prolong the growing season as much as possible, so that your plants mature sooner and continue producing vegetables and fruit later into autumn. This involves protecting your plants from spring frosts and autumn chills, allowing you to start them off earlier and to keep them growing for as long as possible. This is simple to achieve, especially if you grow hardier crops and those that reach a harvestable size quickly.

SOWING UNDER COVER

A greenhouse or conservatory offers the ideal conditions to sow seeds early and to grow plants on before planting out. Neither is essential however, and you can easily start seeds on your windowsills, where they will germinate quickly at room temperatures. Seedlings can also be grown indoors; turn them every few days to stop them growing towards the light and becoming leggy and crooked. Shade hot windows to avoid scorching the young soft growth.

SIMPLE COVERS

Cold frames and mini-greenhouses offer similar benefits to full-size greenhouses, and can be used to raise hardier crops in spring, or for later sowings of more tender seeds. They are also ideal for acclimatizing seedlings raised on windowsills to outdoor temperatures. Both are good for smaller plots as they can be taken apart and stored when not in use. Unlike cold frames, mini-greenhouses are often tall enough to grow mature crops, such as tomatoes and peppers. Remember that plants under cover must be kept well ventilated and watered.

GARDEN CLOCHES

Cloches are temporary covers that trap heat and protect plants from cold. They can also be used to warm the soil before

sowing outside and to encourage early growth. They are often made from rigid plastic, or polythene, but you may prefer to use glass cloches to reduce the amount of plastic in your garden. Dome cloches are used for single plants and different types of tunnel cloches to cover rows. Place them over seeds sown directly outside to promote quick germination or use them to protect newly planted crops from the cold. You can also use them to protect late-sown summer crops during cold nights in autumn.

PROTECTIVE FLEECE

Garden fleece is lightweight fabric, used to protect tender seedlings and plants from frost damage. It is useful for spreading across larger areas, such as whole beds or drills, but can also be wrapped around individual plants. To be effective however, the fleece needs to be held away from the leaves using canes or wire hoops. Fleece should also be held firmly in place, as it can blow away. For extra protection, use several layers but remove them once the risk of frost has passed.

(above) **A greenhouse** extends your growing season, enabling you to keep crops such as tomatoes and tender herbs such as basil cropping longer, as the nights get cooler.

(above left) **Starting plants under cover** gives them a valuable head start. Some varieties of pea and bean can be sown in autumn and will be ready to plant out in spring.

DIY PROTECTION

Although you can buy cloche and cold frame kits, it's often just as easy to make your own. That way, you can tailor them exactly to your site and the crops you grow. It will also be cheaper, especially if you reuse materials or objects you already have.

1 Windowsill growing Group seedlings together in trays on your windowsill to keep them warm and moist. If you want to provide more light, make a reflector using cardboard and tin foil. This will encourage seedlings to grow straight and promote stronger stems.

2 Cold frames These are easy to make using old window frames. Use bricks or blocks to build up the sides, or make a simple wooden base, placing the window on top. These can be permanent or temporary features.

3 Simple shelters Small squares of glass, Perspex, or clear plastic make excellent cloches, and can be leant together at the top or propped up on canes to form more open shelters. Any clear glass will do, such as that from old windows. Take care with sharp edges.

4 Bottle cloches Extend the life of any single-use, clear plastic bottles that you may come across by cutting off their bases and using them as cloches for individual plants. Remove the tops to provide air flow. With the base removed, the cloches stack and store easily, ready to be used again and again.

FEEDING

Keeping your fruit and vegetable plants well-watered and fed is essential for a good harvest, especially in smaller plots where every plant matters. Regular care also promotes strong, healthy growth, which makes plants more resistant to pests and diseases. Crops in pots and raised beds are almost totally reliant on you for protection, nutrition, and water.

HOW AND WHEN TO WATER

Growing fruits, herbs, and vegetables closely together in a small space, especially in containers, limits the amount of root space these plants have. This high concentration of roots needs continual access to moisture if it is to grow well. The ideal would be to install a drip irrigation system set at a level that ensures your soil or compost is evenly and consistently moist, but this is a luxury. Watering cans and hosepipes are more the norm; a thorough soak of beds every few days will ensure water penetrates to the deepest of roots, not just those near the surface. Pots may require a daily drench. Do this in the evening or morning to reduce evaporation, rather than in the heat of the day. Keep all plants well-watered when they are in flower or setting fruit. Dry spells will cause flowers and young fruits to wither, reducing the harvest.

MAKE THE MOST OF MOISTURE

To help your soil retain moisture better, especially if it is light, regularly dig in well-rotted organic matter, which acts like a sponge. If you grow crops in

(above) **Mulching plants** helps to retain moisture in the soil by preventing evaporation. Organic mulches will also feed your plants.

(left) **Automatic micro-irrigation** is a worthwhile investment if you grow lots of crops in containers but have limited time to water them.

(far left) **Young plants** are especially vulnerable to drying out. Water them regularly, at least until they are planted out and fully established.

containers, add water-retaining granules before planting. Set up water butts in your garden to collect rainwater, and consider recycling the household water you use to wash and prepare vegetables and salads.

If you are going on holiday, group potted crops together in a shady spot, water them well, and stand them in trays. Alternatively, ask a neighbour to water while you are away. Doing this is actually better than an automatic watering system, as crops can be harvested at the same time to ensure repeated cropping. (It also serves as a reward for the temporary waterer.)

FEEDING YOUR CROPS

Growing crops takes a great deal of nutrients from the soil or compost, which can become exhausted, so it is essential to replenish them regularly.

There are three main nutrients that plants need most: nitrogen for leaf growth; phosphorus for healthy roots; and potassium (potash) for flowers and fruits. They also require small amounts of "trace" elements for overall health, including magnesium, iron and boron. When feeding your crops, choose a feed that meets your crops' needs. Root crops benefit from a fertilizer that is high in phosphorus to encourage root growth; leaf crops require feeds rich in nitrogen; and fruiting crops such as tomatoes need lots of potash. The wrong type of fertilizer can encourage the wrong type of plant growth, for example, a wealth of foliage and little fruit. Your soil type will dictate to some degree how often you should feed your plants: light, sandy soils lose nutrients quickly while clay soils are retentive.

FERTILIZER TYPES

There are two types of garden fertilizer to use: natural feeds based on organic plant and animal matter, and artificial ones made from chemicals. Both can be applied in various ways and each offers its own advantages. Most are allocated an "N:P:K" value, which is the general ratio of nitrogen (N), phosphorus (P) and potassium (K) within a fertilizer, to help you choose the right feed for your crop. Whichever you use, avoid over-feeding in the hope of bigger harvests as you are more likely to damage plant roots.

1 Granular fertilizers This type of fertilizer breaks down slowly in the soil and provides plants with long-term nutrition, often lasting all season. They are easy to handle and apply, and are available as natural or artificial feeds.

2 Liquid fertilizers These are quick-acting feeds, ideal for giving crops a boost. Natural and artificial types are available, sold as soluble powders or liquid concentrates. Dilute them according to the instructions given.

3 Compound fertilizers Rather than supplying a balanced feed, these chemical or natural fertilizers are used to supply specific nutrients, such as iron sulphate to increase iron in the soil, or bone meal to boost levels of phosphorus.

4 Well-rotted organic matter This is used to add natural nutrients to the soil, as well as to improve its structure. There are many types you can use, from home-made garden compost to horse manure.

YOUR PLOT

MAKING A
START

A three-metre square plot is a good size for most first-time fruit and vegetable growers. It provides ample space for a useful selection of crops yet is small enough to look after easily. To illustrate this, we created, planted, and harvested the plot featured throughout this chapter in a single growing season to show exactly what you can achieve. To help you get started and decide what to grow, follow the planting guides (pp.46–53) for different summer combinations to suit different needs: easy-to-grow, the family plot, a scheme for gourmet crops, and a plan for those with little or no garden at all. The first three plans are for a 3 x 3m (10 x 10ft) square plot, but you can adapt them to the space you have, whether it's a small bed, or pots and troughs on the patio.

PREPARING YOUR PLOT

The most important task between autumn and early spring is to prepare the area for future sowing and planting (see pp.26–27). Exactly what this will involve depends on your soil and site, but it's worth spending time now to ensure a good harvest and to prevent problems later. Provide the best conditions you can by enriching the soil with nutrients, and by resolving problems, such as poor drainage, perennial weeds, or areas of compacted soil. If you are growing in containers, warm them up in your sunniest spot before introducing seeds and plants (see pp.28–29).

Dig the soil well, breaking up large clumps and removing any weed roots. Avoid treading on newly dug areas.

Add rotted organic matter such as garden compost to the soil to improve fertility and moisture retention.

Rake the surface to leave a fine and level surface for sowing seeds directly. Remove any weed seedlings.

Use fabric membrane to help control weeds if you are unable to sow seeds straightaway.

OUR PLANTING PLAN

This combination of vegetables is aimed at beginners who are growing crops for the first time. It includes reliable crops that are quick to grow and can be picked over several weeks. Speedy salad leaves and herbs can be picked a few weeks after sowing, either as cut-and-come-again leaves or as whole plants. The beans will last through summer and the potatoes and kale will provide a welcome harvest in autumn.

TOP ROW sweetcorn x 9 • summer squash x 1 • runner beans x 8
• French beans x 6 • maincrop potatoes x 4

MIDDLE ROW dwarf bush tomatoes x 5 • cucumbers x 3
• kale x 4 • courgettes x 2

BOTTOM ROW beetroots x 20 • carrots x 40 • radishes x 40
• Swiss chard x 8 • kohl rabi x 12 • oriental greens x 20
• lettuces x 20 • coriander x 6 • parsley x 4

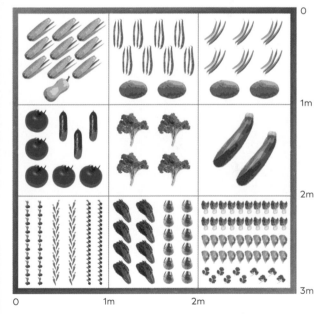

Other jobs to do

• Weed regularly to prevent weeds competing with your seedlings
• Fork in granular fertilizer before sowing seeds directly
• Keep the soil free from plant debris, which can harbour diseases
• Start sowing seeds under cover to plant out in spring
• Chit early seed potatoes (see p.146) to give them a head start

Warm the soil with cloches so your seeds germinate more quickly. Use them to protect young plants.

Use garden canes to mark out your planting plan. Indicate where to sow, and where to put supports..

PLANTING
THE BED

Once the soil is prepared you can turn your attention to sowing and planting. Hard frosts are likely in early spring, making it too soon to plant tender crops which could be damaged. Instead, sow hardier vegetables, such as carrots, peas, beetroots, and radishes, directly into the soil. These will germinate more quickly in soil that has been warmed first with cloches and plastic sheeting. To encourage stronger growth, protect the seedlings with cloches and thin them as they develop. This will ensure good air flow and prevent competition between the young plants.

Frosts become fewer and less severe in late spring when you can start to acclimatize tender crops such as sweetcorn, French and runner beans, tomatoes, and courgettes that have been sown under cover or bought in. To do this, put seedlings outside during the day and bring them in at night for about ten days. Plant them out in early summer when the risk of frost has passed.

Plants grow rapidly as the weather warms making this a busy time on your plot. Keep on top of maintenance to ensure your plants get the best start. Weak or dead plants can easily be replaced at this stage.

French and runner beans twine up their supports once established. Tie in any young, wayward shoots.

Water seedlings well when planting out to encourage deep rooting, which makes them more resilient.

Some hardy seeds can be sown directly in spring. Prepare your soil well first and keep it evenly moist.

Thin direct-sown crops as soon as they develop so that the remaining plants grow unhindered.

Biodegradable pots mean less root disturbance when planting out. Keep them moist to help them rot away.

Keep garden fleece handy in case the weather turns cold. Cloches can also be used.

Other early-season jobs

- Be vigilant against slugs and snails – use pellets around seedlings
- Cover seeds with newspaper for a short spell to boost germination
- Sink flower pots into the soil next to squash plants to make watering down to the roots easier later on
- Hoe between crops to keep on top of weeds

THE CROPS

Growth rates will increase as temperatures rise in early summer, so it's important to keep on top of crop developments. Quick-maturing crops such as radishes, salad leaves, and herbs may begin to provide you with early harvests, while fruits and vegetables that take longer to mature will benefit from continued care and maintenance. Tie in tomatoes and cucumbers to their stakes and remove any yellowing leaves from plants.

Earth up your potatoes to prevent the tubers becoming exposed to light, which turns them green and inedible.Keeping on top of weeds will discourage unwanted competition; while erecting insect-proof barriers will prevent carrot root flies from attacking and boring holes in crops.

Tie in developing cucumber stems to their supports using soft twine. They grow quickly.

Radish sowings will mature in as little as five weeks. Pick them young before they become woody.

Keep carrots well weeded as competition from unwanted growth can reduce yields.

Erect insect netting, 60cm (24in) high, around your carrots to prevent carrot flies (p.240) laying eggs.

To ensure strong roots that will sustain plenty of pods, keep French and runner beans well watered.

Earth up soil around your developing potato plants to prevent light reaching the tubers.

Check plants for signs of pests and diseases. Remove any diseased growth and control pests promptly.

Salad crops will be developing quickly so harvest leaves from individual plants as needed.

Young growth is a magnet for slugs and snails. Make sure appropriate controls, such as pellets, are in place.

Remove yellowing foliage from plants such as kale, kohl rabi, and courgettes to ensure good hygiene.

Other mid-season jobs

- Thin out Swiss chard plants using the thinnings as a baby salad leaf
- Attach individual tomato plants to a stout bamboo cane
- Harvest basil and coriander regularly to encourage further growth
- Feed fruiting vegetables with liquid tomato fertilizer each week

PLENTY
TO PICK

Mid- to late summer when spring sowings and plantings are ready to harvest is the most productive time on the plot. Pick crops such as French beans, courgettes, salad leaves, and herbs regularly as their individual pods, fruits, and leaves mature. They will provide an almost continuous harvest. Other crops, such as carrots and beetroot, yield one-off harvests; once they are picked, the area they occupied can be re-used. Further sowings or plantings at this time will ensure that your plot's productivity doesn't fizzle out.

Some long-season crops, such as sweetcorn, tomatoes, and runner beans, will begin to mature in late summer. Look after them well to encourage good harvests into the autumn.

Train wayward squash stems as they will be putting on plenty of strong stem growth now.

Cucumbers reach their peak over a few days. Check regularly and cut them as soon as they are ready.

Sow seeds direct in bare patches of soil for continuous crops. Keep the drills well watered in hot spells.

Pull up individual carrots as soon as they reach a harvestable size, selecting the largest roots first.

Harvest courgettes regularly or they will soon grow into marrows. Check plants every few days.

Pull up whole lettuce plants or leave the cut stalk in the ground to re-sprout fresh loose leaves.

Keep sweetcorn well watered after the silks and tassels emerge, to encourage the greatest yields.

Other peak-season jobs

- Pull up baby beetroot regularly
- Check for pests and diseases
- Water crops thoroughly
- Apply liquid feeds routinely

ENDING
THE SEASON

This is the time when late crops come into their own. Sweetcorn, winter squashes and tomatoes require ample growing time and sunshine to reach their best and will be at their sweetest in autumn. Now that their skins have formed, maincrop potatoes are ready for harvesting and storing.

Bare patches will become more common as spent crops are pulled up. Sow these with quick-growing microgreens or hardy salad leaves for a late crop, or start preparing the area for next year. Either cover the soil with mulch to prevent weed growth or leave it bare to allow frost to penetrate and expose pests. Your compost heap will fill up as crops are cleared. Turn the contents during autumn to move material on the outside to the centre.

Focus your watering on crops that are still maturing, such as late pumpkins and salad leaves.

Cut winter squashes before the first frosts and lay them in a sunny position so that the skins harden.

Mulch bare soil with organic matter that will break down in time for spring planting.

Squeeze in late sowings of hardy crops such as salad leaves. These can be covered with cloches.

French and runner beans will keep on bearing pods until the first frosts if they are picked regularly.

Gently pull back the outer leaves of sweetcorn cobs to check if the kernels are mature enough to pick.

Leave maincrop potato tubers on the soil surface to dry for a few hours before storing them.

Courgette plants will be coming to the end of their life now – make a final harvest then compost them.

Harvest the leaves and seed pods of coriander. Dry the seeds and freeze any surplus leaves until required.

Pull up spent crops and put them on the compost heap. Chop them up to speed up decomposition.

Other late-season jobs

- Continue to harvest Swiss chard through the winter
- Cover over any new sowings with bell or tunnel cloches
- Stop watering tomato plants; this will encourage fruit to ripen
- Store surplus root crops in a frost-free shed or garage

EASY-TO-GROW PLOT

If you are new to growing your own food, this mix of vegetables, plus some strawberries, will provide a steady supply for your kitchen. Many crops are ideal for beginners, either because they are easy to care for and suffer from few pest and disease problems, or because they yield reliable harvests with little input. By growing just one or two different crops per square metre, you can easily get to grips with their cultivation. As your confidence and experience grow, try adding more of the crops listed below to the overall plan to tailor the plot to your specific needs.

GROWING IN CONTAINERS

Low-maintenance vegetables are ideal for containers, windowboxes, and even hanging baskets. You can grow a wall of summer strawberries by planting one plant per 20cm (8in) pot and fixing them to a fence or some trelliswork in a sunny spot. Shallow-rooted salad crops are perfect for smaller containers, whereas onions and French beans need pots with a minimum depth of 25cm (10in). Choose large tubs or even sacks for potatoes and courgettes.

ALTERNATIVE EASY-TO-GROW CROPS

Tomatoes
pages 54–57

Garlic
pages 162–163

Runner beans
pages 72–73

Sweetcorn
pages 166–169

Broad beans
pages 78–79

Winter squashes
pages 88–91

Carrots
pages 138–139

Turnips
pages 140–141

EASY-TO-GROW MIX

This combination of crops will provide you with all the basics, giving quick results and high yields if grown on a well-prepared, fertile soil. The large patch of strawberries will ensure a bumper crop throughout the summer months; easy-to-grow French beans will crop reliably right through to autumn; and just two courgette plants will supply more than you can eat. Sow fast-growing radishes in regular batches for a steady supply, sowing your next crop as soon as a row has been cleared.

TOP ROW maincrop potatoes x 4
- new potatoes x 6 • onions x 60

MIDDLE ROW spinach x 16
- beetroot x 30 • courgettes x 2
- French beans x 12

BOTTOM ROW radish x 40
- lettuce x 8 • radish x 40
- strawberries x 12

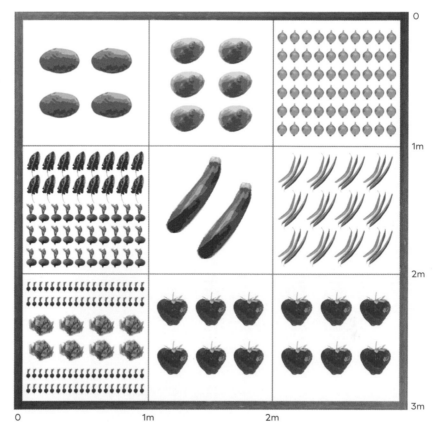

0

1m

2m

3m

0   1m   2m

Swiss chard
pages 126–127

Oriental greens
pages 122–123

Autumn raspberries
pages 202–203

Lettuces
pages 114–117

Shallots
pages 156–157

Plums
pages 218–219

Also consider growing:
- Chillies (pp.62–65)
- Endive (pp.130–131)
- Kohl rabi (pp.170–171)
- Rhubarb (pp.186–187)
- Coriander (pp.194–195)
- Parsley (pp.194–195)
- Mint (pp.190–193)
- Chives (pp.190–193)
- Cabbage (pp.96–101)
- Blackcurrants (pp.208–209)
- Blueberries (pp.212–213)
- Blackberries (pp.204–205)

FAMILY PLOT

There are plenty of delicious fruits and vegetables on the family shopping list that can easily be grown in the garden. A 3 x 3m (10 x 10ft) plot is large enough for a range of crops, and, if space is tight, many of these plants will grow in containers too. Consider giving each family member responsibility for a crop to encourage a friendly rivalry that will result in a better-maintained garden. Sharing the experience and passing tips and techniques down the generations may make growing fruit and vegetables second nature to the whole family.

GROWING IN CONTAINERS

If you don't have a lot of space, or you simply fancy growing in containers, choose large pots and fill them with high-yielding family favourites. Baby parsnips and carrots can be sown in deep containers, while lettuce and beetroot will flourish in shallower pots. Soft fruits such as strawberries are ideal; bush fruits such as blueberries, and even a small apple tree, will thrive in a roomy pot. Ensure that crops such as French beans, tomatoes, squashes, courgettes, and sweetcorn are given a warm, sunny spot to encourage their pods and fruits to develop.

ALTERNATIVE FAMILY CROPS

Peas
pages 70–71

Cabbages
pages 96–101

Pumpkins
pages 92–93

Cucumbers
pages 82–83

Radishes
pages 134–135

Brussels sprouts
pages 108–109

Swiss chard
pages 126–127

Kohl rabi
pages 170–171

FAMILY MIX

Designed for maximum productivity, this planting scheme includes the most popular crops that will be ready to harvest in summer, autumn, and early winter. Make full use of the space by underplanting a triangle of slower-growing sweetcorn with a fast-growing squash, which will cover the ground under the sweetcorn. Winter crops like calabrese and purple-sprouting broccoli occupy the ground for a long period and so are planted together where they won't be disturbed.

TOP ROW early potatoes x 6
- beetroot x 30 • lettuce x 8
- bush tomatoes x 4

MIDDLE ROW calabrese x 8
- sprouting broccoli x 2 • squash x 1
- sweetcorn x 9 • French beans x 12

BOTTOM ROW carrots x 45
- parsnips x 8 • onions x 30
- leeks x 10 • courgettes x 2

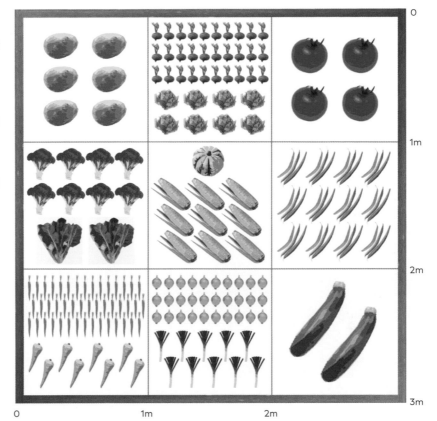

Chicory
pages 128–129

Peppers
pages 60–61

Strawberries
pages 200–201

Annual herbs
pages 196–197

Aubergines
pages 66–67

Redcurrants
pages 206–207

Also consider growing:
- Chillies (pp.62–65)
- Runner beans (pp.72–73)
- Broad beans (pp.78–79)
- Cut-and-come-again salads (pp.118–119)
- Spinach (pp.124–125)
- Turnips (pp.140–141)
- Garlic (pp.162–163)
- Rhubarb (pp.186–187)
- Raspberries (pp.202–203)
- Blueberries (pp.212–213)
- Apples (pp.214–215)
- Cherries (pp.220–221)

GOURMET PLOT

The vegetable and fruit world is a diverse one, and brilliant for adventurous cooks. Crops such as globe artichokes and chicory, unusual varieties such as purple carrots and red gooseberries, and fashionably exotic newcomers add excitement and interest to the garden. Why not embrace them – they're not likely to be found in the average supermarket. These crops are also colourful characters that contribute to an eye-catching garden, as well as a productive one. The saying that you "eat with your eyes as well as your mouth" has never been more appropriate.

GROWING IN CONTAINERS
Fill your pots with moveable combinations of pick-and-mix crops to create a mixture of textures and colours that contrast well with tubs and pots of ornamentals. Unusual salad leaves, herbs, edible flowers, and the feathery foliage of fennel and asparagus are just a few examples. If you are planting bush fruits and perennial vegetables, give them loam-based compost to boost health and longevity and plant them in large troughs or deep pots to accommodate long roots. Thirsty crops such as fennel and celeriac will need plenty of water.

ALTERNATIVE GOURMET CROPS

Kale 'Black Tuscan'
page 110

Carrot 'Purple Haze'
page 138

Cabbage 'January King'
page 100

Tomato 'Tigerella'
page 56

Sprouting broccoli 'Claret'
page 106

Watercress
pages 130–131

Kohl rabi 'Kolibri'
page 170

Swiss chard 'Ruby'
pages 126

GOURMET MIX

The aim here is to fill your plot, no matter how large or small, with produce that is expensive to buy or rarely seen in your local supermarket. Asparagus and redcurrants are luxury crops that are relatively easy to grow. Broad beans, picked young and sweet, are a revelation compared with any you can buy in the shops; and rows of fresh oriental greens will supply enough leaves and stems for your stir-fries and salads all summer.

TOP ROW salad potatoes x 6
- broad beans x 20 • asparagus x 4

MIDDLE ROW celeriac x 9
- strawberries x 8 • redcurrant x 1
- Florence fennel x 10 • garlic x 14

BOTTOM ROW squash x 1
- chicory x 6 • shallots x 8
- loose-leaf lettuce x 8 • oriental greens x 10 • loose-leaf lettuce x 8
- oriental greens x 10

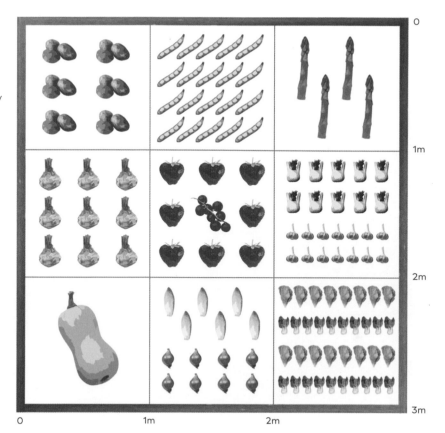

Beetroot 'Chioggia Pink'
page 136

Peppermint
pages 190–193

Peach 'Garden Lady'
page 222

Globe artichokes
pages 182–183

Cauliflower 'Romanesco'
page 102

Blueberries
pages 212–213

Also consider growing:
- Pepper 'Yellow Stuffer' (p.60)
- Chilli 'Ancho' (p.62–65)
- Pea 'Shiraz' (p.70)
- French bean 'Lingua di Fuoco' (p.76)
- Winter squash 'Uchiki Kuri' (p.88)
- Pumpkin 'Rouge Vif d'Etampes' (p.92)
- Jerusalem artichokes (pp.184–185)
- Coriander (pp.194–195)
- Gooseberry 'Hinnonmäki Röd' (p.210)
- Gage 'Coe's Golden Drop'

NO-GARDEN PLOT

With many of us now living in apartments and shared homes, an outdoor growing area is no longer a given. But it's perfectly possible to grow your crops indoors, and you will be surprised by the wide variety of edible plants you can cultivate. In the protected environment of windowsills and bright indoor areas, you can control growing conditions precisely. That's a huge advantage when it's blowing a gale or below freezing outside. Plant breeders are responding to the trend with an ever-increasing range of compact crops. The no-garden revolution begins right here.

GROWING IN CONTAINERS

The no-plot garden is dominated by containers, allowing you to become expert in this modern growing method. Large 30cm (12in) pots, and window boxes inside or out, give you access to stalwart crops, such as tomatoes, carrots, and peas, whereas indoor containers lend themselves perfectly to supporting flavour-packed leafy herbs like coriander and basil. A simple seed tray lined with moist kitchen paper opens the door to adventurous microleaf and sprouted seed cultivation.

ALTERNATIVE NO-GARDEN CROPS

Beetroot 'Forono'
pages 136-137

Dill
pages 194-195

Carrot 'Parmex'
pages 138-139

Sweet pepper 'Snackbite Mixed'
pages 60-61

Turnip 'Snowball'
pages 140–141

Rocket
pages 118-119

Baby kale 'Midnight Sun'
pages 110–111

Spring onion 'Ishikura'
pages 158-159

NO-GARDEN MIX

This design illustrates that you can produce an abundance of home-grown food with no garden and minimal outdoor space. Pots, window boxes, and windowsills are surprisingly productive once you choose the appropriate crops.
As an added bonus, the weather has little effect on this protected space, allowing year-round harvests.

3 POTS chilli peppers x 1
● dwarf tomato x 1 ● dwarf peas x 12

WINDOW BOX thyme x 2
● rosemary x 1 ● sage x 1
● strawberries x 3 ● Swiss chard x 3

WINDOWSILL loose-leaf lettuce x 6
● chives x 1 ● sweet basil x 4
● pak choi x 6 ● mint x 1

SEED TRAY pea shoots x 25
● shiso microleaf x 40 ● coriander microleaf x 40

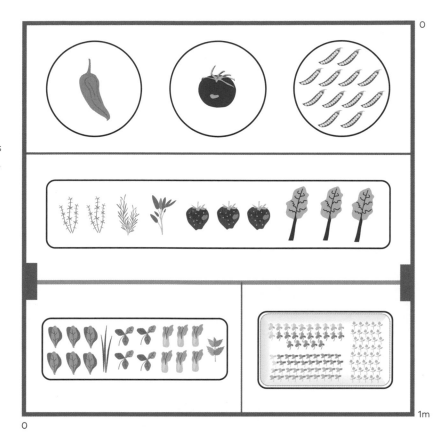

Amaranth microleaf
pages 120-121

Radish 'French Breakfast'
pages 134–135

Aubergine 'Calliope'
pages 66–67

Celery microgreen
pages 120–121

Chinese Cabbage
pages 122-123

Coriander
pages 194–195

Also consider growing:
● Mustard 'Red Russian' (pp.122–123)
● Spinach 'Bordeaux' (pp.124–125)
● Mooli radish 'Neptune' (pp.134–135)
● Flat-leaf parsley (pp.194–195)
● Land cress (p.118)
● Shiso (pp.122–123)
● Oregano (pp.190–193)
● Tatsoi (pp.122–123)
● Corn salad (pp.118–119)
● Mizuna (pp.122–123)

GROW YOUR OWN

VEGETABLES

TOMATOES

Tomatoes are easy to grow under cover or outside in a sunny spot, and produce a reliable harvest from mid-summer. There are many varieties to choose from, and now grafted plants are freely available. Tomatoes fall into two main types: cordon tomatoes that are usually trained up tall canes or strings, and bush varieties that are grown more freely. There are also dwarf varieties to grow in containers, and tumbling tomatoes for hanging baskets.

	SPRING	SUMMER	AUTUMN	WINTER
SOW				
HARVEST				

TIME TO HARVEST: 16-18 WEEKS

SUITABLE FOR: BEDS AND CONTAINERS – UNDER COVER OR OUTSIDE

11 plants

3M (10FT) ROWS
Plant 30cm (12in) apart, depending on the variety

CONTAINERS
1 plant in each

1 SOWING SEEDS

Sow tomatoes under cover in mid-spring. Fill a pot or tray with compost, water well, then sow the seeds on top, spacing them about 1cm (½in) apart. Cover lightly with compost and place the tray in a heated propagator set at 18°C (72°F) for a week or two, or until they germinate. Prick the seedlings out into individual pots when they develop their first pair of leaves. Grow them on under cover for a few weeks until you are ready to plant them in their final positions.

Sowing seeds individually into modules removes the need to prick them out as seedlings. This minimizes root disturbance of young plants.

Grow the seedlings on until roots appear at the base of the modules. They can then be potted on into larger pots or planted out if conditions allow.

Tomatoes need deep soil so choose a generously sized container. Add a cane to support cordon varieties and tie the stem in.

Support tomato plants as they grow, especially those trained as cordons. Vertical strings are practical and flexible for indoor crops.

2 GROWING INDOORS

Tomatoes crop best under cover in greenhouses or growing frames where they can be planted into beds or containers. They need a bright spot, shaded from hot sun, with good airflow, and should be watered daily in warm spells and fed regularly. Cordon varieties, trained as a single stem with the sideshoots removed, are best for growing this way as they require less space than bush-types.

TIP Buy plants grafted onto a vigorous rootstock to elevate yields.

3 GROWING OUTSIDE

To grow tomatoes outside, choose a sunny site and prepare the soil by digging in well-rotted organic matter. Alternatively, plant into large containers. Water plants during dry spells and feed regularly with tomato fertilizer. Bush tomatoes have more room to spread outside; support them with several canes encircled with twine.

Plant out tomatoes at the same depth as they were in their pots and firm them in gently.

Insert canes near the plants after planting. Outdoor cordons require only a single support.

Tie in the tomato stems as they grow to help support the developing trusses of fruit.

4 TRAINING

Cordon tomatoes are grown as single stems trained up a cane or string. Keep checking the plants for sideshoots in the leaf joints and pinch them out. The sideshoots on bush-types can be left to grow. Once cordon plants have formed four or five flower trusses, cut out the tops to stop further growth.

5 ROUTINE CARE

Water all plants regularly (perhaps daily for under-cover crops) and once the first flowers appear, feed them every week with a high-potash tomato fertilizer. Avoid letting plants dry out, which can cause the fruit to abort and may lead to the nutrient disorder, blossom end rot (see p.246).

Use your fingers to pinch out sideshoots as soon as they appear on cordon tomatoes. Use a sharp knife to remove older, thicker shoots.

Tomato plants are especially thirsty when they are in flower or fruit. It is important to keep plants in containers constantly moist.

6 HARVESTING

Tomatoes ripen from midsummer onwards; for the best flavour wait until each fruit is evenly coloured. Smaller tomatoes ripen quickly, but larger fruits, like those from beefsteak-types, can take several days. Picked tomatoes keep for a few days but if you can't use them soon, cook and freeze surpluses. Underripe fruits will ripen indoors if kept in the sun.

To harvest fruit, place your thumb on the stalk "knuckle" and bend the tomato upwards.

TOMATOES

1 'Totem' This dwarf bush variety should be planted in a container or windowbox, and won't need pinching out. The cherry-sized red fruits are produced in abundance.

2 'Tumbling Tom Yellow' This compact, cascading bush tomato is ideal for growing in sunny hanging baskets. Pick the cherry-sized, golden fruits throughout summer.

3 'Crimson Crush' Producing large, round, red fruits, this variety is suitable for growing outside. It has a strong tolerance of blight and shrugs off infections.

4 'Marmande' This beefsteak variety bears large, deep red fruits with few seeds. Grow this cordon-type outdoors; support it with a stake and remove any sideshoots.

5 'Sungold' One of the sweetest-tasting, this hybrid bears cherry-sized, deep-orange fruits. It is suitable for growing indoors or out, and should be trained as a cordon.

6 'Sweet Aperitif' This variety can produce hundreds of delicious, small, shiny-red fruits in a greenhouse over a long season and can be grown outside in a sunny, sheltered spot.

7 'Sweet Olive' A hybrid "baby plum" tomato, it yields oblong-shaped red fruits, each about 4cm (1½in) long. It is suitable for growing inside or out, but should be staked for support.

8 'Moneymaker' A traditional cordon variety that can be grown indoors or out, it bears red, medium-sized tomatoes. Train the stem up a cane or vertical strings.

9 'Tigerella' This unusual, early variety bears medium-sized, red fruits with distinctive yellow stripes. It can be grown under cover or outside, and should be trained as a single cordon.

OTHER VARIETIES
'Black Opal'
'Folia'
'Ferline'
'Green Sausage'
'Yellow Stuffer'
'Black Russian'

PEPPERS

Ideal for growing in containers, just two or three pepper plants will supply you with plenty of sweet, delicious fruits, particularly if they are grown under cover. There are many different varieties to choose from, with fruits in a range of shapes and colours – including purple, orange, and even black. You can harvest while the fruits are still green to encourage others to form, or leave the peppers to colour up and mature and develop their full sweet flavour.

	SPRING	SUMMER	AUTUMN	WINTER
SOW				
HARVEST				
TIME TO HARVEST: 20–26 WEEKS				

SUITABLE FOR: BEDS AND CONTAINERS – UNDER COVER OR OUTSIDE

0   1m   2m   3m

8 plants

3M (10FT) ROWS
Plant out 40cm (16in) apart

0   30cm

CONTAINERS
1 plant in each

1 GETTING STARTED

Peppers are tender plants that require a long growing season, so it's important to sow them under cover early in the year to give them time to mature and produce fruit. Alternatively, you can buy young plants later in the season. Plants will grow well in large containers as long as they have fertile compost and space to develop.

'Snackbite Mixed' has sweet, "snack-sized" fruit and is suitable for growing indoors.

'Marconi' fruits are long, thin, and tapered. They mature to a rich, glossy red colour.

'Gourmet' is a compact plant that bears good yields of sweet, bright orange peppers.

'Redskin' is compact with green fruit that turn red when mature. It is ideal for containers.

If you have just a few seeds, sow them singly in small pots. Cover with a thin layer of soil and put in a heated propagator.

Plant strong seedlings into 9cm (3½in) pots and continue to grow them on under cover. Keep the young plants well watered.

Once the plants' roots fill their pots they can be planted on again. Choose a large pot so the pepper has space to grow.

2 SOWING SEEDS

Fill pots with seed compost, firm gently, water well, and allow to drain. Sow seeds 1cm (½in) apart on the top, pressing them gently into the surface. Cover with a 5mm (¼in) layer of compost, water lightly, and place on a sunny windowsill. Once germinated and large enough to handle, remove from the propagator and prick out the seedlings into individual pots. When plants reach 20cm (8in) in height, start feeding them regularly with a liquid tomato fertilizer.

TIP To boost yields and speed ripening, purchase grafted peppers as plants.

GROW YOUR OWN VEGETABLES **FRUITING CROPS**

3 PLANTING OUT

If you plan to position peppers outside, harden them off in early summer by placing them outside during the day and inside at night for two weeks. Plant in a sunny, sheltered site, spacing plants 40cm (16in) apart, or plant into containers with a minimum diameter of 30cm (12in), filled with multi-purpose compost. Water in well.

Pepper plants will be ready to transplant in early summer when all risk of frost has passed. Give them a warm, sheltered site.

Firm the plants in well as they will become quite heavy over time. Water thoroughly and keep the plants moist during all stages of growth.

Insert a stout bamboo cane 60cm (24in) in height beside each plant and tie the plant in. The large fruits become heavy as they develop.

When the first fruits appear feed the plants every two weeks. Feeding and regular watering will ensure a succession of fruits.

4 GROWING INDOORS

Peppers can be grown under cover or on a sunny windowsill indoors. You will need to pollinate the flowers, either by transferring pollen from one flower to another with a soft paintbrush, or by gently watering from above to dislodge pollen. Opening the greenhouse door will give access to pollinating insects.

5 ROUTINE CARE

Keep plants well watered and feed regularly with a high-potash liquid fertilizer such as tomato feed, to encourage flowers and fruit to form. Often plants will produce one main fruit before developing others; it is best to pick this one small so that subsequent fruits are given the chance to mature.

6 HARVESTING

Individual fruits will begin to colour up from green, through to either yellow, orange, red, or purple, depending on the variety. Either harvest them while green, or wait for them to mature when their flavour becomes sweeter. Cut individual fruits off with a pair of secateurs or scissors; pulling them off can damage the plant. Cover outdoor plants with a cloche in autumn to help speed up ripening.

Cut the peppers regularly once they begin to ripen to encourage more fruits to form.

CHILLIES

These tiny peppers add real colour to the plot and are very easy to grow. To crop well, all they need is a bright, sunny position in the smallest plot, on a patio, or even on a windowsill. They are available in red, green, yellow, orange, and purple, and with a huge array of "heats" – from mild to atomic – making it easy to find a variety to suit your taste. Many are excellent for drying, which means that one plant can provide you with a supply of chillies for up to a year.

	SPRING	SUMMER	AUTUMN	WINTER
SOW				
HARVEST				

TIME TO HARVEST: 20-26 WEEKS

SUITABLE FOR: BEDS AND CONTAINERS – UNDER COVER OR OUTSIDE

0   1m   2m   3m

11 plants

3M (10FT) ROWS
Plant out 30cm (12in) apart

0   25-30cm

CONTAINERS
1 plant in each

Chilli seeds are quite large and easy to handle. Sow 5mm (¼in) deep, and if sowing into trays, space the seeds roughly 2cm (¾in) apart.

Thin the seedlings as they grow to one per pot. If using biodegradable pots (as above), the plants can be planted out in them and the pot will soon rot.

1 SOWING UNDER COVER

Chillies need a long growing season and should be sown under cover in early spring. Fill small pots or module trays with seed compost, water well and allow to drain. Sow the seed, water again, and place the trays or pots in a heated propagator set at 20–24°C (68–75°F). Once seedlings appear, after 7–21 days, take them out of the propagator and grow them on under cover in a warm position.

> **TIP** Instead of sowing seed, you can buy young plants later in the year.

2 GROWING ON

Grow the seedlings on under cover in a bright position, making sure they are no cooler than 18°C (64°F), even at night. Pot up module-raised plants into 10cm (4in) pots as soon as their roots fill the cells. When seedlings reach 10cm (4in) tall, start feeding them using a high-potash liquid fertilizer such as tomato feed. Plants may branch naturally, but to encourage fruiting stems, pinch out their tops when they are 20cm (8in) tall.

Pot on plants as they grow to prevent them becoming pot-bound, which will check their growth. Use a multipurpose compost.

Grow on under cover until frosts have passed and plants can be planted out. Pot indoor crops into their final containers once large enough.

3 PLANTING OUT

If you plan to grow your chilli plants outside, begin hardening them off in early summer. Once they are ready they can be potted up into containers or hanging baskets, or planted into free-draining soil in a sunny spot.
If you are growing your plants on under cover, ensure that you pot them up into containers at least 25cm (10in) wide.

Plant chillies out at the same depth as they were in their pots and water them in well. Protect from slugs with a scattering of organic pellets.

Support the plants by inserting a sturdy cane next to each one and tie it in with soft string. Use several canes to support large-fruited varieties.

Keep plants well watered all summer to encourage a good crop. Dry spells can result in stunted growth and lower yields.

Chillies crop over many weeks, and you can freeze or dry any surplus fruits. Take care not to touch your eyes after handling hot varieties.

4 ROUTINE CARE

Water plants regularly during the growing season, especially those under cover or in containers, and feed often with a liquid tomato fertilizer. If the plants are under cover, hand-pollinate the flowers using a soft paintbrush, or open doors on sunny days to give access to pollinating insects.

5 HARVESTING

Chillies mature over several weeks and can be harvested as soon as they are large enough, whether still green or fully coloured. At the end of the season, outdoor plants can either be covered with cloches or pulled from the soil and hung in a warm dry spot for any remaining fruits to ripen.

DRYING THE FRUIT

Chillies can be dried when they are green or fully ripe. The most suitable varieties for drying are those with thin skins – the fleshier types tend to decay. Lay the fruits out under cover on wire racks in a warm, dry, well-ventilated place. Fruits can also be strung together and hung up. Chillies take about a week to dry, after which they can be stored on strings or in jars.

CHILLIES

1 'Apache' This compact variety is ideal for patio containers and windowboxes as it only reaches 45cm (18in) tall. The red fruits have a medium heat and grow to 4cm (1½in) long.

2 'Alma Paprika' A mild-tasting variety, this chilli is suitable for growing in cooler areas. The rounded fruit grow to about 5cm (2in) long, and can be sliced and used in salads. The fruits are best used fresh.

3 'Hungarian Hot Wax' This is a good choice for cooler areas, producing large, pointed, mild-tasting fruits. These ripen from pale yellow to red, and when they are fully grown can be up to 11cm (4in) long.

4 'Prairie Fire' This is a prolific variety, and gives a steady crop of small, brightly coloured fruits throughout summer – they are very hot. Suitable for containers and for drying.

5 'Aji Amarillo' Bearing long, slender fruits that are particularly hot-tasting, this variety needs a warm position to grow well and usually does best under cover. The fruit can be picked green or red.

6 'Padron' This chilli produces a good crop of 5cm (2in) long fruits over several weeks that can be picked when mild and green, or left to ripen fully and heat up. It is suitable for drying.

7 Cayenne This is a type of chilli, rather than a distinct variety, and bears long curling fruit, up to 30cm (12in) long. It has thin skin, making it ideal for drying, and a hot, fiery flavour.

8 'Trinidad Perfume' This chilli has medium-sized, fruity, yellow peppers without the intense spice. The plant is compact and ideal for growing indoors or in a container.

9 'Demon Red' This variety gives a large crop of small red fruit that are thin-skinned and very hot. It is a compact plant, suitable for containers, and grows well in cooler areas.

OTHER VARIETIES
'Heatwave'
'Lemon Drop'
'Inferno'
'Ring of Fire'
'Tabasco'

AUBERGINES

Ideally, aubergines need a warm, sheltered spot but the introduction of modern hybrids and grafted plants means that they can crop well in cooler climates. One plant can produce between four and eight fruits; they fare best when they are grown in well-enriched soil in a sunny site in a greenhouse. There are many different types of aubergine available, from the classic large-fruited purple-skinned varieties to tiny, green- or white-skinned types used in Asian cooking.

	SPRING	SUMMER	AUTUMN	WINTER
SOW				
HARVEST				

TIME TO HARVEST: 24–28 WEEKS

SUITABLE FOR: BEDS AND CONTAINERS, UNDER COVER OR OUTSIDE

11 plants

3M (10FT) ROWS
Plant 30cm (12in) apart

CONTAINERS
1 plant in each

1 GETTING STARTED

Aubergines are commonly raised from seed but they can also be bought as young plants in spring. Grafted plants crop very heavily, and consist of a named fruiting variety grafted onto the vigorous root system of another. These plants are available from mail-order seed suppliers and garden centres.

'Moneymaker' is a reliable, large-fruited variety to grow under cover or outside.

'Calliope' produces a good yield of small rounded fruit. It is a good choice for pots.

'Black Enorma' is grown for its very large, dark, glossy fruit. It crops heavily and reliably.

White-fruiting plants are not widely sold but gave rise to the American common name, eggplant.

Fill small pots or modules with seed compost. Firm it in gently, water well and leave it to drain before sowing.

Sow one seed in each pot and put them in a warm propagator. Germination takes about a week, but check the pots every day.

Remove from the propagator and grow the seedlings on. They don't need pricking out, just pot them on as they grow.

2 SOWING SEEDS

Start seed under cover in early spring. Fill small pots with seed compost, firm gently, water well and allow to drain. Sow seeds on the surface, spacing them 2cm (¾in) apart and lightly press them into the surface using a pencil or dibber. Cover the seed with a little more compost, water them in, and place the pots in a heated propagator. Once seedlings are large enough to handle, prick them out into individual 10cm (4in) pots of multi-purpose compost and grow them on under cover. Feed regularly with a balanced liquid fertilizer to encourage healthy growth. Alternatively, sow individually (see left).

3 GROWING INDOORS

When roots appear through the base of the pots, repot the plants individually into containers at least 30cm (12in) wide, filled with multi-purpose compost. If you have several aubergines, plant three plants per 1-metre trough. Grow them in a sunny position under cover, such as in a greenhouse or cold frame.

Root disturbance checks growth so keep the root ball intact when potting on plants. Also avoid letting young plants become pot-bound.

4 GROWING OUTSIDE

Once all risk of frost has passed, plant aubergines out in a sunny, sheltered spot. Plant directly into the soil or grow outside in containers. Support all plants with canes and pinch out the main shoot when they reach 30cm (12in) tall to promote bushier growth.

5 ROUTINE CARE

Keep plants well watered, and as soon as the first flowers appear, switch from a general-purpose liquid feed to one high in potash to encourage fruiting. The flowers require pollination so open greenhouse doors on sunny days if growing plants under cover.

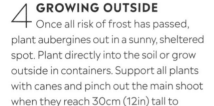

Outdoor plants should be hardened off fully before being planted out. Gradually acclimatize them to outdoor conditions over a few weeks.

Aubergine fruits become heavy as they develop. Support fruiting plants with canes and string to prevent the stems snapping.

6 HARVESTING

Harvest fruits as soon as they are large enough. The skins should still be shiny; if they are dull then the aubergines are over-ripe. Pick regularly to encourage fruiting and remove very young fruits at the end of the season to help those that remain to develop fully.

Cut ripe aubergines from the plants using secateurs. The stems can be tough and woody.

TIP Aubergines don't keep well so use them as soon as possible once picked.

FRUITING CROPS

Warmth-loving crops such as tomatoes and peppers revel in the sunniest, most sheltered spot your plot can offer, be that in the ground, a pot, or under cover. New dwarf varieties suit small spaces, while advances in breeding and propagation is helping to thwart pests and diseases and boost yields. That said, watering and good nutrition are as essential as ever.

Q How can I guarantee fruit pollination, especially under glass?

All the fruiting crops in this section are self-fertile, meaning that only one plant is needed to gain fruits. Flowers on outdoor plants are pollinated automatically by the wind shaking pollen from the male "anthers" and depositing it on the female "stigmas", and also by visiting pollinating insects. For indoor crops, gently tapping the plants in bloom or watering them overhead has the same effect, and opening windows and doors will allow access to pollinating insects.

Q My plants are very slow-growing. How can I speed them up and be sure of a good crop?

Tomatoes, peppers, chillies, and aubergines are all heat-loving, tender plants so it's crucial to provide them with sun and shelter. Some chilli peppers (especially very hot varieties) grow slowly so consider sowing these very early in the year (January or February). Also watch out for grafted plants for tomatoes and aubergines; these are named varieties that are propagated onto a vigorous rootstock. They have improved disease resistance, vigour, and consequently, produce better yields.

Q Can I overwinter my chilli plants?

Some chilli varieties, such as 'Hungarian Hot Wax', are annuals in that they are derived from *Capsicum annuum*. Others (e.g. *C. pubescens* 'Rocoto' and *C. chinense* 'Dorset Naga') have a perennial parentage and these are the ones that will overwinter. Choose pot-grown plants that are healthy (otherwise you risk overwintering pests and diseases too). Trim them back by half, keep them somewhere frost-free (minimum temperature 10°C/50°F) and well-lit, and keep the compost just moist until spring. Then re-pot and gradually increase watering and feeding.

Q What's the best way to grow fruiting crops in my tiny garden?

There are now dozens of naturally compact varieties that lend themselves perfectly to pot culture. Tomato 'Totem', chilli 'Prairie Fire', sweet pepper 'Redskin', and aubergine 'Pinstripe', are just a few of those available. Some varieties, such as tomato 'Losetto' and chilli 'Basket of Fire' also have a cascading habit, making them ideal for hanging baskets. If you have vertical space, try training a single cordon tomato such as 'Sungold' up a wall. One plant can easily grow to 1.5m (5ft) tall yet is only about 30cm (12in) wide.

PEST AND DISEASE WATCH

Here are some of the most common pests and diseases affecting fruiting crops.

- If seedlings are cut off at the stem, check the soil for creamy brown grubs called cutworms (see p.242).
- Tomatoes, peppers, and aubergines grown under cover are prone to attack from whitefly (see p.240). and aphids (see p.242), which cause sooty mould.
- Red spider mites (see p.242) cause mottled, pale leaves.
- Distorted, holey new shoots of peppers and chillies can be a sign of capsid bug damage (see p.242).
- Sunken black bases of tomato fruits indicate blossom end rot (see p.246).
- Narrow, distorted foliage can signal cucumber mosaic virus (see p.244).
- Yellowing older tomato foliage can imply a magnesium deficiency (se p.248).
- Brown blotches on tomato leaves are symptoms of blight (see p.244).
- Ghost spot (see p.248) causes white spots on the skins of tomatoes.

PEAS

All vegetables taste better when picked fresh but that is especially so with peas, which are almost like a different crop from shop-bought pods. Peas are very easy to grow, with dwarf and climbing forms that are ideal for smaller plots. Sown little and often, you can enjoy fresh peas from late spring to mid-autumn. As well as traditional podded peas, try your hand at premium types like sugar snaps and mangetout, which are expensive to buy in the shops.

	SPRING	SUMMER	AUTUMN	WINTER
SOW				
HARVEST				

TIME TO HARVEST: 12-14 WEEKS

SUITABLE FOR: BEDS AND CONTAINERS

60 plants

3M (10FT) ROWS
Sow or plant out 5cm (2in) apart

CONTAINERS
20 plants in each

1 GETTING STARTED

Peas are easy to raise from seed and come in two forms: those with smooth seeds and those with wrinkly seeds. Smooth-seeded varieties are hardier and can be sown early. Those with wrinkly seeds are sweeter tasting, and are best sown in late spring and summer. Check the packet before deciding which to sow.

'Oregon Sugar Pod' is a sugar snap variety that should be harvested as whole pods when young.

'Shiraz' is a mangetout variety with striking, purple pods and good mildew resistance.

'Meteor' produces a generous crop of sweet-tasting peas on compact plants. It is good in pots.

'Hurst Greenshaft' produces a sweet-tasting, high yield of peas over a sustained period.

In small pots, sow three seeds in each but don't thin them. Sow seeds singly in "growing tubes". Seeds should be sown 5cm (2in) deep.

Keep seedlings cool and well watered until planted out to encourage a strong root system. Their growth can be checked by poor care at this stage, reducing the eventual yield.

2 SOWING UNDER COVER

Peas can be sown in spring to plant out when the weather warms. Alternatively, for an earlier crop, they can be sown in autumn and kept under cover through the winter to plant out as larger plants in spring. Sow into cardboard "growing tubes" or deep pots filled with seed compost. Water the seeds in and they will germinate without additional heat within two weeks. Grow them on, harden them off, and plant out when the plants reach about 20cm (8in) tall.

TIP Make your own "growing tubes" using old newspaper or rolls of cardboard.

3 SOWING OUTSIDE

When the soil starts to warm up in spring, make a drill 10cm (4in) wide and 5cm (2in) deep. Water it well then space seeds 5cm (2in) apart along its length. Cover the seeds with soil, firm in gently, and water. If you are sowing in summer, water the soil well the day beforehand, and sow seed deeper than normal, at 8cm (3in).

Pea seeds need warm soil, around 10°C (50°F), in order to germinate and may fail to grow or rot off if it is too cold or wet. Space the seed evenly.

Thin any seedlings growing closer than 5cm (2in) apart. These plants can be cropped as tasty pea shoots rather than composted.

4 PROVIDING SUPPORT

Most peas are climbing plants and need support as they grow. Just after sowing or planting out, insert twiggy sticks along the row, tall enough to suit the variety you are growing (check the packet). You can also use garden twine or chicken wire held upright using sturdy canes.

5 ROUTINE CARE

Keep the plants well watered throughout summer, especially when in flower or pod. Pigeons adore pea foliage and pods, and can quickly strip plants bare. If they are a problem in your area, cover young plants with fine netting, held taut to prevent birds becoming snagged. Check for gaps.

Insert canes or pea sticks next to the young seedlings for support, or stretch lengths of jute twine along the length of the row.

Water pea plants thoroughly, especially when the flowers appear as this well help the developing pods to swell more fully.

6 HARVESTING

Tender young peas should be ready to harvest from early summer onwards. Pick them as they mature and eat them as soon as possible to enjoy them at their sweetest. If your plants produce a glut, it is better to pick them regularly and freeze them – peas store particularly well this way. Leave a few pods on the plants to dry and turn yellow at the end of summer if you want to collect your own seed.

If picked regularly, plants will crop for several weeks. Check your plants every few days.

RUNNER BEANS

One of the most productive crops you can grow, runner beans will supply a ready harvest of tender pods for most of the summer; the more you pick, the more will grow. Most runner beans are climbing plants and take up little bed space, making them a good choice for smaller plots and well-suited to vertical growing spaces on patios and balconies. The easiest way to grow them is up a wigwam of canes, which can easily be incorporated into flowering borders.

	SPRING	SUMMER	AUTUMN	WINTER
SOW				
HARVEST				
TIME TO HARVEST: 12–16 WEEKS				

SUITABLE FOR: BEDS AND CONTAINERS

15 plants

3M (10FT) ROWS
Sow direct or plant out 20cm (8in) apart

CONTAINERS
4 plants in each

1 GETTING STARTED

You can grow your own plants from seed, sowing them under cover or directly outside. Runner beans are also sold as plants in spring, which is ideal if you only want a few. As well as climbing varieties, there are also dwarf bush-types that are ideal for growing in patio containers. Position them in a sunny sheltered site.

'Moonlight' is a reliable, easy-to-grow, self-pollinating variety that has white flowers.

'White lady' has white flowers that are less attractive to birds, which may eat them.

'Lady Di' produces long, stringless pods during summer. It is a reliable variety for beginners.

'Firestorm' is a self-pollinating variety that produces long, stringless pods.

Prepare the soil by digging in well-rotted organic matter before sowing. Runner beans do best in rich, moist soil.

Insert canes either in two rows to join at the top, which can then be linked as a row, or in circles of four or five to create wigwams.

Wait until the soil is warm enough before sowing directly. It needs to be at least 12°C (54°F) for them to germinate.

2 SOWING OUTSIDE

Runner beans are tender plants and should only be sown outside once the risk of frost has passed. Before sowing, prepare the soil well by digging a trench or large circle (for wigwams) in spring, and filling it with well-rotted organic matter, such as compost or well-rotted manure. Insert canes where the plants are to grow, and sow one or two seeds 5cm (2in) deep at the base of each one. Cover the seeds with soil, firm in gently and water well. The seeds can take a couple of weeks to germinate, after which they should be thinned to the one healthy plant per cane. Protect the seedlings from slugs with a light sprinkling of organic pellets.

3 SOWING INSIDE

In cooler areas, start seeds off under cover – seed will germinate earlier and more reliably. Sow the seeds individually into pots or "growing tubes" filled with seed compost and water them well. Grow them on under cover in a bright position for a few weeks. Plant out once all risk of frost has passed. Keep them well watered.

Sow the seeds 5cm (2in) deep and water well. It's worth sowing more than you need in case some fail to come up.

Harden off the seedlings by standing them outside during the day and bringing them in at night for about two weeks.

Plant out seedlings at the base of your canes, one per support. Water the plants in well and twist the stem up the cane.

Mulch plants with plenty of well-rotted manure or garden compost. This will help to keep the root area moist and encourage the best crop.

Runner bean roots grow deep into the soil. Ensure you give your plants a good soaking so the water penetrates right down to them.

4 MULCHING

Runner beans are hungry and thirsty plants. To help conserve moisture and to feed your crop, mulch the plants in summer with well-rotted organic matter, such as garden compost. This is particularly valuable for container-grown crops.

5 ROUTINE CARE

Plants must be kept well watered once the flowers appear for the beans to set; dry spells can cause the flowers or beans to wither and fall. Pinch out the growing tips of the bean plants when the stems reach the top of the canes to promote cropping sideshoots.

6 HARVESTING

Pick the pods as soon as they are large enough. Check plants every two or three days – regular picking promotes a prolonged harvest. Beans become tough if left to grow for too long, so pick them young and tender and freeze any surpluses, or make runner bean chutney.

 TIP If you are going away in summer, ask neighbours to pick the beans for you.

To save your own seed, leave a few pods to develop fully on the plants at the end of summer. Dry and save them to sow next year.

FRENCH BEANS

Otherwise known as filet or snap beans, French beans are an easy crop for beginners and can be harvested for their plump pods or for the beans themselves. They are a good choice for smaller plots, with climbing varieties that can be trained up space-saving rows of wigwams and trellises, and bushy dwarf varieties that can be grown in containers. If you have a warm greenhouse you can even grow a batch of French beans under cover for an extra-early spring crop.

	SPRING	SUMMER	AUTUMN	WINTER
SOW				
HARVEST				

TIME TO HARVEST: 12–16 WEEKS

SUITABLE FOR: BEDS AND CONTAINERS

3M (10FT) ROWS
Sow or plant out 25cm (10in) apart

12 plants

CONTAINERS
4 plants in each

1 SOWING OUTSIDE

The simplest way to grow French beans is to sow seed in the soil in late spring. Prepare the site by digging in well-rotted organic matter, such as garden compost (this can also be done in the autumn), and remove weeds. Firm the soil and rake it level. Insert canes, 25cm (10in) apart, where climbing plants are to grow, and sow two seeds, 5cm (2in) deep, at the base of each one. Thin the seedlings to one per cane.

French beans are hungry plants and need moist soil, rich in organic matter to crop well.

Sow seed directly once the soil has warmed up in spring. Use cloches to speed up this process.

2 SOWING UNDER COVER

For an early start in cooler areas, sow under cover. Sow seed 3cm (1¼in) deep, two per pot or "growing tube" filled with seed compost. Keep them moist and germination will take about one week at 15–18°C (59–64°F).

Paper "growing tubes" are easy to make and ideal for accommodating the deep roots of bean plants.

Seedlings grow quickly so don't sow them too early unless you plan to grow them under cover.

3 GROWING ON

Grow the seedlings on under cover in a bright position until the risk of frost has passed. As they grow, thin plants sown in pots to leave the strongest seedling per pot. Once the plants reach 8cm (3in) tall, harden them off by standing them outside during the day and bringing them in at night. Any seedlings sown directly outside should be kept well watered and protected from slugs. Use bottle cloches to encourage strong growth.

Seedlings become tangled if they are not thinned early. The roots will also be hard to separate.

4 PLANTING OUT

For climbing French beans, plant out indoor-raised seedlings at the base of their canes, water them in well, and gently twine the main stem around its cane. If space is limited, it is easier to insert the canes after planting. Dwarf beans can also be planted in large pots and troughs (allowing space of at least 25cm (10in) between plants).

Carefully ease pot-raised beans from their pots. Plants raised in biodegradable tubes are planted in their tubes, which will quickly rot away.

Plant at the same depth as the plants were in their pots, firm gently and water well. Twine the young stem around the cane after planting.

Use canes at least 2.5m (8ft) tall for climbing beans, pushing them 30cm (12in) into the soil. Use soft string, such as jute, to attach the plants.

Weeds compete for water and slow down growth, so keep them under control. Remove weeds between plants by hand or hoe carefully.

5 PROVIDING SUPPORT

Climbing beans are self-clinging once established and will wrap themselves around their supports, although new growth and the occasional wayward stem may need tying in. Dwarf varieties have a bushy habit and do not require additional support or tying in.

6 ROUTINE CARE

Once the plants start to flower, keep them well watered and feed them regularly with a balanced liquid fertilizer. Dry spells may cause the flowers and young beans to drop. Protect young plants from slug and snail damage with a light scattering of organic pellets.

7 HARVESTING

Tender young pods can be picked as soon as they are large enough. Check plants every few days to harvest them at their best; picking often also encourages a larger crop. If you want to grow and keep some pods for seeds, leave them on the plant until fully mature.

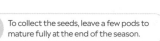

TIP To collect the seeds, leave a few pods to mature fully at the end of the season.

Pinch off the young pods before they become old and tough using your fingers.

FRENCH BEANS

1 'Selma Zebra' An heirloom climbing variety, it matures early, bearing green pods that are heavily streaked. The distinctive purple colour disappears during cooking.

2 'Borlotto' This dwarf variety produces flat pods that are heavily speckled with red. The beans can be used fresh or dried. Support the plants to keep the pods off the soil.

3 'Rocquencourt' A dwarf variety that freely bears vivid yellow pods. It is cold-tolerant and matures quickly, so is ideal for early and late sowings, if given protection.

4 'Stanley' This high-yield, dwarf variety produces straight, green pods about 14cm (5½in) long. It can be sown either early or late in the season.

5 'The Prince' Widely grown, this is a productive dwarf variety. The uniform green pods are borne steadily over a long season, which is unusual for a dwarf variety.

6 'Speedy' Quick to mature, this variety takes in the region of 60 days to produce green pods on stocky, dwarf plants. It is a good choice for early or late crops.

7 'Cobra' This climbing bean bears a long succession of tender, stringless, green pods. It also produces attractive purple flowers, making it a good choice to grow in an ornamental bed.

8 'Amethyst' Ideal for patio pots, this dwarf variety is especially compact. The purple pods are slender and stringless, and are borne over a long harvesting period.

9 'Delinel' This popular dwarf, green-podded variety bears tender pods that are totally stringless and have an excellent flavour. It is suitable for containers if watered well.

OTHER VARIETIES
'Cornetti Meraviglia di Venezia'
'Yin Yang'
'Barlotto Lingua di Fuoco'
'Cannellino'
'Polka'

BROAD BEANS

These small, tender beans are a must-grow crop because shop-bought pods just don't compare to those picked fresh from the plant. Autumn sowings are one of the first vegetables to harvest in spring, which makes them a good choice for smaller plots as they can soon be replaced with other summer crops. If space is limited, they can also be grown in containers. As well as the mature beans, the young tips and pods are also edible, so make the most of their versatility.

	SPRING	SUMMER	AUTUMN	WINTER
SOW				
HARVEST				
TIME TO HARVEST: 12–28 WEEKS				

SUITABLE FOR: BEDS AND CONTAINERS

0   1m   2m   3m

12 plants

3M (10FT) ROWS
Sow direct or plant out 25cm (10in) apart

0   40cm

CONTAINERS
6 plants in each

1 GETTING STARTED

Broad beans are usually raised from seed, although you can also buy young plants in spring. They can be grown in most soil types, although those sown directly outside in autumn need good drainage or cloche protection to prevent them rotting off in the cold and wet. Check the packets for varieties suitable for autumn sowing.

'The Sutton' can be sown in autumn or spring, and crops early on sturdy dwarf plants.

'Super Aquadulce' gives an early crop of flavoursome beans. Sow autumn or spring.

'Stereo' is best sown in spring and can be picked as whole young pods or as mature beans.

'De Monica' is one of the earliest broad bean varieties to mature from spring sowings.

2 SOW INSIDE

In cooler areas, seeds can also be started off under cover in autumn or spring to plant out later, but don't give them too much warmth. Broad beans have long tap roots, so sow the seeds individually into taller pots or "growing tubes". Germination takes a week; grow them on in a cool, light spot, keeping them frost-free.

TIP Plants grown in blocks help to hold each other up.

Tall "growing tubes", which you can buy or make, are ideal for sowing beans under cover.

3 SOWING OUTSIDE

Broad beans can be sown directly into the soil during autumn or early spring. Fork the soil over first, add compost or well-rotted manure, and either sow into drills or into a grid pattern of individual holes, 25cm (10in) apart.

Broad beans absorb nitrogen from the air and fix it in the soil. They don't require heavy feeding.

Sow the seed 5cm (2in) deep directly into beds or pots. Cover with soil, firm gently, and water in well.

4 PLANTING OUT

When indoor-sown plants are showing strong growth, harden them off for a week or two to acclimatize them to outdoor temperatures. Dig over the site thoroughly, and plant them out 25cm (10in) apart each way. If you are planting them in blocks, additional support is not usually necessary, except on more exposed sites.

Harden off plants before planting them out in autumn or spring. Stand them outside in the day, bringing them in at night.

Seedlings in biodegradable "tubes" can be planted as they are; the roots will penetrate and the tube will rot away.

Protect seedlings with fleece if hard frosts are due straight after planting. Direct-sown plants don't require protection.

Young plants should be well-watered at first but soon develop a deep tap root. On lighter soils, mulch plants with compost to retain moisture.

Pinching out tips encourages the bean pods to develop, and also provides an early crop of tasty leaves, which are delicious when steamed.

5 ROUTINE CARE

Broad beans require little care once they are growing strongly, and need only watering in summer when plants are flowering. Plants should be kept well weeded until they establish. Broad beans in rows may need support from strings staked on each side of the row.

6 PINCHING OUT

When the first flowers begin to set pods, pinch out the soft growing tip of each plant. This causes the plants to focus on developing pods rather than leafy growth, and also deters blackfly (see p.242), which feed on the shoots during late spring and summer.

7 HARVESTING

Crops sown in autumn are ready to harvest in late spring. Pods are best harvested before the developing beans create visible swellings in the pods. All broad beans are best picked while young, so pick and freeze any that you can't use straightaway. After harvesting, you can cut the plants to the ground but leave the roots in the soil to break down. They will release their stored nitrogen for the next crop to use.

Broad beans are best eaten fresh but will keep well in their pods in the fridge for a few days.

PODDED CROPS

Hardier peas and broad beans thrive in autumn and spring, and as soon as conditions warm up, French and runner beans join them. Vigorous climbers make use of vertical space, and for smaller gardens compact varieties are available. Feed established plants to produce generous yields, and pick regularly, even daily in high summer, to encourage more pods to form.

Q My broad bean flowers are being eaten by bees – what can I do?

You're witnessing "robbing" on your broad beans, where short-tongued bumblebee species (e.g. buff- and white-tailed) create a hole at the flower's base to reach the nectaries more easily. This method of nectar gathering bypasses the anthers so that the flower isn't pollinated. Don't worry – there should be enough long-tongued bees pollinating your broad bean flowers for sufficient pods to set.

Q After I planted out my pea seedlings, they disappeared almost overnight – what happened to them?

Pea seedlings are as delicious as podded peas, so it's likely that slugs, mice, or birds gorged on your transplants. Slugs leave silvery slime trails on remaining seedlings and the surrounding soil – a scattering of organic pellets will deter them in future. If you plant out larger, more robust plants, they will be less vulnerable. Mice nip off seedlings at their base with a clean cut; setting humane traps will help to catch them (sultanas and chocolate are good baits). Birds such as pigeons can quickly shred a row of peas – you may still see tattered foliage if these were the culprits. Netting the plants will thwart them.

Q After giving a good initial harvest, my peas seem to have stopped cropping. Why?

Peas, like many other podded plants, will regulate the amount of flowers they develop. If plants are large and healthy they'll set generous numbers of pods. Pick these before they mature because harvesting peas while they're young gives you the most tender crop and will encourage your plants to produce more flowers. Seeds that are allowed to mature on the plant demand excess resources and trigger the plant to cease flowering.

Q The beans that I see on allotments are often large plants. Is it possible to grow them in containers on my patio?

While climbing beans can become sizeable plants, there are plenty of dwarf and compact varieties. For dwarf runner beans that grow to only 50cm (20in) tall, look for varieties such as 'Millionaire' and 'Hestia'. 'The Sutton' and 'Robin Hood' are compact broad beans that only grow 40–50cm (16–20in) tall. The numerous varieties of dwarf French beans include purple-podded 'Amethyst', yellow-podded 'Golddukat', and green-podded 'Safari'. Finally, 'Little Marvel' and 'Half Pint' are excellent dwarf varieties of peas.

PEST AND DISEASE WATCH

Once established, podded crops can tolerate a degree of damage, but watch out for the following.

- Slugs (see p. 242) can devour seedlings at the sowing and transplanting stage.
- Seedlings may collapse or damp off (see p. 248) if overwatered and/or chilled.
- Watch young growing tips in case they become smothered by blackfly (aphid) colonies (see p. 242).
- If you find maggots within pea pods (pea moth, see p. 240), sow early next time.
- Small, semi-circular notches cut around the edge of pea and broad bean leaves is indicative of pea and bean weevil (see p. 242).
- Powdery mildew (see p. 246) affects peas – look for white coating on the leaves and try resistant varieties.
- Climbing beans can be vulnerable to leaf scorch (see p. 246) if they are grown on windy sites.
- Rust (see p. 244) can be troublesome on broad and runner beans, as can chocolate spot (see p. 248) on broad beans, although mature plants will still crop.

CUCUMBERS

These summer salad stalwarts are easy to grow in any garden, and although some varieties require a greenhouse to crop well, "ridge" varieties are perfectly happy outside. These can be left to sprawl over the ground, or where space is limited, they can be trained up stout canes or trellises, making good use of vertical surfaces. Small-fruited "snacking" cucumbers are particularly productive and convenient, with fruit just large enough for a lunch box.

	SPRING	SUMMER	AUTUMN	WINTER
SOW				
HARVEST				

TIME TO HARVEST: 16-20 WEEKS

SUITABLE FOR: BEDS AND CONTAINERS, UNDER COVER OR OUTSIDE

11 plants

3M (10FT) ROWS
Plant 30cm (12in) apart

CONTAINERS
1 plant in each

1 GETTING STARTED

Cucumbers can be raised from seed, which is ideal if you want a large crop. They can also be bought as seedlings in spring, which may be a better choice if you only want a few plants. Cucumbers are productive, and depending on the variety, just two or three plants will be enough for most families all summer.

'Mini Munch' is a heavy-cropping, "snackbox" variety. Fruits are harvested small.

'Passandra' grows indoors and gives a large crop of small, single-serving fruits.

'Marketmore' is reliable with good disease resistance and is suited to being grown outside.

'Crystal Apple' bears a good crop of small, round, juicy fruits. It is easy to grow outside.

Cucumber seed can be expensive. Sow one seed per pot and keep them warm, 22-25ºC (72-77ºF), to encourage germination.

Check the seed regularly until they germinate, which should take a week or two. Remove them from the propagator and grow them on indoors.

2 SOWING SEEDS

Cucumber seeds should be started off under cover because plants are very sensitive to the cold and need a long growing season to fruit well. Hybrid seeds may be more expensive but they result in more vigorous, productive plants, so are worth the extra expense. Fill 10cm (4in) diameter pots with seed compost, water well and allow to drain. Sow one seed per pot, 2cm (¾in) deep, water them lightly, and put them in a heated propagator to germinate.

TIP Cucumbers require constantly high temperatures, so don't sow too early.

3 PLANTING OUT

Once they are large enough, plant cucumbers out in early summer – enrich the soil thoroughly in advance. Outdoor "ridge" varieties can be planted directly into the soil in a sunny spot and left to trail across the surface, or can be trained up canes. Greenhouse-types can be planted one per 30cm (12in) pot.

Outdoor varieties should be hardened off for a few weeks before planting to acclimatize them to outdoor conditions.

Insert canes to train plants upwards where space is limited. This also keeps the fruit clean and away from crawling pests.

Containers are ideal for greenhouse crops but they can also be used outside. Allow the soil to warm up before planting.

4 POLLINATION

Outdoor varieties have both male and female flowers; the latter must be pollinated to set fruit. Many modern greenhouse varieties are "all female" and must not be pollinated because they then produce bitter-tasting fruits. Grow these well away from varieties that produce male flowers.

Female flowers have an embryonic fruit behind the petals. These must be pollinated unless the variety is "all female". Check before you buy.

5 ROUTINE CARE

Keep plants well watered, and apply tomato fertilizer regularly, as directed. Indoor plants thrive in high humidity, which you can achieve by watering the ground around the plants. This also helps to deter red spider mite (see p.242) and powdery mildew (see p.246), which are both common.

Swelling cucumbers become heavy, especially on mature plants with several fruits, so make sure the stems are attached to their supports,

6 HARVESTING

As soon as individual fruits are large enough, cut them from the plants using secateurs. Cucumbers grow quickly and their quality declines if they are left too long on the plant. To enjoy them at their best, check plants daily and harvest them as soon as they are ready. The fruit can be stored in the fridge until needed. If you expect a glut, very young fruits can be harvested as gherkins and used for pickling.

Some cucumbers are smooth-skinned, others have small prickles but both types taste just as good as each other.

COURGETTES AND MARROWS

Courgettes are notoriously productive – just two or three plants are all you need to be self-sufficient in them throughout the summer. They require a rich soil but are extremely easy to grow either directly in the ground or in containers. There are many varieties to choose from; their green or yellow fruits can either be round or elongated. Left to mature, your courgettes will develop into marrows, ideal for autumn stews and bakes.

	SPRING	SUMMER	AUTUMN	WINTER
SOW				
HARVEST				

TIME TO HARVEST: 14 WEEKS

SUITABLE FOR: BEDS AND CONTAINERS, UNDER COVER OR OUTSIDE

11 plants

3M (10FT) ROWS
Plant 90cm (36in) apart

CONTAINERS
1 plant in each

1 GETTING STARTED

Courgettes are very easy to raise from seed, which is the best choice if you want to grow a particular variety. Alternatively, young plants are widely available to buy during spring. Courgettes crop very quickly, so consider yellow-fruited varieties as the fruits are much easier to spot amongst the dense foliage.

'Parthenon' doesn't require pollination, so sets early and reliably even in poor conditons.

'Defender' is resistant to cucumber mosaic virus (see p.244) and crops very heavily.

'Jemmer' produces attractive yellow fruits that stand out clearly among the dense leaves.

'Shooting Star' is a golden-skinned, climbing variety suited to smaller spaces.

Sow seeds into 10cm (4in) wide pots part-filled with seed or multi-purpose compost. Cover the seeds lightly with more compost and water them in.

Direct sow seeds in pairs 3cm (1¼in) deep, 90cm (36in) apart, in early summer. Water well and cover them with mini cloches. When seedlings are large enough to handle, thin each pair to one seedling.

2 SOWING SEEDS

Courgettes are tender plants, and it is useful to sow seeds under cover to give them a head start after the frosts pass. Sow seed singly in pots, 2.5cm (1in) deep, and place them in a heated propagator set at 20°C (68°F) until germinated. Seed can also be sown directly outside in early summer, and provide a useful second flush of crops to follow indoor-raised plants. Choose a sunny, sheltered site, and dig in some organic matter before sowing.

TIP Non-fruiting, male courgette flowers can be harvested and cooked.

3 GROWING ON

Grow the plants on under cover at a temperature of 18°C (64°F). Keep them well watered and begin feeding them with a balanced liquid fertilizer after two weeks. Plants will grow quickly and may need potting on if roots appear at the base of the pots. Harden them off and plant out in beds, or one plant per 50cm (12in) pot.

Seedlings sown early may need to be potted on if they outgrow their pots when it is still too early to plant them out.

Plants sown in later spring can be hardened off during the daytime as soon as the risk of frost has passed.

After planting out your hardened-off plants, you can cover them with cloches to help them establish more quickly.

4 WATERING

Courgettes are quick growing and fruiting, and should be kept well-watered throughout summer. To make this easier, create a well around individual plants for water to collect in, or plunge a funnel (an upturned bottle with the base cut off works well) next to each plant for direct watering.

5 ROUTINE CARE

Young plants need weeding until established when their dense canopy of leaves will smother other competing plants. Most courgettes form a large rosette of leaves but some newer varieties have a trailing habit and can be trained up canes. On older plants, regularly remove any yellowing leaves.

Courgettes plants need regular watering while they are developing to produce a broad canopy of leaves and a steady supply of fruit.

Powdery mildew (see p.246) can develop on the foliage and weaken plants. Remove heavily affected leaves and water more regularly.

6 HARVESTING

Using a sharp knife, harvest traditional courgettes when they measure between 8–15cm (3–6in) long; round-fruited varieties should be picked when 7–12cm (3–5in) in diameter. Check over the plants daily as the fruit develop very quickly in summer. Alternatively, leave the fruits on one or two plants to develop fully. These plants will then give a smaller crop of thick-skinned marrows to harvest in late summer.

Keep harvesting young fruits – if they are allowed to grow on, they will become marrows but fewer fruit will be produced as a result.

SUMMER SQUASHES

A close relative of courgettes, summer squash are very easy to grow, and some can be trained upwards, making them ideal for smaller plots. They come in a wide selection of shapes and sizes, including scallop-edged "patty pans" and crook-necked, vase-shaped varieties; all are extremely free-fruiting. The fruits are either harvested when small and thin-skinned to eat whole, or can be left to grow large enough to stuff and roast whole.

	SPRING	SUMMER	AUTUMN	WINTER
SOW				
HARVEST				

TIME TO HARVEST: 14–20 WEEKS

SUITABLE FOR: BEDS AND CONTAINERS

3M (10FT) ROWS
2–3 plants
Plant 1–1.5m (3–5ft) apart, depending on variety

CONTAINERS
1 plant in each

1 GETTING STARTED

Only a few varieties of summer squash are commonly sold as young plants, so they are best raised from seed. The plants crop heavily – two or three will give a good supply of fruit all summer, so don't grow more than you need. The fruits can be harvested while young to help you to keep on top of summer gluts.

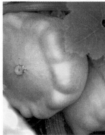

Patty pan is a type not a variety, and there are yellow, green, and white forms to grow.

'Sunburst' can be picked as young fruit or left to grow on. It crops freely if harvested often.

'Tromboncino' is best harvested when 30cm (12in) long, but can reach 1m (3ft) if left to grow on.

'Rolet' gives a good crop of round, cricket ball-sized fruits, that have sweet-tasting flesh.

Sow seed under cover into 10cm (4in) wide pots, 2cm (¾in) deep and cover with compost. Water them in and place the pots in a propagator.

To sow direct, first prepare a seedbed and sow the seeds 2cm (¾in) deep, 90cm (36in) apart. Position each seed on its side to help prevent it rotting.

2 SOWING SEEDS

For an early start, sow seeds under cover into individual pots and place them in a heated propagator set at 20°C (68°F) until they germinate. Once the seedlings emerge, grow them on under cover at 18°C (64°F) in a bright spot. After about a fortnight start feeding weekly with liquid fertilizer. Seeds can also be sown directly into the soil in early summer. Sow seeds in pairs, water them in, and cover with a cloche. When seedlings emerge, thin each pair and leave the stronger plant to grow on.

TIP Summer squash prefer rich soil, so dig in organic matter before planting.

GROW YOUR OWN VEGETABLES **CUCURBITS**

3 GROWING ON

Plants raised under cover should be grown on until the risk of frost has passed, then hardened off before they are planted out. Space them 1–1.5m (3–5ft) apart, and water them in well. To get water to the roots when watering, bury a flower pot next to each plant to act as a funnel. Plants can also be grown one per 50cm (12in) container.

Harden off seedlings for a few weeks before planting out, placing them outside during the day but bringing them back under cover at night.

Trailing summer squash varieties can be planted beneath taller crops, such as sweetcorn or tomatoes, or near rows of climbing beans.

4 ROUTINE CARE

Summer squashes are vigorous plants, and should be watered well and fed regularly with tomato fertilizer. To help conserve soil moisture, mulch around plants with a thick layer of compost or similar organic material. The mulch will gradually break down and release nutrients to the plants.

Mulch to help maintain moisture – if fruiting plants are allowed to dry out or are watered irregularly, fruits may be aborted.

5 TRAINING

Most varieties are trailing plants and can be left to creep across the soil. To make harvesting easier, gradually remove the surrounding leaves as they grow, to provide access to the fruit. If space is limited, the stems can also be looped into circles on the ground or trained vertically up cane wigwams.

Train trailing squash stems along the edges of beds or paths so the fruits are easy to pick. This will also free up bed space for other crops.

6 HARVESTING

Squashes produce separate male and female flowers on the same plant, but only the female flowers fruit. The flowers wither as soon as they are pollinated and the fruit begins to develop. Young, tender squash will be ready to harvest after four to seven days, depending on the weather. They can be left to grow longer for larger fruit that are ideal for stuffing and roasting.

Squashes that develop a thick skin before harvesting in summer will keep longer in storage.

WINTER SQUASHES

Winter squashes are available in a huge range of shapes and colours, and provide a delicious feast in late autumn and winter, especially when roasted or in soups. Easy to grow, they can be left to trail across the ground and make good use of the space between your other crops. They can also be grown in containers, with the stems trained to make a feature of the decorative fruit. If you have space for storage, the fruits will keep and last well into the winter months.

	SPRING	SUMMER	AUTUMN	WINTER
SOW				
HARVEST				

TIME TO HARVEST: 18–20 WEEKS

SUITABLE FOR: BEDS AND CONTAINERS

2–3 plants

3M (10FT) ROWS
Sow or plant 1–1.5m (3–5ft) apart

CONTAINERS
1 plants in each

1 SOWING UNDER COVER

Winter squash are tender but can be sown under cover in spring to plant out when any danger of frosts has passed. Fill 10cm (4in) pots with seed compost, water them well, and then leave them to drain. Sow one seed per pot at a depth of 3cm (1¼in). Place the pots in a heated propagator set at 20°C (68°F) for a week or two. Once the seedlings emerge, grow them on in a warm, bright position.

Sow the seeds individually at a depth of 3cm (1¼in), cover lightly with soil, and place in a heated propagator for one or two weeks.

Winter squash seedlings grow quickly but can only be planted out after the last frosts, so don't sow them too early. Pot them on if necessary.

Direct-sow seed at the base of a sturdy support if you plan to train your squash plants as climbers. Seed can also be sown beneath tall crops.

Thin surplus seedlings to leave the strongest. If you have unfilled gaps, transplant spare plants to where they are needed. Water in well.

2 SOWING OUTSIDE

Sow seeds direct in late spring. First, prepare the soil by digging in plenty of well-rotted manure or compost, and remove weeds. Then firm and rake level. For an earlier crop, warm the soil first with cloches. Sow seeds in pairs, 3cm (1¼in) deep and 1m (3ft) apart, water well, and cover with a cloche. As each group of seedlings emerges, thin them to leave only the strongest plant. Protect plants from slugs and snails.

TIP Placing a tile under large squash helps to prevent them rotting on wet soil.

3 PLANTING OUT

Plants sown under cover can be planted out into their final positions in early summer. Before doing so, harden them off to acclimatize them to outdoor conditions. Place them outside during the day for two weeks, bringing them back in each night. Plant out at 1m (3ft) apart and water them in well. Protect young plants from slugs.

Water the plants well before planting them out to help their roots establish successfully.

Plant out at the same depth as the plants were in their pots and firm them in gently.

Water in well and keep plants moist until they are growing well, especially on lighter soils.

4 ROUTINE CARE

Plants require plenty of water during the summer months; to make watering easier and get water down to the roots, push a plant pot vertically into the soil beside each plant. Feed plants with a regular application of a general-purpose liquid fertilizer, as directed on the instructions.

Mulch plants with well-rotted compost to help retain moisture, especially on lighter soils. The mulch will break down, feeding your plants.

5 TRAINING

Winter squash are either bushy, or trailing. Bush-types form neat clumps of leaves, whereas trailing plants send out long, winding stems. These can be trained into loops if space is limited, or allowed to ramble among other plants. You can also train smaller-fruited varieties up trellis work or canes.

Trailing stems can be looped around canes to form circles, or trained up supports. Both methods will contain the plants' spread in smaller gardens.

6 HARVESTING

In mid-autumn the leaves will start to die back and the fruits should be colouring up well. Fruits need to be harvested before the first frosts. Cut them from the plant, leaving a short length of stem attached to act as a handle. Leave them in a warm, dry sunny spot for two weeks to harden the skins – windowsills are ideal. The fruits can then be stored indoors until needed.

Colourful fruits can be used for temporary seasonal decoration until needed in the kitchen.

WINTER SQUASHES

1 **'Sweet Dumpling'** This trailing variety bears slightly ribbed, white-skinned fruits with green vertical stripes. Each fruit grows 12–15cm (5–6in) in diameter, with yellow flesh.

2 **'Uchiki Kuri'** Also known as the "onion squash", this trailing variety bears delicious fruits with intense orange flesh. Expect to harvest five or six fruits per plant.

3 **'Queensland Blue'** This heirloom Australian variety bears heavily-ribbed grey-blue fruits. They reach 25cm (10in) in diameter, and have intensely nutty, orange flesh.

4 **'Butternut'** These classically shaped squashes are borne on trailing plants. With deep orange flesh and few seeds, they are ideal for roasting or stuffing. They also store well.

5 **'Marina di Chioggia'** This Italian heirloom variety produces fruit of up to 5kg (10lb) in weight. Fruits have yellow–orange flesh and can be stored for up to six months.

6 **Turk's Turban** A trailing-type with sweet flesh, it bears unusually shaped orange fruits with bold green and white stripes. The fruits grow to 20–25cm (8–10in) in diameter.

7 **'Crown Prince'** This trailing plant bears round, squat, grey-blue fruits, 20–25cm (8–10in) in diameter. The deep orange flesh has a very good nutty flavour when cooked.

8 **'Harlequin'** With its highly coloured fruit, this is an attractive variety to grow where space is limited and plants need to look, as well as produce a good harvest.

9 **Vegetable spaghetti** When steamed, the mild-tasting flesh of this trailing crop separates into spaghetti-like strands. Expect three or four large fruits per plant.

OTHER VARIETIES
'Butterbush'
'Butternut Harrier'
'Celebration'
'Sunshine'

1

2   3

6

PUMPKINS

Mammoth pumpkins take up a lot of space in the garden, but there are plenty of varieties with smaller fruits that are ideal where space is limited – some can even be planted in containers. Pumpkins are reliable and easy to grow. All they need is a good supply of water and fertile soil, and some protection against slugs and snails. Although pumpkins are associated with lantern-carving at Halloween, the fruits have tasty sweet flesh and store well into winter.

	SPRING	SUMMER	AUTUMN	WINTER
SOW				
HARVEST				

TIME TO HARVEST: 18–22 WEEKS

SUITABLE FOR: BEDS AND CONTAINERS

0 1m 2m 3m
2–3 plants

3M (10FT) ROWS
Plant 1–1.5m (3–5ft) apart, depending on variety

0 50cm

CONTAINERS
1 plants in each

1 GETTING STARTED

Pumpkins may be sold as plants in spring but they are usually grown from seed, and there are many varieties to choose from. If you want large fruits for carving, pick a suitable variety and thin the fruits to one or two per plant. For edible fruits, choose your variety and let each plant develop four or five fruits each.

'Atlantic Giant' is one of the largest fruiting varieties and can be eaten if picked early.

'Jack be Little' bears small, brightly coloured fruits that are tasty as well as decorative.

'Rouge Vif d'Etampes' is an heirloom variety, with large fruits, good for eating or decoration.

'Baby Bear' is a compact variety with thin-skinned fruits, each the size of a football.

Sow seed individually 2cm (¾in) deep into 10cm (4in) wide pots and place them in a warm propagator set at 20–25°C (68–77°F).

Check the seeds daily until they germinate, which takes between one and two weeks. Remove the pots from the propagator and grow them on under cover.

2 SOWING UNDER COVER

Large pumpkins need a long growing season to develop full-size fruits. Start them off under cover in spring, especially in cold areas, and then harden them off and plant outside when the frosts have passed. Part-fill small pots with seed compost, sow one seed per pot, water well, and allow to drain. Place pots in a heated propagator at 20°C (68°F) and keep the compost moist. When seeds germinate, grow seedlings on under cover for a few weeks in a bright spot.

TIP Sow smaller-fruited pumpkins direct into the soil in early summer.

3 SOWING OUTSIDE

In early summer, seeds can also be sown directly into the soil. Well before sowing, improve the soil with well-rotted organic matter, such as garden compost, then sow the seeds 3cm (1¼in) deep and 1m (3ft) apart. Water them well, and when seedlings start to emerge, cover them with a cloche. Keep the plants well-watered as they grow on.

Sow outdoor seed in groups of two or three in case any fail to grow. You can then thin to the strongest seedling as they start to develop.

Carefully transplant stronger spare seedlings if they are needed elsewhere on the bed. Lift them with a trowel and water them well once planted.

4 ROUTINE CARE

Pumpkins are hungry plants and will benefit from regular feeding with a liquid general-purpose fertilizer. Young plants need weeding until they establish fully. To keep the fruits clean and off the soil, place a short plank of wood under each one.

5 TRAINING

Most pumpkins produce trailing stems and can be left to ramble over the ground among other plants. Where space is limited, tie the stems to canes set out in a circle and pushed into the soil. Small-fruited varieties can also be trained up sturdy supports.

Mulching plants with well-rotted organic matter, such as garden compost, will help retain moisture in summer. It will also feed your plants.

Where space is limited, train pumpkin plants vertically, using nets to support the swelling fruit. Tie the stems in as they grow.

6 HARVESTING

In mid-autumn your fruits will be ready for harvest. Cut them with a short length of stalk attached to prevent the stem from rotting back into the fruit, and to provide a handy carrying handle. Unless you plan to use them straightaway, dry or "cure" the skins by leaving them in a sunny spot outside for at least a week. If rain is predicted, move them to a bright position under cover. The fruit will store well for months.

Small pumpkins can be cooked whole; larger fruits should be cut into manageable pieces.

CUCURBITS

Quick-to-grow with generous foliage, cucurbits thrive in warm, moist soils. The huge yellow flowers attract pollinating insects, and regular feeding satisfies the voracious appetite of these plants. Pest attacks are often tolerated by mature plants, and diseases such as powdery mildew manifest only after a respectable harvest has been gathered.

Q My pumpkins are producing male flowers but no female ones, why is that?

This phenomenon often occurs at the beginning of the growing season. It can cause frustration for gardeners because only the female flowers (which have a tiny embryonic fruitlet behind them) bear fruit. Usually, as the season progresses plants develop a balance of female and male flowers. However, excess male blooms can occur if plants are in too much shade, are being fed too much high-nitrogen fertilizer, or are weak and stressed, so these issues should be remedied.

Q Why are my courgette fruitlets rotting off before they get to a harvestable size?

Fruitlets rotting at the flower end can signal that the plant has set too much fruit, and this triggers the plant to abort some of its crop. Regular harvesting before the courgettes get too large can reduce the problem. Rotting fruitlets may also be caused by incomplete pollination by bees and visiting insects: fertilization often fails in windy or wet weather. If the problem persists, grow courgette 'Parthenon' which can set fruit without pollination.

Q Why has one of my greenhouse cucumber plants wilted and collapsed, despite being full of fruits?

Greenhouse cucumbers thrive in warm, humid environments. These growing conditions can, however, encourage fungal rots (especially *Fusarium* species) to form on the plant's root system. Perhaps your plant became chilled, or excessively hot – both conditions would cause root stress, making plants especially vulnerable to fungal rots. Once the main stem rots the whole plant can quickly collapse. Deter by ventilating well on hot days, shutting vents on cool nights, and avoiding overwatering. Consider changing your greenhouse border soil if the problem recurs annually.

Q I've been told that my winter squash 'Crown Prince' will store well into the spring – what should I do to make this work?

'Crown Prince' is a delicious winter squash with excellent keeping qualities. The key to longevity in storage is for fruits to develop an unblemished, well-cured skin. Achieve this by exposing your ripening squashes to sufficient sunlight. Periodically cut off any leaves that shade the fruits during summer. Standing them on a slate or tile can deter skin blemishes. In late autumn (but before the first frosts) cut unblemished fruits from the plant with a short length of stem attached. Keep them somewhere sunny, airy, and frost-free (a heated greenhouse or windowsill is ideal) until needed.

PEST AND DISEASE WATCH

Here are some of the most common pests and diseases affecting cucurbits.

- Slugs and snails (see p.242) can damage plants, especially on moist, warm nights when feeding activity is high. Seedlings are most vulnerable – check for any trace of silvery slime trails.
- Aphids (see p.242) can congregate on growing points, sucking sap and, if populations are large, weakening young plants.
- Tiny yellow and white flecks on the foliage can be indicative of red spider mite (see p.242).
- Yellowing veins and distorted foliage and fruits suggest a cucumber mosaic virus infection (see p.244).
- A white, dust-like coating over the upper leaf surface indicates powdery mildew attack (see p.246) but it can be tolerated if occurring late in the growing season.
- Clouds of tiny white flies appearing when leaves are disturbed signals whitefly infestation (see p.240).

SUMMER AND AUTUMN CABBAGES

Whether you eat cabbage leaves as part of your classic Sunday roast or use them in dishes such as stir-fries, they are a mainstay crop for your vegetable patch. Cabbages can be grown throughout the year, with summer and autumn varieties producing a large, reliable harvest if they are kept well-watered and covered with nets. Once harvested, the stumps can be left in the ground to re-sprout and give a second crop of loose leaves, making the best use of your plot.

	SPRING	SUMMER	AUTUMN	WINTER
SOW				
HARVEST				

TIME TO HARVEST: 18–24 WEEKS

SUITABLE FOR: BEDS AND CONTAINERS

8 plants

3M (10FT) ROWS
Plant 40cm (16in) apart

CONTAINERS
3 plants in each

Sow the seeds thinly and check them daily until seedlings emerge. They don't need additional heat.

Thin seedlings as they develop in their trays; those left can be pricked out into small pots.

1 SOWING UNDER COVER

For an early harvest, sow summer varieties under cover in spring. Fill trays or modules with seed compost, water well, allow to drain, then sow the seeds 2cm (¾in) deep. When the seedlings appear, thin them out to leave the strongest, then prick the remaining seedlings out into small pots. Grow the young plants on indoors in a cool, bright spot for a few weeks longer.

TIP Cabbages, like most brassicas, are prone to club root (see p.246).

2 SOWING OUTSIDE

Although cabbages are often sown under cover, they can also be sown outside directly into the soil. A few weeks before sowing, dig over the soil, remove any weeds, firm it, and then rake the surface level. Excavate a drill 2cm (¾in) deep, water it well, and then sow the seeds thinly along the base. Cover over with soil, firm gently, and water lightly. When the seedlings have a few leaves, thin them out, leaving the strongest. Water regularly and protect plants from slugs and snails.

Carefully tip seeds, directly from the packet or use your fingers to sow them in pinches.

Thin the seedlings to their final spacings or transplant them once they reach 15cm (6in) tall.

3 PLANTING OUT

Once large enough, move the young plants, raised indoors or out, to their final positions. Prepare the area first by digging it over, removing weeds, and applying some high-nitrogen granular fertilizer. Water the young plants well and lift them from the seedbed, or from their trays or pots, and plant them out 40cm (16in) apart.

Transplant young plants carefully to minimize root loss or disturbance, which can check growth. Water in well after planting.

Young plants are vulnerable to attack from various different pests, including aphids (see p.242). Check for damage and infestations.

4 ROUTINE CARE

Keep beds weeded until plants are well established, by which time their foliage will suppress weeds. Water regularly, especially during hot or dry spells, and apply a balanced liquid feed, as directed by the manufacturers, to promote strong, leafy growth.

Water well directing the flow at the base of the plants. On lighter soils, mulch to help retain moisture or lay pieces of cardboard.

5 PROTECTING PLANTS

Fit brassica collars around each plant to deter cabbage root fly (see p.242). At the same time, cover plants with fine netting to protect against cabbage white caterpillars (see p.240) and pigeons. Keep the netting pulled taut and check regularly for holes.

Cover with fine netting to prevent cabbage white butterflies from laying eggs on your plants. Use canes to hold it clear of the leaves.

6 HARVESTING

The plants are ready to harvest from late summer onwards, once they have fully-formed, leafy heads. To harvest, either cut through the tough stalk with a sharp knife or lift the roots using a fork. Mature plants can be left in the ground for a few weeks but will gradually deteriorate. Trim off the outer, tougher leaves and use only the tender heart. Cut heads can be stored in a fridge for about a week.

Harvest young cabbages, picking every other one in a row, to allow others space to mature.

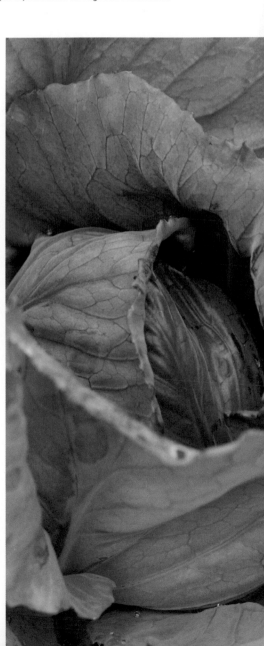

SUMMER CABBAGES

1 'Greyhound' This reliable, fast-maturing variety forms loose leafy heads with few tough stalks. If sown in spring, the first heads can be harvested in early summer.

2 'Derby Day' An early summer variety, this cabbage produces rounded heads, tightly packed with tender leaves. It is the earliest "ball" cabbage to mature during the season.

3 'Kalibos' This heirloom variety develops small, pointed heads, packed with deep red leaves. It can be used raw in salads if chopped finely, or eat it lightly boiled instead.

4 'Duncan' This quick-maturing variety forms loose, pointed heads. It is a versatile choice that can be sown in spring to harvest in autumn, or sown in autumn to crop in spring.

5 'Red Jewel' This variety produces dense, round heads, tightly packed with dark red leaves that retain their colour well when cooked. It is good for storing and also keeps well in the soil.

6 'Tinty' This variety has the shape and colour of a red cabbage, but the flavour and softer, thinner leaves of a green cabbage.

7 'Stonehead' These mid-size, compact plants can be grown closely together, making best use of smaller plots. The heads will last well in the soil during autumn until needed.

8 'Dutchman' This variety produces pointed heads with great flavour. It is compact, so works well in a small space. Harvest from late summer to early autumn.

9 'Hispi' This cabbage is very quick to mature, and can also be sown in autumn to harvest in spring. It forms neat, pointed heads of tasty leaves, and is a good choice for smaller gardens.

OTHER VARIETIES
'Elisa'
'Excel'
'Kilaton'
'Primo'
'Green Express'
'Golden Acre'

WINTER AND SPRING CABBAGES

From deep green, crinkle-leaved savoys to pointed, dense-hearted spring cabbages, these hardy brassicas are invaluable during the leaner months of the year. Spring-cropping plants can be packed tightly together, making efficient use of small plots. They also give a useful secondary crop of loose leaves in spring if the cut stumps are left to grow back. Always cover your crops with netting to protect them from pests such as pigeons and caterpillars.

	SPRING	SUMMER	AUTUMN	WINTER
SOW				
HARVEST				
TIME TO HARVEST: 26–28 WEEKS				

SUITABLE FOR: BEDS

0   1m   2m   3m

7–11 plants

3M (10FT) ROWS
Plant out 30–50cm (12–20in) apart, depending on variety

1 GETTING STARTED

The best way to raise both winter and spring cabbages is from seed, sown under cover in late spring. You can also sow seeds indoors in summer and then plant out or sow them directly into the soil outdoors. Alternatively, if you are planning to grow just a few cabbages, you can buy young plants in summer, which is an easier but more costly option.

'Tundra' is a winter variety that can be left in the ground for several weeks until needed.

'Traviata' has dense heads of crinkled leaves with great flavour, and good disease resistance.

'January King' can be cropped in autumn as young heads, or left to mature through winter.

'Kilaton' produces dense, round autumn cabbages and has good resistance to club root.

Cabbage seeds are reliable but sow two to a cell, just in case one fails. They are large and easy to handle, allowing you to sow them accurately.

Grow the seedlings on in a bright position under cover for two or three weeks, until they can be planted out into beds. Keep them cool but frost-free.

2 SOWING UNDER COVER

Raising plants under cover helps reduce the effects of club root disease on your plants (see p.244). Fill module trays with seed compost, water well and allow to drain. Make holes 1cm (½in) deep in each cell, sow one seed in each, then thin to leave the strongest seedling once they emerge. Grow the young plants on under cover until 15cm (6in) tall. Prepare them for outdoor conditions by moving them outside during the day, then back in at night.

TIP Acclimatize plants to outdoor temperatures for about two weeks.

3 SOWING OUTDOORS

Cabbages can be sown outside in summer when the soil has warmed up and transplanted at seedling stage. Prepare a seedbed by digging over the soil, removing weeds, and raking it level. Make drills, 2cm (¾in) deep, water the base well, then sow the seed thinly. Fill with soil, firm, and lightly water again. Seeds will germinate in a week or two.

Prepare the soil before planting out your seedlings. Digging in some well-rotted organic matter will help encourage plenty of leafy growth.

Make drills long enough to suit the size of your plot. To retain moisture during dry spells, cover with newspaper until the seeds germinate.

4 PLANTING OUT

Plant out your winter cabbages in summer and your spring cabbages in autumn. Dig over the site to remove weeds and fork in high-nitrogen granular fertilizer. Plant out or transplant winter seedlings 50cm (20in) apart, and spring types 30cm (12in) apart.

Young cabbage plants are ready to plant out when they are about 15cm (6in) tall. If much larger or smaller, they may be slow to establish.

5 ROUTINE CARE

Water plants regularly, especially during dry spells. To encourage strong growth before winter, apply high-nitrogen liquid feed in late summer, as directed on the packet. Weed the beds regularly and remove any yellowing leaves from the plants.

Cabbages develop a crown of leaves so aim the water directly at the base to ensure it reaches the roots. Use a watering can with a long spout.

6 HARVESTING

When individual cabbage heads are large enough to use, harvest them as needed during winter and spring, using a sharp knife to cut through the stalk. To maximise your crop, leave the stumps of spring cabbages to grow on in the soil. Use a knife to make a cross in the cut end – this will encourage the stumps to produce a crop of fresh, loose leaves which can be harvested a few weeks later.

Loose spring leaves make a useful bonus crop after the cabbage heads have been harvested.

CAULIFLOWERS

It is possible to grow and harvest delicious fresh cauliflowers all year round – there is a wide range of varieties to choose from. As well as conventional white-headed types you can also grow cauliflowers with striking purple, orange, or green heads. Space the plants widely so that the heads can grow to full size, or densely in containers to produce "mini" cauliflowers. They can produce high yields if given enough food and water.

	SPRING	SUMMER	AUTUMN	WINTER
SOW				
HARVEST				

TIME TO HARVEST: 20–26 WEEKS

SUITABLE FOR: BEDS AND CONTAINERS

5–6 plants

3M (10FT) ROWS
Plant 60–70cm (24–28in) apart

CONTAINERS
4 plants in each

1 GETTING STARTED

Cauliflowers that mature from autumn to spring are sown when conditions are warming up: sow direct into warm soils in late spring to early summer. Conversely, cauliflowers that mature in summer are sown in late winter; for these varieties sowing in modules under cover is the best method.

'Snowball' is sown in spring for an autumn harvest; the medium-sized heads keep well.

'Violet Queen' bears purple heads in late summer that turn green when cooked.

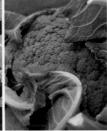
'Graffiti' is a striking, purple-headed variety: the colour intensifies with light exposure.

'Romanesco' has lime-green curds that are both highly ornamental and full of flavour.

2 SOWING UNDER COVER

Fill module trays or pots with compost, water well, and allow to drain. Make a hole 1cm (½in) deep in each cell and sow two seeds into it. Firm over with compost and water in. When seedlings have emerged, thin to leave the stronger seedling.

Summer and autumn varieties are sown in early to midwinter and then placed in a propagator.

Keep seedlings well watered; these thirsty plants require sufficient water at all stages.

3 SOW OUTSIDE

For winter and spring cauliflowers, you can sow the seed direct in late spring. Prepare a seedbed by digging over the ground, incorporating plenty of organic matter. Then excavate a short drill, 2cm (¾in) deep. Water the base thoroughly, sow your seeds, and then cover with soil to level and water in lightly. To prevent a build-up of soil pests and diseases, don't plant cauliflowers where other brassica crops have grown in the past year.

Sow seed thinly along the drill. Once the seedlings develop they can be thinned if necessary.

3 PLANTING OUT

Harden off module-raised seedlings when they are 15cm (6in) tall. Place them outdoors during the day and inside at night for a week. Once seedbed-raised plants reach this height, water them well and then lift gently from the soil. Summer varieties should be spaced 60cm (24in) apart; winter types 70cm (28in) apart.

Hardened-off cauliflowers should be planted promptly. There is a risk of plants bolting if they become root bound.

Plant both module-grown and seedbed-raised seedlings in soil that has had a high-nitrogen granular feed incorporated.

Firm the plants in well. The heads will become very heavy as they grow and will need to be well supported.

4 PROTECTING PLANTS

Water in your transplants, and fit a brassica collar around the base of each. Place netting with a maximum mesh diameter of 5mm (¼in) around plants. This will deter cabbage white butterflies and pigeons. Hoe between young plants; established cauliflowers will smother any competing plants.

5 ROUTINE CARE

It's especially important to keep cauliflowers well watered during the summer months to obtain a good-sized curd. As these develop, bend a few leaves in over the head – this protects summer varieties from being "burnt" by the sun. It also offers winter types some frost protection.

Ensure that netting reaches the ground, leaving no gaps for pests to fly underneath – peg the netting down or bury it in the soil.

Covering the cauliflower head with its leaves will prevent white varieties from yellowing in the sun. Secure the leaves in place with string.

6 HARVESTING

As soon as the curds reach a harvestable size, cut them from the plant; they will keep better if you cut them with a few leaves attached. The heads are best eaten fresh but can be stored in the fridge for a few days. Blanch and freeze surplus heads.

 TIP Grow in pots for "mini" 6cm (2½in) wide curds. Space 15cm (6in) apart.

Make sure you harvest cauliflowers when they are at their best. The heads will be tight and composed of tiny, firm buds.

CALABRESE

It's well worth growing your own calabrese because home-grown crops are much more tender and flavourful than shop-bought types. The plants produce one main central head and then numerous smaller sideshoots, which prolong the harvest period; the florets also freeze well, so any gluts can be preserved for later. If you're too short of space to sow in pots or modules indoors, direct sowings in summer outdoors will perform extremely well.

	SPRING	SUMMER	AUTUMN	WINTER
SOW				
HARVEST				

TIME TO HARVEST: 12–16 WEEKS

SUITABLE FOR: BEDS

8 plants

3M (10FT) ROWS
Plant out 40cm (16in) apart

0   40cm

CONTAINERS
3 plants in each

1 GETTING STARTED

Calabrese prefer rich, well-drained soil, so dig in plenty of organic matter such as well-rotted manure or compost in the season before you intend to plant. Make sure that no other members of the brassica family have been planted in the same location in the previous year; this will help to prevent the build-up of soil pests and diseases.

'Fiesta' produces large, well-rounded heads and a good crop of secondary sideshoots.

'Ironman' produces a reliable crop of dome-shaped, blue-green heads with fine buds.

'Belstar' keeps well once cut and is worth growing for its tasty blue-green heads.

'Kabuki' can be harvested when young for a second crop. Good for small spaces.

Calabrese can be overwintered in a frost-free greenhouse for harvests in early spring. Sow two or three seeds in each individual pot in late summer or early autumn.

After germination seedlings will need to be thinned to one per pot or module as they develop. When they are about 15cm (6in) tall they will be ready to plant out.

2 SOWING SEEDS

Calabrese can be sown under cover in pots or large modules to transplant later. Fill the container with seed compost, firm gently, water well, and make two holes per pot or module, 1cm (½in) deep. Drop a seed into each hole, cover with compost, and water in lightly. Once emerged, thin to leave the stronger seedling. Alternatively, seed can be sown directly into the final position outside. Create a seedbed: mark out rows 30cm (12in) apart and sow a cluster of three seeds every 20cm (8in), into holes 2cm (¾in) deep. Thin the seedlings to the strongest and use organic pellets for slug protection.

3 PLANTING OUT

Once indoor-sown plants are 15cm (6in) tall, harden them off and plant out 20cm (8in) apart, in rows 30cm (12in) apart. Don't let them become root-bound as this can cause the premature formation of small heads. Keep the plants well watered and well weeded. Put a brassica collar around each plant to deter cabbage root fly.

Divide up your plot using bamboo canes and string – this will help you work out your plant spacings and will provide support for netting.

Young plants should be hardened off and planted out as soon as possible in spring, as they cope best with being moved if the weather is not too warm.

4 ROUTINE CARE

As the heads of the plants begin to develop, draw soil around the base of the stems to stabilize them – this is called "earthing up". At this point a liquid high-nitrogen fertilizer can be applied to boost the main head size and to encourage the production of sideshoots for subsequent harvests.

5 PROTECTING PLANTS

Erect a frame of netting over your plants to deter birds – especially pigeons and cabbage white butterflies. Ensure the net is fine, with a maximum mesh diameter of 5mm (¼in) to stop the adult butterflies reaching your plants, and keep it taut to reduce the risk of birds becoming entangled in it.

Tall varieties may need staking if earthing up does not provide sufficient support. Tie the plants in to sturdy bamboo canes as necessary.

Mealy cabbage aphids target brassica crops and can swarm plants, disfiguring the leaves. Aim to protect crops at an early stage.

6 HARVESTING

The first cutting can be expected approximately 3–4 months after sowing, depending on the variety and time of year. Cut the main head off first and when the smaller sideshoots appear, harvest these. Young, tender leaves of calabrese can also be eaten.

 Calabrese plants spaced closely (15cm/6in apart) give a flush of small heads.

Use a knife to cut the heads whole before the tight flower buds begin to open. This encourages a second crop.

SPROUTING BROCCOLI

This hardy crop is one of the most eagerly awaited in winter and spring; it bears a profusion of tender stems tipped with tasty white or purple florets when few other crops are available. Traditional varieties form large plants that mature slowly and are best suited to bigger gardens. If you enjoy broccoli but can't wait until winter, there are now faster-growing varieties that can be harvested throughout the summer and autumn months.

	SPRING	SUMMER	AUTUMN	WINTER
SOW				
HARVEST				

TIME TO HARVEST: 16–36 WEEKS

SUITABLE FOR: BEDS

0   1m   2m   3m

4 plants

3M (10FT) ROWS
Plant out 80cm (32in) apart

1 GETTING STARTED

Traditional broccoli is easy to raise from seed and can also be bought as young potted plants or plugs in spring. Summer-maturing broccoli plants are not as widely available, so this crop is best raised from seed. Sow the seed in several batches, from late winter to mid-spring, and harvest florets from early summer to mid-autumn.

'Claret' is a reliable variety that produces succulent heads from mid-spring onwards.

'Purple Sprouting' is very hardy and bears an abundance of dark shoots in early spring.

'White Star' crops in late spring, producing attractive white heads that can be eaten raw.

'Summer Purple' is a hardy variety that bears a high yield of purple heads in summer.

Sowing into modules means the seedlings don't need to be pricked out, reducing root disturbance. They can also be sown in trays.

Thin the seedlings, leaving only the strongest one per module. If you have gaps, carefully replant stronger thinned seedlings into vacant cells.

2 SOWING UNDER COVER

Broccoli is a hardy crop, and most varieties need a long growing season. Give crops a head start by sowing under cover in spring. Fill module trays with seed compost, water well, then leave to drain. Make one hole per cell, 2cm (¾in) deep, and sow two seeds in each. Cover with compost and water in lightly. The seeds won't need additional heat and will germinate within two weeks. Grow the seedlings on under cover until planted out.

TIP Raising plants under cover reduces the effects of club root disease (see p.246).

3 SOWING OUTDOORS

Seed can be sown into seedbeds, and the seedlings transplanted when large enough, or sown directly into their final growing positions. For seedbed sowing, dig the soil over, and rake it fine and level, then sow into drills 2cm (¾in) deep. Alternatively, sow pinches of seeds at 80cm (32in) intervals, and thin to the strongest seedling per station.

To sow longer rows, carefully pour the seeds directly from the packet, tapping the top so they drop out at regular intervals.

Sowing direct in clusters takes away the need to transplant your seedlings, and means less root disturbance for the crop.

4 PLANTING OUT

Harden off indoor-raised plants before planting them out. Water seedbeds well so that outdoor-sown plants are easy to lift. Prepare the soil by forking in granular high-nitrogen fertilizer, as per the instructions on the packet. Plant out seedlings 80cm (32in) apart and water well.

Fit brassica collars snugly around the base of each plant soon after planting to stop cabbage root flies from laying their eggs at soil level.

5 ROUTINE CARE

Water and weed plants regularly to ensure steady growth. As the plants become taller, earth soil up around the base of their stems to help stabilize them. If your garden is fairly exposed, you might need to insert a stout cane at the base of each plant for support during autumn gales.

Net plants against pigeons and cabbage white butterflies. Keep the netting taut to avoid snaring birds and check it regularly for gaps.

6 HARVESTING

As plants mature in winter and spring and begin to develop their florets, pick them over daily to ensure you harvest the heads while still tightly closed. Cut them with a length of stem roughly 10cm (4in) attached; both the stem and the leaves are tender to eat. Continual picking promotes new sideshoots to grow, leading to a longer harvest. The florets are best eaten soon after picking but can be frozen.

Tender florets should be picked before the tiny flower buds open. Cut them off close to their base with a sharp knife.

BRUSSELS SPROUTS

A winter plot would be incomplete without Brussels sprouts, and there is a range of varieties that will crop from mid-autumn right through until early spring. Individual "buttons" develop over a long period, meaning that two or three plants can provide a steady supply through the winter months. In addition to the tasty sprouts is a further treat: the sprout "top" – a loose rosette of leaves that has a deliciously mild flavour. These are high in quality if not in quantity.

	SPRING	SUMMER	AUTUMN	WINTER
SOW				
HARVEST				

TIME TO HARVEST: 30–36 WEEKS

SUITABLE FOR: BEDS

0   1m   2m   3m

6 plants

3M (10FT) ROWS
Thin out or plant to 60cm (24in) apart

1 GETTING STARTED
For a large crop, Brussels sprouts are worth raising from seed, although they can also be bought as plants in spring. Prepare your site by digging in plenty of well-rotted manure or compost during the season before planting. Brussels sprouts prefer a pH of at least 6.8, so apply lime to the soil if yours falls well below that.

'Crispus' produces small, dark green sprouts with fantastic flavour. Good standing ability.

'Kalette' produces unusual-looking, sweet, nutty sprouts from October to March.

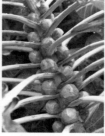
'Trafalgar' bears heavy crops of reliable, firm, flavourful sprouts from midwinter to early spring.

'Maximus' is a high-yielding variety, bearing sweet green sprouts over a long season.

Sprinkle the seed evenly along the base of a short drill, with a view to transplanting them later. This makes best use of limited space.

If you are sowing under cover, sow the seed into holes spaced 5cm (2in) apart. Prick the seedlings out when they are strong enough to handle.

2 SOWING SEEDS
To sow seed in the ground, dig over the soil to remove any weeds, firm it well, and rake it level. Either sow a short drill, 2cm (¾in) deep, from which seedlings will be moved to their final position, or sow clusters of seed at 60 x 60cm (24 x 24in) apart – this allows you to thin each cluster to the strongest seedling, minimizing root disturbance. You can also start plants off in modules under cover. Fill a module tray with seed compost, firm gently, and water. Sow two seeds per cell, 2cm (¾in) deep, before covering them with compost. Water lightly and, once germinated, thin out to leave the strongest seedling per module.

3 PLANTING OUT

Once tray-grown plants reach 10–12cm (4–5in) in height, harden them off ready for life outside. Prepare seedbed-raised sprouts for transplanting by watering the bed thoroughly. Dig over the soil ready for planting, rake it level, and firm well. Space the seedlings 60 x 60cm (24 x 24in) apart, and water in well.

Transplant the healthiest of your seedlings once they have reached 10–12cm (4–5in) tall and have four or five true leaves.

Ensure that the seedlings are planted 60cm (24in) apart so that the plants remain well ventilated. Plant Brussels sprouts in firmly.

Use brassica collars to deter cabbage root fly, which is a common brassica pest that can cause the young plants to die.

4 PROTECTING PLANTS

Fit brassica collars around the base of each seedling to prevent attack from cabbage root fly (see p.242), and erect a frame of netting over plants to deter pigeons and cabbage white butterflies. Brussels sprouts can grow to at least 80cm (32in) in height, so ensure the frame is tall enough.

Netting should be pulled taut to prevent birds becoming snagged. Regularly check for gaps at the base where birds or butterflies could get in.

5 ROUTINE CARE

Keep the top-heavy plants stable by earthing up soil around their bases or stake them with canes. The lower leaves will yellow as they age, and should be picked off to encourage good air flow around the developing buttons. Keep plants well watered and fed using a high-nitrogen liquid fertilizer.

Older leaves near the base of the stems yellow naturally and die off ; they are not a sign of poor health. They should snap off easily.

6 HARVESTING

Harvest sprouts when large enough by firmly twisting them off; older cultivars mature from the bottom of the stem upwards. Newer hybrids mature more evenly, and can be cut as whole stems. Stand them indoors in water in the cool and harvest as needed.

TIP Harvest the delicious leafy "top" before picking the sprouts themselves.

Sprouts taste especially sweet from late winter, once they have been frosted a few times.

KALE

Packed with vitamins, kales are robust plants and fare extremely well over winter, providing a generous harvest in otherwise lean times. The plants are highly ornamental and are not as prone to the common pests and diseases that affect other members of the brassica family. Leaves should be harvested little and often to ensure they remain tender and to keep the plant cropping. Two or three plants can provide ample pickings if used as cut-and-come-again crops.

	SPRING	SUMMER	AUTUMN	WINTER
SOW				
HARVEST				

TIME TO HARVEST: 24–28 WEEKS

SUITABLE FOR: BEDS

0   1m   2m   3m

7 plants

3M (10FT) ROWS
Plant out 50cm (20in) apart

1 GETTING STARTED

Kale plants prefer a rich, well-drained, firm soil and need plenty of space to develop. There is a good selection available, including savoy-leaved and crinkled types, dwarf forms, and varieties with striking purple foliage. All are highly ornamental and look great in a mixed border as well as in a traditional vegetable plot.

'Cavolo Nero' has a rich flavour and its dark green, savoyed leaves are tender when cooked.

'Midnight Sun' has stunning pink veins. The leaves can be eaten when young or mature.

'Redbor' makes an attractive border plant thanks to its purple-stemmed frilly leaves.

'Starbor' has heavily frilled leaves that are best harvested while young and tender.

Seeds can also be sown into pots using a dibber or pencil to make holes in the compost. Sow two seeds into each planting hole.

Sow clusters of two or three seeds in a grid pattern then thin the seedlings to the strongest. Protect the young plants against slugs using organic pellets.

2 SOWING SEEDS

Crops can be sown under cover in mid-spring. Fill module trays with seed compost, water well, allow to drain, and then make holes, 1cm (½in) deep, in each cell. Drop two seeds in each cell, cover with compost and water in lightly. Thin to leave the stronger seedling per cell and grow on under cover. Kale can also be sown outside in early summer. Dig over a seedbed, removing any weeds, and work in some high nitrogen granular fertilizer. Firm the soil gently and rake it level. You can either sow a short drill to transplant later, or sow two or three seeds at their final spacings: 50 x 50cm (20 x 20in) apart.

3 PLANTING OUT

Plant out or transplant the kale seedlings spaced 50 x 50cm (20 x 20in) apart during early summer. Water plants in well and place cabbage root fly collars around the base of each plant. These small discs prevent the adult female fly laying her eggs next to the stem at soil level (see p.242). Hoe between plants regularly to keep weeds at bay.

As soon as their roots fill their module cells or pots, begin hardening seedlings off ready for transplanting outside.

Seedlings should be firmed in well when they are planted, as the soil will help to support the eventual weight of the plants.

Kale plants can become large so it is vital to plant them with enough space to develop: about 50cm (20in) is ideal.

4 PROTECTING PLANTS

Keep seedlings fed and well watered to help them recover from flea beetle attack, which can check their growth. If cabbage white butterflies (see p.240) or pigeons are a problem, use canes to erect some taut netting over the plants. Use a maximum mesh size of 5mm (¼in). Check for gaps.

5 ROUTINE CARE

As plants continue to grow they can become tall and top-heavy – some cultivars can reach up to 1m (3ft) high. Give them some support by staking the plants individually using stout canes or sticks. Older leaves at the base of the plant that begin to turn yellow should be removed and composted.

Keep plants well weeded, especially when they are young and vulnerable to competition. Pull out weeds by hand, or use a hoe.

Cabbage white butterflies lay tiny yellow eggs on the underside of leaves. Grow the plants under fine mesh netting to deter attacks.

6 HARVESTING

The inner leaves of each rosette are the most tender while the outer ones are a bit tougher. Harvest the leaves when they are large enough but bear in mind that removing all the young leaves will weaken the plant. Pick over the plants every few days to ensure a steady supply.

 TIP Pull up plants and compost them once they develop flowers in spring.

Kales develop one main rosette of leaves and, occasionally, offsets of smaller rosettes.

TROUBLESHOOTING
BRASSICAS

These leafy greens supply us with sizeable curds, heads, and buttons, and this generosity requires good nutrition. Pests and diseases that weaken or devour foliage can be troublesome, so be vigilant and step in at an early stage. The range of pests, diseases, and disorders looks intimidating, but growing crops under fine mesh is a wise precaution against many of them.

Q The foliage of my winter cabbages is narrow and almost stripped back to the veins – what is causing that?

Pigeons will strip succulent foliage but leave the tougher midribs and veins in place. If plants are tattered, and damage occurs overnight, these are your culprits. Cabbage white caterpillars will cause similar damage but over a longer period; you will see yellow and black, or pea-green caterpillars on the leaves. Netting prevents all these pests. Plants affected by whiptail (caused by molybdenum deficiency) develop narrow leaves over time. This micronutrient becomes unavailable in acidic soils so add lime to correct it.

Q How can I tell when my cauliflowers and calabrese are ready to harvest?

The most obvious sign of maturity is the size and appearance of the calabrese head (for cauliflowers, this is called a "curd"). A head that is about 20cm (8in) in diameter is a good harvestable size, but will often be smaller as size varies with plant quality and variety. Each head or curd is composed of hundreds of tiny buds – if these begin to expand into individual "bobbles" or florets, this indicates over-maturity so harvest quickly. Luckily, gluts of both crops freeze well if blanched (briefly plunged into boiling water) first.

Q Why do my Brussels sprouts look like loose, tiny cabbages instead of tight buttons?

This problem (called "blowing") tends to occur on buttons at the base of the plant and is often attributed to planting into freshly dug, uncompacted soil. However, blowing can still occur when plants have been firmed in well. Open pollinated varieties seem more affected by it, so opt for F1 hybrids such as 'Maximus' and 'Trafalgar'. Your blown sprouts are still edible: in fact, a kale–Brussels sprout hybrid, 'Petit Posy', has this trait bred into it and is marketed as a flower sprout.

Q Is it possible to grow sizeable brassicas in a small garden, or even in pots?

While it is not usually practical to cultivate larger brassicas, such as sprouting broccoli and Brussels sprouts in pots, some crops such as cauliflower and calabrese can be successful. Their root systems are extensive, so opt for a large tub rather than a small pot. Fill it with a loam-based compost for optimum nutrition, weight, and structure. Don't expect large yields – the size of individual heads and curds will be small. However, this can be advantageous if you have just a small household to feed.

PEST AND DISEASE WATCH

Being a large group of plants, brassicas have an impressive list of associated ailments:

- Seedlings are prone to slug and snail damage – check for silvery slime trails (see p.242).
- Watch for flea beetle attack (see p.240), where tiny black beetles pepper holes in seedling leaves.
- Pigeons and cabbage white caterpillars (see p.240) can quickly defoliate plants – protect them by growing plants under a cage of netting.
- Plants wilting, even when well watered, can be indicative of either clubroot fungus (see p.244) or cabbage root fly larvae (see p.242).
- Distorted blister-like foliage is symptomatic of mealy cabbage aphid colonies (see p.240).
- Clouds of tiny white flies appearing when foliage is disturbed indicates whitefly infestation (see p.240).
- Yellowing on the upper leaf surface combined with grey powdery patches on the underside can indicate downy mildew (see p.244).
- Distinct yellow-brown foliar spotting implies fungal or bacterial leaf spots (see p.244).

LETTUCES

Fast-growing and attractive, lettuces are ideal for pots, tubs, and windowboxes if you don't have space elsewhere. Choose from dense-headed "hearting" types or frilly loose-leaf varieties that can be harvested as cut-and-come-again crops (see pp.118–119) or allowed to develop to full size and cut whole. You never need to be short of this excellent salad staple, as sowing under cover allows you to harvest fresh leaves all year round.

	SPRING	SUMMER	AUTUMN	WINTER
SOW				
HARVEST				
TIME TO HARVEST: 6–8 WEEKS				

SUITABLE FOR: BEDS AND CONTAINERS

3M (10FT) ROWS
Plant 15–35cm (6–14in) apart
9–20 plants

CONTAINERS
3 plants in each
0   30cm

1 SOWING UNDER COVER

Early sowings can be made under cover between late winter and early spring, to be planted outside once weather conditions are suitable. Fill modules or trays with seed compost, firm gently, water well, and allow to drain. Make a 1cm (½in) deep hole in each pot or module and drop two seeds into each. Alternatively, sow seed in trays at the same depth. Cover the seeds with compost, then water in lightly. Place in a warm, 12°C (54°F), light place.

Sow two or three seeds per small pot or module and once they emerge, thin them out leaving the strongest to grow on.

Sow seed thinly in larger seed trays and prick the seedlings out once they develop. Plant them into individual pots or modules for growing on.

Germination can be erratic outside, so sow seed in clusters every 10cm (4in) along the dril in case some fail to germinate.

As seedlings develop, thin to leave the strongest per cluster, then later to 30cm (12in) between plants. The thinnings can be eaten.

2 SOWING OUTSIDE

Outdoor sowings of summer varieties can be made from early spring until midsummer; winter-hardy lettuces should be sown in late summer. Dig over the soil to remove any weeds, firm it gently, and rake it level. Create drills 2cm (¾in) deep and 30cm (12in) apart, and sow seeds in clusters of four or five every 15cm (6in). Cover the seeds over with soil and water lightly. Protect the seedlings against slugs.

TIP Leave cut stumps in the soil to produce a second crop of smaller leaves.

3 PLANTING OUT

Once indoor-raised seedlings are large enough to handle, gradually harden them off by placing them outside during the day and inside at night for seven to ten days. Prepare the soil by digging it over to remove any weeds. Plant the seedlings out 15–35cm (6–14in) apart and cover them with a cloche or cold frame in cool weather.

Module-raised seedlings are ready to be hardened off and planted out once their roots fill their cell. Water them well before planting out.

Firm the soil in well around the heads after planting. Ensure that the lettuces have adequate room by spacing the rows 30cm (12in) apart.

4 ROUTINE CARE

Keep plants well watered in dry, warm weather so that they bulk up quickly. If the plants become too dry in the last few weeks before harvesting, they will be prone to bolting. Keep on top of the weeds that pop up between rows and compete with the lettuces for light, nutrients, and moisture.

5 PROTECTING PLANTS

Slugs and snails (see p.242) are the most common pest, especially during periods of warm, wet weather. Lay bait traps or organic pellets for them, or use grit to create a barrier around your crops. Aphids can also be a problem, so check over plants regularly for signs of damage.

Regularly weed lettuces used as a cut-and-come-again crop to avoid harvesting unwanted growth by mistake. Weeding by hand is easiest.

Lay a sand or grit ring around the plants to keep slugs away. Check it regularly to ensure that the circle has not been breached.

6 HARVESTING

Pick individual leaves from loose-leaf lettuces when they mature, or harvest the leaves all at once. Varieties that form a dense head of leaves, or "heart", can be cut whole once mature. Sow seeds little and often for a regular supply. Although some types will mature faster than others, a good rule of thumb is to sow a new batch when the previous one is ready to be planted out or thinned for a second time.

Harvest lettuces whole as soon as they are large enough, or pick the leaves individually.

LETTUCES

1 'Amaze' This improved red gem lettuce with uniform growth produces a good crop within just a few weeks. Grow it in the ground or in containers.

2 'Tom Thumb' A butterhead variety, it produces tender green leaves, which are sweet, with little bitterness. Compact, it is useful for windowboxes or containers.

3 'Freckles' This cos lettuce is unusual as its deep green, glossy leaves are splashed with burgundy. The upright plants have sturdy growth and are slow to bolt.

4 'Winter Density' Widely-grown, this gem lettuce is popular for it hardiness and its dense hearts. It also has good heat tolerance, and is ideal for early or late crops.

5 'Sioux' An iceberg-type, its crisp, green leaves flush an attractive red as they mature, especially in sunny sites. It has good mildew resistance; sow it repeatedly in summer.

6 'Lollo Rosso' Well-known, this loose-leaf variety has red-flushed, crinkled leaves that can be harvested as and when needed. Alternatively, whole heads can also be cut.

7 'Catalogna' This loose-leaf, "oak-leaf" lettuce works well in salads. Use it as a baby leaf, cut-and-come-again, or harvest the entire head once it has matured.

8 'Little Gem' A popular semi-cos variety, it produces small, dense hearts, and is ideal for sowing in containers. It is slow to bolt in summer, and is cold resistant.

9 'Mazur' A loose-leaf, "frisée" lettuce, this variety has sweet, textured leaves. It does not bolt, has a good resistance to powdery mildew, and stores well.

OTHER VARIETIES
'Arctic King'
'Red Salad Bowl'
'Cocarde'
'Lobjoits Green'
'Marvel of Four Seasons'

CUT-AND-COME-AGAIN SALAD

This is a method of growing salad leaves, rather than an actual vegetable, and is extremely quick and productive. It is ideally suited to growing crops in containers, and on small plots it allows you to make the most of bare patches for short periods. Useful crops can even be raised on windowsills or indoors. Often these salad leaves are sold in blends, such as a hot and spicy mix or stir-fry mix, but you can make up mixtures to suit your particular tastes.

	SPRING	SUMMER	AUTUMN	WINTER
SOW				
HARVEST				

TIME TO HARVEST: 4–6 WEEKS

SUITABLE FOR: BEDS AND CONTAINERS – UNDER COVER OR OUTSIDE

0   1m   2m   3m

60 plants

3M (10FT) ROWS
Sow and thin to 5cm (2in) apart

0   30cm

CONTAINERS
20 plants in each

1 GETTING STARTED
These salad plants are raised from seed and can be sown in batches through the year. Lettuce is commonly used but most salad crops can be grown this way. They are mainly grown outside in summer but you can also grow smaller crops under cover, even on the windowsill, to harvest in spring or autumn.

Corn salad is a useful leaf crop to grow during winter. It is very hardy and crops regularly.

Lettuce crops reliably as young leaves and there are many good varieties to grow.

Land cress has a spicy flavour. It is a good choice to grow under cover for an early crop.

Rocket has a peppery flavour and combines well with milder-tasting leaves like lettuce.

Sow the seed according to the spacings given on the packet. Some salads are sown deeper or more thickly than others.

Pick leaves individually as soon as they are large enough to use. The plants will continue growing and produce more.

Cutting the plants off checks their growth and they will take a week or two to recover. Water them to promote re-growth.

2 UNDER COVER CROPS
If you don't have outdoor space, or just want an extra early or late harvest, grow plants under cover. Use troughs or fill pots or seed trays with compost, water well, and leave to drain. Sow seeds on the surface and cover lightly with compost. Keep moist until the seeds emerge in a week or so, then harvest the leaves once large enough, leaving the bases to re-grow. Expect two or three similar harvests before the plants run out of steam.

TIP Feed indoor crops with balanced liquid fertilizer to encourage new growth.

3 SOWING OUTSIDE

For larger crops, sow direct into the soil in summer. First dig it over to remove weeds, firm it gently, then rake it level. Mark out drills 1–2cm (½–¾in) deep and water the base well. Sow the seeds, cover with soil, then water again. If sowing in warm weather, temporarily cover the soil with sheets of newspaper to help retain moisture.

Sow into drills to help you distinguish weeds from your crop. On smaller plots, you can sow directly into pots or troughs.

4 ROUTINE CARE

Seedlings will emerge in a few days (if your drills are covered with newspaper, check underneath every day and remove it as soon as the seeds germinate). Keep the rows well weeded, and water regularly to promote quick growth. Protect your plants against slugs with a sprinkling of organic pellets.

Crops in containers will dry out more quickly than those grown directly in the soil and will need more regular watering.

5 HARVESTING

These salad crops can be ready for harvest in as little as three weeks in the height of summer. You can either pick individual leaves as they become large enough to eat, or you can cut back whole rows using scissors. Either use the leaves fresh or bag them and store them in the fridge for a few days.

Plants picked for individual leaves live longer than plants harvested to the base; they will keep growing until they wear out.

GROWING ON

Salad plants that have been cut to the base need to be given time to recover and to be encouraged back into growth. Water them well, adding a dilute liquid fertilizer to the can, and they should be ready to harvest again within two weeks. The plants will wear out after a few crops, so sow new batches to provide a steady flow of replacement leaves.

MICROGREENS

This tasty, trendy crop often features on fine restaurant menus, and is amazingly easy to grow. Harvested as tiny seedlings, the plants are ready to crop in little more than a week. You don't need a garden or any outdoor space: microgreens grow well in pots on bright windowsills, and can even be sown on damp cottonwool. There are dozens of vegetables and herbs that can be grown in this way. Pick and mix and sow them together for different flavour combinations.

	SPRING	SUMMER	AUTUMN	WINTER
SOW				
HARVEST				
TIME TO HARVEST: 7–10 DAYS				

SUITABLE FOR: BEDS AND CONTAINERS, UNDER COVER OR OUTSIDE

0   1m

3,000 plants

1M (3FT) ROW
Sow and thin to 1cm (½in) apart

0   40cm

CONTAINERS
300 plants in each

1 GETTING STARTED

Microgreens are raised from seed and there are many different types. Ready-mixed combinations are available or you can mix your own. Most of the vegetables grown as microgreens are the same as conventional crops; they are just harvested as seedlings instead of as fully-grown crops. If you have spare seeds left over from sowing your main crops, try sowing them as microgreens with a fast turnaround, rather than storing seed until next year.

Basil Like many culinary herbs, the young seedlings have a rich, sweet taste.

Beetroot Although normally grown as a root crop, the tasty leaves are also edible.

Kale All brassica seedlings are edible, and have a delicious peppery flavour.

Coriander Full-grown plants often bolt, so use it as a fresh-tasting seedling instead.

Amaranth The mildly flavoured leaves add contrasting colour to homemade dishes.

Celery Enjoy the delicious taste of this late-season stem crop throughout the year.

Mustard These eye-catching microleaves have a punchy, peppery flavour.

Pak choi This useful crop can be harvested at almost any stage, including as seedlings.

Chives These tender leaves have a sweeter flavour than full-grown plants. Use as a garnish.

Pea shoots These have the familiar pea flavour and are ideal added to salads and stir-fries.

2 SOWING UNDER COVER

Fill seed trays with moist compost and sow the seeds on top. Cover them with a little more compost and water lightly. The seeds will germinate in a few days and should be grown on in a bright position until large enough to harvest. Seeds can also be sown uncovered on trays of moist kitchen paper or cotton wool.

Sow seeds thickly to give a good crop, and sow more every few days for a constant supply. Keep them handy on your kitchen windowsill.

3 SOWING OUTSIDE

Microgreens are best suited to small-scale growing, but if you wish to sow outside, weed the area and rake the soil level and fine. Water the soil, sow the seed 5mm (¼in) deep in blocks or rows, cover lightly and water again. Protect from slugs with organic pellets.

Seed can be sown outside directly in the soil, but is sown more often in small batches in containers, trays, and windowboxes.

4 ROUTINE CARE

Crops grown under cover need little care, other than watering them once or twice until they are harvested. If crops are sown outside, weed seedlings may come up among your microgreens. Remove weeds early in case they are harvested by mistake.

If you have trouble differentiating weed seedlings from your crop, sow in lines rather than blocks to make weeds easier to spot.

5 HARVESTING

Depending on the temperature and light levels, seedlings can be ready for harvest in as little as a week. Ensure they are kept well-watered during this period. Pinch off individual leaves with your fingers, or cut whole clumps of seedlings with scissors.

TIP Use cut seedlings before they have a chance to wilt; within the hour ideally.

Harvest microgreens when the seedlings develop their first pair of "true" leaves.

STEP-BY-STEP
ORIENTAL GREENS

The majority of Oriental greens are leafy brassicas most of which are brilliant in stir-fries and salads. There is a plethora of crops in this group, and great variety within each crop: for example, pak choi ranges from large, tall types grown for their crunchy stems, to tight, squat plants with disc-like leaves. Oriental greens are ideal for filling gaps in the vegetable garden in summer as they benefit from a mid- to late summer sowing and grow quickly.

	SPRING	SUMMER	AUTUMN	WINTER
SOW				
HARVEST				
TIME TO HARVEST: 6–8 WEEKS				

SUITABLE FOR: BEDS, CONTAINERS, AND GROWING BAGS

15-20 plants

3M (10FT) ROWS
Plant 10–20cm (4–8in) apart

CONTAINERS
3 plants in each

1 GETTING STARTED

It is important not to sow Oriental greens too early in the year as the cold temperatures and increasing day length make these crops prone to bolting (running to seed). Waiting until mid-spring to sow helps to avoid the problem, but be aware that high temperatures and dry spells can also cause plants to bolt in summer.

Pak Choi has large rounded leaves with excellent flavour, good eaten raw or cooked.

'Red Giant' mustard leaves are red-flushed with a mild, peppery, flavour. Good in salads.

Mizuna has mild-flavoured, serrated leaves that look attractive in salads or as a garnish.

Chinese Cabbage has firmly packed, crinkly leaves that are good in salads and stir-fries.

2 SOW INSIDE

From mid-spring onwards, and at routine intervals, fill trays or modules with seed compost, firm gently, water thoroughly, and then allow it to drain. Sow the seeds lightly across the surface and cover with compost to a depth of 1cm (½in). Firm the surface again, water in lightly, and keep at 15°C (59°F) or above. The seeds will germinate in about a week. When large enough, harden them off before transplanting them outside.

Plan your sowings so that you don't end up with a glut. Sow a fresh batch every fortnight.

3 SOWING OUTSIDE

Oriental greens do well sown directly. Dig over the site, remove all weeds, and apply high-nitrogen feed. Firm the soil and then rake level, before marking out 1cm (½in) deep drills 15–30cm (6–12in) apart, depending on the crop.

Water the drill, then sow seeds 2cm (¾in) apart. Cover with soil and firm with the back of a rake.

Seedlings will need thinning as they appear. Pull them out gently and space 10–20cm (4–8in) apart.

GROW YOUR OWN VEGETABLES **SALADS AND LEAVES**

4 PLANTING OUT

Prepare the soil well: dig it over to remove any weeds and apply high-nitrogen fertilizer. Once the indoor-grown seedlings are large enough to handle, harden them off by placing them outdoors during the day and bringing them indoors at night for two weeks. Some greens can become quite large, so check the spacing before planting.

These are quick-growing crops and can be grown in the gaps left when other vegetables are harvested, making good use of the space.

5 ROUTINE CARE

Oriental greens are prone to brassica pests, such as cabbage root fly (see p.242) and flea beetle, so deter them by covering rows with a fine insect-proof mesh. Keep plants weed-free and water frequently to encourage quick growth. Doing this will also help prevent sudden bolting.

6 PICK YOUNG LEAVES

When they are large enough to eat, cut individual leaves or shoots from your crops, or shear back whole plants. Oriental crops grow quickly so it's best to sow small batches frequently during the summer. Sowing seed every fortnight will give you multiple harvests all summer, rather than one big crop.

Oriental greens are thirsty plants and will resent competition for moisture from weeds. Remove any that appear by hand.

These are ideal crops for cut-and-come-again leaves, especially when sown in repeated batches. Plants can be cropped for weeks.

7 HARVESTING

You can also let plants mature by thinning the seedlings or transplants as the season progresses. When individual heads reach a good size, cut them whole at the base or, for broccoli-type plants, pick individual shoots as they appear.

TIP In hot sites, sow seed slightly deeper and keep the soil moist at all times.

Whole plants such as pak choi can be cut off at the base once the heads mature.

SPINACH

Delicious harvested young and used in salads or allowed to mature for cooking, spinach is an easy-to-grow crop that will quickly yield armfuls of large, tender leaves. Sow seed in short drills, little and often, tend and water your plants well, and you will be guaranteed a constant supply all summer. Spinach matures quickly, making it a useful crop in smaller plots as it can soon be replaced. It can also be used for a quick crop in temporary gaps and spaces.

	SPRING	SUMMER	AUTUMN	WINTER
SOW				
HARVEST				

TIME TO HARVEST: 6–12 WEEKS

SUITABLE FOR: BEDS AND CONTAINERS

0   1m   2m   3m

20–45 plants

3M (10FT) ROWS
Plant 7–15cm (3–6in) apart

0   40cm

CONTAINERS
7–15 plants in each

1 GETTING STARTED

This versatile, easy-to-grow crop will tolerate cool weather and a shady site. Even a small patch devoted to spinach will be extremely productive; the leaves will also grow well in containers. Spinach needs rich, well-drained soil, so dig in organic matter, such as well-rotted manure or compost, in the season before you start growing it.

'Bordeaux' is both attractive and tasty. It has dark green leaves and bright red stems.

'Medania' produces high yields of large, succulent, dark green leaves. It is slow to bolt.

'Toscane' is a bolt-resistant cultivar that bears high yields of thick, tender leaves.

'Perpetual' is vigorous and easy to grow, producing new leaves after each picking.

Sow directly outdoors from mid- to late spring onwards. The last batches can be sown as late as mid-autumn if plants are covered with cloches.

Once seedlings are large enough to handle, thin them out 7–15cm (3–6in) apart along the drill leaving the strongest to grow on.

2 SOWING OUTSIDE

Spinach is sown directly, either into the soil or in containers and windowboxes, so there is no need to raise plants in seed trays or modules. Direct sowing makes plants less prone to bolting, which can be a problem. Dig over the soil, firm gently, and rake level. Mark out drills 2cm (¾in) deep and 20cm (8in) apart, and water the base thoroughly. Sprinkle seeds roughly 1cm (½in) apart along the drill, cover with soil, firm gently, and water in well.

TIP Sow in batches every few weeks for a constant supply of leaves.

3 WATERING

All spinaches are thirsty, fast-growing crops so make sure that your plants are watered generously and regularly. During spells of hot, dry weather this may mean watering them as frequently as once a day. Regular weeding is also important to keep the crop pure and eliminate competition for moisture, light, and space.

Ensure plants are kept well watered, as annual spinach can quickly "bolt" (run to seed) if it experiences any disruption in its growth.

Remove any weeds close to the plants by hand to avoid damaging the leaves. Use a hoe to remove weeds between the rows.

4 ROUTINE CARE

Net plants to deter birds. Downy mildew can be a problem, but resistant varieties are available. Crops will benefit from a top-dressing of a high-nitrogen granular fertilizer, such as pelleted poultry manure, or from regular doses of a high-nitrogen liquid feed.

Birds may target young plants so net rows as a precaution. Slugs can also be a problem, so apply a light sprinkling of organic pellets.

5 CUTTING SALAD LEAVES

Annual spinach can be harvested as a salad leaf while still small; cut individual leaves from plants as and when they become large enough. These can also be cooked as a milder-tasting, more tender leaf than those picked from mature plants.

Use a pair of scissors to harvest the young, tender leaves as a cut-and-come-again crop. Cut the outer leaves first and work inwards.

6 HARVESTING

If you prefer larger plants, leave them until about 10–12 weeks after sowing and then cut all the leaves off at about 2.5cm (1in) above the base, discarding any yellowing ones. If the harvested row is well fed and watered, you should get a smaller flush of leaves to be harvested again within two weeks. Discard the plants afterwards. An alternative way to harvest is to dig the plants up whole and strip the leaves.

Cut leaves as soon as they are ready, and use them promptly. The leaves do not store well and will soon wilt and spoil.

SWISS CHARD

Although this crop is a larger vegetable than most spinach varieties, it offers similar benefits to spinach. It can also be harvested for much of the year, cropping well into autumn and winter. It is easy to grow for beginner gardeners, and is useful for small plots because its colourful stems allow it to double-up as an ornamental in beds and pots. The foliage can be harvested as needed, either as young tender leaves for salads or as mature leaves and crisp stems for steaming.

	SPRING	SUMMER	AUTUMN	WINTER
SOW				
HARVEST				

TIME TO HARVEST: 6–16 WEEKS

SUITABLE FOR: BEDS AND CONTAINERS

0   1m   2m   3m

11 plants

3M (10FT) ROWS
Thin to 30cm (12in) apart

0   40cm

CONTAINERS
8 plants in each

1 GETTING STARTED

Swiss chard is often sold as young plants in spring, and sometimes also as a winter bedding plant. However, it is easy to grow from seed, which is the best way to raise several plants, especially if you want to harvest baby leaves. Swiss chard is also known as "seakale beet" and "silver chard"; they are all the same crop.

'Bright Lights' is a colourful mix of red- and yellow-stemmed plants. It is good for containers.

'Bright Yellow' can be harvested as baby leaves or left for its mature yellow stems.

'Lucullus' produces thick white stems that are delicious lightly steamed or braised.

'Rhubarb Chard' is grown for its purple-tinted green leaves and dark red stems.

Swiss chard seed are large and easy to handle. Sowing into modules, rather than in pots or trays, minimizes disturbance to seedlings because it does away with the need to prick them out later.

Plant out the young seedlings into well-prepared soil, 10cm (4in) apart, and water them well. Protect them from slugs and snails with traps or a thin scattering of organic pellets.

2 SOWING UNDER COVER

Although hardy, Swiss chard can be sown under cover to give an early crop. Fill modular trays with seed compost, firm gently and water well. Using a dibber or pencil, make holes 2.5cm (1in) deep per cell, drop one or two seeds into each, then cover with compost and water well. The seed won't require heat and should germinate in a week or two. Thin the seedlings to one per module and grow them on under cover in a bright, frost-free place for a few weeks until large enough to handle. Harden them off for a couple of weeks to acclimatize them to outdoor conditions, then plant them out, 30cm (12in) apart.

GROW YOUR OWN VEGETABLES **SALADS AND LEAVES**

3 SOWING OUTSIDE

Seeds can also be sown directly where they are to grow, and will give a later crop. Prepare the soil by digging it over and work in some granular high-nitrogen fertilizer. Rake the soil to a fine tilth and make drills 2.5cm (1in) deep, 30cm (12in) apart. Water the base well, sow seeds 5cm (2in) apart, then cover over with soil.

Space the seed carefully to save sowing more than you need. Unused seeds can be stored for later sowings if kept somewhere cool and dry.

4 THINNING OUT

Direct-sown seedlings should be initially thinned to 10cm (4in) apart, then thinned again to give an eventual spacing for mature plants of 30cm (12in). Use the thinnings as early-season salad leaves. Water the rows after thinning to settle the soil.

5 ROUTINE CARE

Water the plants well and feed regularly with a liquid high-nitrogen fertilizer to promote leafy growth. Keep them well-weeded to prevent competition. For harvestable new leaves in winter, cover plants with a glass or fleece tunnel cloche.

Don't leave the seedlings too long before you thin them out. They will become harder to pull, which increases root disturbance.

Swiss chard should be kept moist. If growing it on a lighter soil, mulch around plants with some well-rotted organic matter in summer.

6 HARVESTING

For salads, plants can be harvested when they are about 10cm (4in) tall. Either pick leaves individually or cut off whole plants near the base (they will grow back). To cook the leaves in the same way as spinach, let them reach full size and cut them off as needed.

TIP White-stemmed varieties are the hardiest type for overwintering.

When cutting leaves for salads, leave the base of the plant in the soil to grow back.

CHICORY AND ENDIVE

This robust duo is an asset to any plot. They are highly ornamental, take up relatively little space, and can be grown in containers too. All varieties are easy to grow, and most are hardy. They have a pleasant, slightly bitter taste, which can be moderated by blanching. Witloof chicory can be forced in winter to produce "chicons" – a unique crop of fleshy shoots with mild-tasting leaves.

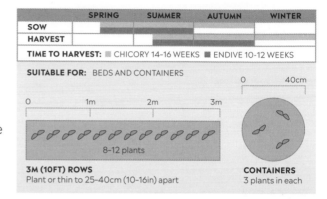

	SPRING	SUMMER	AUTUMN	WINTER
SOW				
HARVEST				

TIME TO HARVEST: ■ CHICORY 14–16 WEEKS ■ ENDIVE 10–12 WEEKS

SUITABLE FOR: BEDS AND CONTAINERS

8–12 plants

3M (10FT) ROWS
Plant or thin to 25–40cm (10–16in) apart

CONTAINERS
3 plants in each

1 GETTING STARTED

There are three types of chicory: Witloof, which has a deep root and elongated, green heads, and can be forced to produce "chicons"; radicchio, which forms a heart, much like lettuce; and sugarloaf types, which have a loose head of green leaves. The two main types of endive are "frisée" and "Batavian".

Chicory 'Treviso Precoce Mesola' is a radicchio-type with white-ribbed, red leaves.

Chicory 'Palla Rossa' has bitter, red leaves. This radicchio-type is good in salads.

Chicory 'Pan di Zucchero' is a sugarloaf type, ideal as a cut-and-come-again crop.

Endive 'Frenzy' is a self-blanching frisée endive with dense heads and fine leaves.

2 SOWING SEEDS

Early sowings in spring for summer and autumn crops can be started off under cover, as can autumn sowings for cut-and-come-again leaves or for spring-maturing crops. Fill trays or modules with compost, water them well, and allow to drain. Make holes 1cm (½in) deep, 5cm (2in) apart in each cell and sow one seed in each hole. Cover with a little more compost and water them in lightly. Germination rates are usually high.

Seed can be sown in trays, after which you will need to thin out the seedlings, leaving the stronger plants, once they are large enough to handle.

Water the seeds using a can fitted with a fine rose to prevent the seeds becoming washed to the edges of the tray, or into clusters.

Prick out the seedlings as soon as they are large enough to handle, planting them on into small pots or individual modules.

TIP "Blanching" endive by covering its heart with a plate makes it taste less bitter.

3 SOW AND PLANT OUT

To sow direct, dig over the site and remove any weeds. Create drills 1cm (½in) deep, water well, then sow seeds thinly along them. Cover with soil and water in. If you have raised seedlings under cover, these can be planted outside as soon as their roots fill the individual cells. Plant them 25–40cm (10–16in) apart. Water in well.

Seed will do well if sown direct, as long as the soil has warmed up enough; the plants are more at risk of bolting if they are sown too early.

Thin out the seedlings as they develop, leaving the strongest to grow on 25–40cm (10–16in) apart. The thinnings can be used as salad leaves.

4 ROUTINE CARE

Keep the plants well watered while they develop and weed regularly. The plants don't have high nutritional requirements but plants grown on light, sandy, or chalky soils, or those in pots, may benefit from a fortnightly dose of general-purpose liquid fertilizer.

Keeping plants well watered will deter them from bolting. Give them a thorough soak in dry spells to make sure that water reaches the deeper roots.

5 HARVESTING

Harvest chicory when plants are a good size. Leave the stump, cut a cross in the top and remove any remaining leaves. Within a few weeks new shoots will appear. Cut endive leaves when the plant is mature and leave in the ground to re-sprout for an autumn crop.

Harvest the crop either by lifting the whole head at once (as shown) or by snipping leaves off individually as they are needed as a cut-and-come-again crop.

FORCING "CHICONS"

In winter, witloof chicory can be forced into producing "chicons". Lift mature roots in mid-autumn, remove the leaves, and plant them in a deep pot or box of compost. Water them well, then place an upturned pot over the top to block out the light. Keep them in a warm spot. Cut the "chicons" after two or three weeks, when they are about 10–15cm (4–6in) tall.

WATERCRESS

Watercress has steadily become a must-have ingredient, adding crisp texture and a fresh, peppery kick to salads and many other summer dishes, or enjoyed in sandwiches or on its own. Although it usually grows in streams and running water, it doesn't have to: it can be grown easily in containers, providing it is kept well watered. Watercress grows quickly, and if harvested regularly, a few pots will be enough to meet your needs throughout the summer.

	SPRING	SUMMER	AUTUMN	WINTER
SOW				
HARVEST				

TIME TO HARVEST: 8–18 WEEKS

SUITABLE FOR: CONTAINERS

0   40cm

0   1m

10 plants

TROUGHS
Plant or thin to 10cm (4in) apart

CONTAINERS
16 plants in each

1 SOWING UNDER COVER

Watercress is hardy but can be started off under cover. Fill individual pots with seed compost, firm gently and water well. Sow seeds thinly on the surface, cover with compost 5mm (¼in) deep, and water lightly. Keep the pots on a bright windowsill or in a warm greenhouse, stood in saucers of water, 5cm (2in) deep. Thin the seedlings to leave the strongest and grow them on outside, repotting into containers at least 30cm (12in) wide.

Seed can be sown into small pots which can be thinned for small crops or potted on.

Keep the compost moist at all times. The seeds won't need additional heat to germinate.

Seedlings grow quickly once they germinate. Grow them on in a bright position under cover.

An old sink is ideal for growing watercress, sow seed across the surface and cover with compost, or sow into shallow drills. Water well.

Thin seedlings as they grow, keeping them well-watered at all times. Protect the plants from slugs with a light sprinkling of organic pellets.

2 SOWING OUTSIDE

After the risk of frost has passed, fill containers, at least 30cm (12in) wide, with multipurpose compost. Sow seed across the surface, 5mm (¼in) deep, and water in. Stand the pots outside in a sunny position in trays of water 5cm (2in) deep, and keep them topped up at all times. The seeds will germinate in about two weeks. Thin the seedlings to 10cm (4in) apart, leaving the strongest. Sow batches regularly.

TIP Use the thinned seedlings as an early crop, treating them as microgreens.

3 TAKING CUTTINGS

Instead of sowing seed, you can also raise plants by rooting cuttings. Buy fresh watercress from a supermarket, stand a few stems in water and leave them on a windowsill. The stems will develop roots after 10–14 days, when they can then be potted up into a shallow tray of moist compost. Grow them on under cover and harvest.

Stand the cuttings in a bright position and change the water every few days to keep it fresh. Remove leaves or stems that turn yellow.

4 ROUTINE CARE

Feed the plants with a high-nitrogen liquid fertilizer to encourage a large crop, and keep them well-weeded to prevent harvesting weeds by mistake. Plants will start to deteriorate after a few harvests and should be replaced by sowing a fresh batch.

5 HARVESTING

Start harvesting the plants once they have grown to 10–15cm (4–6in) in height. Begin by pinching out the main stems to encourage new sideshoots, and to prevent the plants becoming straggly. Pick over each plant lightly so that none are over cropped.

Watercress grows quickly but the plants need replacing after a few harvests. Sow more seeds every few weeks for a steady supply.

Pick over plants every few days and harvest the young shoots. Take only a few stems per plant and allow them to grow back.

GROWING LAND CRESS

An alternative to watercress is land cress, which has similar tasting leaves and can be used as an alternative in many recipes. It is easier to grow than watercress because it doesn't require such wet growing conditions. Land cress can be sown directly into the soil or grown in large containers. Plants are hardy and crop throughout winter.

SALADS AND LEAVES

Leafy crops are often quick-to-mature, and their shade-tolerant nature makes them useful for winkling into small spaces on the plot. Ample moisture is key to the rapid development of tender foliage – otherwise plants run the risk of flowering ("bolting"), which makes them bitter and inedible. Good hygiene helps to ensure the lush foliage remains free from rots and pests.

Q I'm struggling to sow neat, even drills of miniscule, fiddly seeds. Are there any tips?

Some seeds, such as watercress, rocket, and mustards, are tiny. If sowing them directly into the soil, mix them with some dry sand. Blend together thoroughly then sprinkle this evenly along the base of your drill. Some seeds are sold in tapes with the seeds embedded at regular intervals in a strip of biodegradable paper. Just bury this in your drill and water it in. Many salads (for example, corn salad, lettuce, and watercress) can be sown into modules and transplanted into rows later.

Q I sowed Swiss chard, and annual and perpetual spinach in spring, but half the plants bolted. What went wrong?

Bolting, which is the term used to describe premature flowering, is a nuisance in leafy crops because the large flower spike makes plants tough and unpalatable, and they produce fewer and smaller leaves. Many leafy veg are annual or biennial, naturally running to seed at the end of their life cycle. However, stress can cause this to happen prematurely, sometimes because the crops have become too dry, or because they are too closely planted, which induces root congestion. Fluctuating high and cold temperatures can also trigger bolting.

Q What can I do to prevent my seedlings rotting off after autumn sowings of salad leaves in the greenhouse?

Most salad crops are surprisingly hardy, and the protection of a greenhouse encourages lush, palatable growth. However, falling temperatures in autumn can encourage rots such as grey mould and damping off. Reduce the risk by sowing into a heated propagator (10–15°C/50–59°F is sufficient) and sowing more thinly than you would in summer to encourage good air flow and reduce humidity. Also consider your greenhouse soil – it may need changing if rots reoccur.

Q Every year in warm wet weather, my lettuce plants get destroyed by slugs. Is it worth trying to grow them again?

Slugs are a major enemy of leafy vegetables, with plants being especially vulnerable to damage at the seedling stage. Feeding activity is highest at night, especially on warm, wet nights. Scatter organic slug pellets based on ferric phosphate around vulnerable plants. Night-time patrols with a torch allow you to pick off and dispose of the pests. Consider using a biological control (microscopic nematodes) or installing a pond for predatory amphibians.

PEST AND DISEASE WATCH

These crops come from diverse backgrounds so can suffer from a variety of ailments:

- When sown in large numbers, salad seedlings are vulnerable to damping off disease (see p.248) where seedlings suddenly wilt and collapse.
- Aphids (see p.242) can quickly build in vast numbers with colonies clearly visible on leaves and shoots.
- Root aphids (see p.242) cause seedlings to wilt and can be confirmed if white powdery colonies are visible on the roots.
- Collapsed seedlings can imply cutworm damage (see p.242) – seedlings are cut off at the base.
- Slugs and snails (see p.242) eat jagged holes in leaves, and leave slime trails. (Often whole rows of seedlings can be devoured overnight.)
- Grey, fuzzy fungal growth on plants that are chilled and/or congested indicates botrytis (see p.246).
- White-yellow blotches on leaves is a sign of downy mildew (see p.244).
- Peppered holes in leaves implies flea beetle damage (see p.240), especially at the seedling stage.

RADISHES

In the height of summer, quick-growing radishes can be ready to harvest in as little as five weeks, which makes these small tasty roots handy for filling gaps in small plots. Radishes are available in a range of colours, sizes, and shapes, making them an attractive addition to salads. The leaves and seed pods of some varieties can also be eaten. Where space is very limited, they can also be sown direct into patio containers and windowboxes.

	SPRING	SUMMER	AUTUMN	WINTER
SOW				
HARVEST				

TIME TO HARVEST: 5–8 WEEKS

SUITABLE FOR: BEDS AND CONTAINERS

0   1m   2m   3m

60 plants

3M (10FT) ROWS
Sow or thin to 5cm (2in) apart

0   40cm

CONTAINERS
32 plants in each

1 GETTING STARTED

Radishes are adaptable plants and will grow in most soils and sites, even in partial shade. Because radishes mature very quickly it is important to sow seed little and often if you want to obtain regular supplies and avoid a glut. Sow a new batch once your existing plants have reached 8cm (3in) in height.

'Cherry Belle' is a fast-growing variety. The round, cherry-red roots are ideal in salads.

'French Breakfast' has fast-growing, white-tipped, elongated roots with a sweet flavour.

'Scarlet Globe' is an easy-to-grow variety that produces attractive, round, bright red roots.

'Sparkler' is a reliable variety, known for its round red roots, which have a peppery flavour.

When sowing in seed trays you can simply create 1cm (½in) deep planting holes with your finger, and drop the seed in.

Alternatively, sow pinches of radish seeds into modules. Once germinated, thin these to leave the strongest four to six seedlings per module.

2 SOWING UNDER COVER

Radishes are hardy plants but can be sown under cover in early spring to give an earlier start in colder areas. Sow seed thinly on the surface in small clusters, and cover with compost. Radish seed doesn't need additional heat to grow, and germinates within a few days. Harden off and plant the modules out when the frosts finish.

TIP Grow radishes alongside slower growing crops, such as parsnips.

3 SOWING OUTSIDE

Radishes mature quickly when sown directly in the ground; this is also the most straightforward way to grow them as the seedlings are simply cropped in the row. Before sowing, prepare the soil by digging it over to remove weeds, firm it gently, then rake to a fine tilth. Avoid sowing where brassicas have been grown recently.

Mark out drills that are about 2cm (¾in) deep. Radishes are relatively small plants, so the rows can be just 10cm (4in) apart.

Water each drill thoroughly then sow seeds 1cm (½in) apart. Cover them over with soil, firming it with the back of your rake. Water in lightly.

4 ROUTINE CARE

Thin out the seedlings carefully as they grow, and keep the plants well watered. Radishes are quick-growing crops so compete well with weeds. However, weeds can harbour pests and diseases, so it is important to keep on top of weeding around your crops.

5 PROTECTING PLANTS

Radishes are at risk from slugs and snails, and are vulnerable to flea beetle damage, especially in hot, dry weather. You can cover them with fine insect netting, which will also deter cabbage root fly (see p.242). Keep plants well watered to offset any damage.

Once the plants are large enough to handle, thin them out to 5cm (2in) spacing. The thinned seedlings can be used as a peppery salad leaf.

Flea beetles create ragged holes in the leaves. The best way to deter them is to cover crops with fine mesh netting..

6 HARVESTING

Pull up the roots as soon as they reach a harvestable size. Pick the radishes daily, checking the row to find the biggest roots. For the best taste and texture, eat radishes while they are young and tender. Don't leave them in the ground for too long because summer radishes can become spicy and pithy if they are left to grow large and over-mature. Plants are also prone to bolting.

Sow radish seed successionally and pull the roots gently from the ground as required.

BEETROOTS

One of the most popular crops on the vegetable plot, beetroot plants are highly productive, trouble-free, and great for small gardens because they also grow well in containers. Beetroot is very versatile, and can be harvested as baby roots a few weeks after sowing, or left until they are full size and are ideal for storing. Gone are the days when beetroot was simply preserved in vinegar. Modern cooks roast the roots, purée them, grate them into salads, and add them to cakes.

	SPRING	SUMMER	AUTUMN	WINTER
SOW				
HARVEST				

TIME TO HARVEST: 12–16 WEEKS

SUITABLE FOR: BEDS AND CONTAINERS

0   1m   2m   3m
30 plants

3M (10FT) ROWS
Sow 4cm (1½in) apart, thinning to 10cm (4in)

0   40cm

CONTAINERS
12 plants in each

1 GETTING STARTED

Beetroot can be bought as plug plants in spring for a head start, but is easily raised from seed. Most beetroot "seed" is actually a cluster of three or four true seeds, which germinate as a clump, and should then be thinned out. The exceptions to this are "monogerm" varieties that produce one seedling.

'Red Ace' produces large, dark red roots that are easy to grow and are good for storing.

'Chioggia Pink' has red-skinned roots with pink and white flesh. It has a sweet flavour.

'Boltardy' is widely grown and produces firm, round roots. It is resistant to bolting.

'Forono' is a reliable variety to grow for tender baby roots. It is suitable for containers.

Beetroot seeds are large and easy to handle, allowing you to sow one per module. Keep the soil moist after sowing.

Thin the seedlings as they grow to leave the strongest per module. Monogerm seed, sown singly, won't require thinning.

Plant out the seedlings as soon as possible so the plants develop fully in the soil. Try to avoid disturbing the roots.

2 SOWING UNDER COVER

To give them a head start, beetroot can be sown under cover. Fill modular trays with seed compost, firm gently, water it well then allow it to drain. Make a 2cm (¾in) deep hole in each module using a dibber or pencil, and drop one seed into each. Firm the compost, water lightly and place the tray in a propagator. As soon as roots start growing through the base of the cells, harden off the seedlings and plant them out 10cm (4in) apart.

TIP Soak seeds in warm water for 30 mins before sowing to help germination.

3 SOWING OUTSIDE

Beetroot can be sown directly in the soil, provided it is warm enough. Dig over the site to remove any weeds then rake it to a fine tilth. Along a garden line, create drills 2.5cm (1in) deep using the edge of a hoe or rake. Water the base, then sow the seeds roughly 4cm (1½in) apart. Cover with soil, firm gently, and water in lightly.

Sow the seed at regular intervals, spacing it by hand. The soil should be at least 8°C (46°F) before sowing, otherwise germination will be slow.

Thin the seedlings to 10cm (4in) apart by pulling them up or pinching them off completely. The "thinnings" can be used as salad leaves.

4 WEEDING

Beetroot are fairly pest- and disease-free, but remember to keep hand-weeding around the plants to prevent weeds establishing. If left, weeds will compete against your crop for moisture and nutrients, and will slow their growth. Weeds also attract pests.

Carefully weeding by hand close to the plants is safer than using a hoe, which can easily damage the top of the swelling roots.

5 ROUTINE CARE

Seedlings should be watered regularly. Mature plants are fairly drought-resistant, but the roots are more tender if the soil is kept moist. Avoid overwatering because this will encourage the production of excess leaves at the expense of roots.

Water plants at the base and avoid splashing the leaves, which can encourage disease. Plants on lighter soils should be watered more regularly.

6 HARVESTING

Roots can be harvested as soon as they reach a usable size, or can be left in the soil to grow larger for later use. To harvest, carefully lift them from the ground, wash off any soil, and twist off the leaves. Surplus, undamaged roots can be stored in wooden boxes lined with newspaper. Place 2.5cm (1in) of sharp sand in the base, then a layer of roots. Add more layers to fill the box, then store in a cool, dry shed or garage.

Young roots are best enjoyed fresh, so only harvest them on the day you intend to eat them.

CARROTS

This ever-popular root crop is just as happy growing in a container as it is in the soil, more so if your soil is stony. Carrots are a useful crop that can be enjoyed for almost 12 months of the year – with baby "pullings" in early spring and substantial maincrop roots that store well into winter. Their high sugar levels and crunchy texture make carrots a children's favourite. They are also rich in vitamin A, an essential nutrient for good health.

	SPRING	SUMMER	AUTUMN	WINTER
SOW				
HARVEST				

TIME TO HARVEST: 12-20 WEEKS

SUITABLE FOR: BEDS AND CONTAINERS

3M (10FT) ROWS
24-150 plants
Depending on variety, grow 2-12cm (1¾-5in) apart

CONTAINERS
50 plants in each

1 GETTING STARTED

Carrots come in a wide variety of shapes, sizes, and even colours. They are grown from seeds, and if they are harvested young, they can be ready in a matter of weeks. Round varieties are the best choice for growing in containers or in shallow or stoney soils; larger maincrop varieties need deep, moist beds.

'Resistafly' has good resistance to carrot root fly. It produces sweet, cylindrical roots.

'Parmex' produces bite-size, sweet-tasting, round carrots. It is ideal for container growing.

'Purple Haze' crops early, yielding unusual purple-skinned roots with contrasting flesh.

'Sugarsnax' produces long roots with an extra sweet flavour and high beta-carotene levels.

2 SOWING SEEDS

To sow direct, dig over the soil to remove weeds, firm it, then rake it level. Make drills with a hoe, water the base, and sow the seed. Then cover it with soil and water in. Carrots can also be sown into short drills in deep containers.

Make seed drills 2cm (¾in) deep, 10-20cm (4-8in) apart, depending on the variety. Check the packet first.

Sow the fine seeds thinly, roughly 5mm (¼in) apart. Tip them from the packet or sprinkle them along the row with your fingers.

3 GROWING ON

Carrot seed can be notoriously slow to germinate, so be patient. While you wait, it is important to keep the soil or compost well watered until seedlings emerge. If you are sowing early crops outside or in containers in spring, you can cover them with garden fleece to provide insulation. Where space allows, seed sown in containers can also kept under cover until it has germinated, then moved outside to grow on.

Remove garden fleece on milder days to let in the sunlight. Cover seedlings if hard frost is predicted.

4 THINNING OUT

As they grow, thin the seedlings to the recommended distances for your particular variety. In general, maincrop varieties require much wider spacings than early carrots. Very young seedlings can be pulled but those with developing taproots should be pinched off to prevent leaving holes that are ideal for carrot fly eggs (see below).

Check the seed packet before thinning the seedlings as some varieties require more space, and therefore more thinning, than others.

5 ROUTINE CARE

Water plants during dry spells but don't overdo it, as this promotes leafy growth at the expense of roots. Regularly weed close to plants by hand. Weeding releases the scent of the leaves, which attracts carrot fly, so it is best done at dusk, when the pests are less active.

Weed regularly, as removing fully grown weeds can disturb the crop. As carrots mature, their foliage will help to suppress weeds.

6 PROTECTING PLANTS

Carrot fly larvae (see p.240) can be a troublesome pest, eating into the roots, especially on crops sown in late spring. To prevent the low-flying adults laying eggs at the base of plants, erect a barrier of fine insect mesh, at least 60cm (24in) high, around the beds.

Use canes to support carrot fly netting, and also bury the base 5cm (2in) into the soil, all the way around, to prevent flies sneaking under.

7 HARVESTING

Carrots are ready to pull once they reach the desired size. Early sowings are ready when they are roughly finger-thickness, and are pulled from the soil by hand. Harvest maincrop varieties when they measure about 4cm (1½in) across, easing them out with a fork.

If using a fork to lift carrots, take care not to disturb neighbouring plants left to grow on.

TIP Eat early carrots fresh; maincrop roots can be stored like beetroot (see p.137).

TURNIPS

This vegetable has undergone a revival, with top chefs and gardeners alike rediscovering what these sweet, tender roots have to offer. Baby crops can be harvested in as little as six weeks, or plants can be left in the ground to mature fully. Turnips can also be grown for their leaves, or turnip "tops". These can be treated like a cut-and-come-again crop and will provide several flushes of leafy greens through the leaner months in late autumn and early spring.

	SPRING	SUMMER	AUTUMN	WINTER
SOW				
HARVEST				

TIME TO HARVEST: 6–10 WEEKS

SUITABLE FOR: BEDS AND CONTAINERS

0   1m   2m   3m

30 plants

3M (10FT) ROWS
Plant 10cm (4in) apart

0   40cm

CONTAINERS
12–20 plants

1 GETTING STARTED

Turnips prefer a site with moist, rich, well-drained soil that contains plenty of nitrogen, so dig in plenty of organic matter, such as well-rotted compost or manure, in the season before growing. Consider sowing turnips that will be harvested as baby roots alongside slow-growing crops such as parsnips or sweetcorn.

'Purple Top Milan' should be pulled early at 5cm (2in) wide. The roots have a sweet flavour.

'Snowball' has pure white roots that are sweet and tender. Lift the roots at six weeks.

'Primera' roots have purple tops and should be pulled small. They have sweet, tender flesh.

'Atlantic' produces purple and white roots that can be harvested young or left to mature.

Hardy varieties can be sown under cover at the beginning and end of the growing season, giving you roots during almost every month of the year.

Harden the seedlings off and plant them out, once their roots fill the modules. Space the plants 10cm (4in) apart, with 30cm (12in) between rows.

2 SOWING UNDER COVER

Fill module trays with seed compost, firm gently, and water well. Let the soil drain then make a 2cm (¾in) deep hole in each cell. Sow two seeds per hole, cover over, and water in. Harden them off and plant out when they are large enough to handle. Alternatively, fill large containers with compost and make drills 2cm (¾in) deep. Sow seed thinly along the base or sow a pinch of seeds every 10cm (4in). Thin the seedlings to one per cell, or one every 10cm (4in).

TIP To prevent a glut, sow seed little and often for a small but steady supply.

3 SOWING OUTSIDE

You can sow turnip seed directly outside between mid-spring and late summer. Create a seedbed by digging over a patch of soil to remove any weeds and incorporate a base dressing of high nitrogen granular fertilizer. Firm gently, rake level to create a fine tilth, then create drills 2cm (¾in) deep and 23–30cm (9–12in) apart.

Water the drills well and then sow seeds thinly along the base. Cover them back over with a thin layer of soil and then water them in lightly.

Carefully thin the seedlings to leave a strong specimen every 10cm (4in). Use the thinned turnip seedlings as a leafy green or in salads.

4 ROUTINE CARE

Flea beetle can be a problem, especially in hot, dry weather, so cover drills initially with insect-proof mesh. Keep plants well watered and fed as they grow. Container plants and those on light soils can be fed periodically with a high-nitrogen liquid fertilizer.

Fine insect-proof mesh should be used to protect crops from flying pests such as flea beetle during the early stages of their growth.

5 WEEDING

It is important to keep the young plants weed-free, as weeds compete with the seedlings for light and nutrients and may harbour disease. Weed around the plants by hand to prevent damaging the roots; use a hoe to remove weeds between the rows.

Pull out competing weeds by hand, to avoid damaging the young turnip roots. Check the rows regularly so weeds can be pulled up when young. Weeding is easier when the soil is damp.

6 HARVESTING

Pull individual "baby" roots of fast-growing summer crops once they reach the size of a golf ball; leaving them to grow any larger can result in a woody texture. Hardy winter types can be left to grow larger and then lifted in autumn as and when they are needed. If you have a glut, it is possible to store turnips in boxes of sand, but they are only likely to keep for a couple of weeks as they have fairly thin skins.

Early roots are ideal for harvesting when they reach about 4–5cm (1½–2in) in diameter.

PARSNIPS

A delicious staple of the winter kitchen, parsnips are a worthy addition to any vegetable plot. A respectable number can be grown on just a small patch of ground and they are easy to cultivate – just make sure that you give them plenty of water. Although parsnips take a long time to grow, they are extremely hardy and can be left in the soil well into the winter months. In fact, exposure to frost is thought to make the roots taste sweeter.

	SPRING	SUMMER	AUTUMN	WINTER
SOW				
HARVEST				

TIME TO HARVEST: 32–36 WEEKS

SUITABLE FOR: BEDS

0   1m   2m   3m

11–15 plants

3M (10FT) ROWS
Plant 20–30cm (8–12in) apart

1 GETTING STARTED
Parsnips grow best in light soils that are free from stones and not compacted; this reduces the risk of roots becoming crooked or forked. Pick a site that was manured the previous autumn. Applying manure just before sowing can cause root tips to become scorched, which results in forked roots.

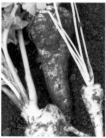

'White Gem' has relatively short roots with white skin and excellent flavour.

'Gladiator' is an exhibition variety, known for its sweet, smooth-skinned roots.

'Javelin' produces a brilliant yield of long slender roots and has good disease resistance.

'Tender and True' roots are large, smooth-skinned, and show some resistance to canker.

Sow the seed in mid- to late spring, as soon as the risk of frost has passed. Seed sown earlier than this may struggle to germinate.

Once the seedlings are large enough to handle, thin them by pulling out or pinching out the weakest, leaving only the strongest to grow on.

2 SOWING SEEDS
Because they develop a long tap root parsnips are best sown direct. Prepare the soil then sow clumps of four or five seeds every 20–30cm (8–12in), 2cm (¾in) deep. Space rows 30cm (12in) apart. Seedlings can germinate slowly – often taking up to 10–14 days – so be patient. Save space and mark your rows by sowing fast-growing salad leaves or radishes between your parsnip seedlings. These crops can be harvested well before the parsnips mature.

TIP Buy new seed each spring because parsnip seed viability is very short.

3 PROTECTING PLANTS

Parsnips are part of the carrot family and similarly prone to carrot fly attack (see p.240). Prevent this by pinching off the surplus seedlings at soil level rather than pulling them, which can leave holes for the female fly to lay her eggs in. Also, erect a barrier of fine insect-proof mesh at least 60cm (24in) tall around your plants.

Bury the insect-proof mesh 5cm (2in) deep in the soil, completely surrounding the plants, so that the carrot flies can't get underneath it.

4 ROUTINE CARE

Keep plants well watered as they develop to ensure good-sized, even roots. Hand-weed around the plants to avoid disturbing their roots until the plants are established and better able to compete with weeds. Parsnips do not require any additional feeding.

Regular watering will encourage the roots to grow evenly. If they are allowed to become dry, later watering may cause the roots to split.

5 HARVESTING

Early parsnip varieties will be ready to lift in early autumn; later types can be harvested during winter. Roots can grow very deep, especially on open, light soils. Lift them by inserting a garden fork next to each root and gently easing the root out of the soil.

Lift parsnips gently to avoid damaging them. In very dry conditions, roots will emerge more readily if the soil is moistened beforehand.

STORING ROOTS

Late-maturing parsnips can be left in the ground until required. In very cold areas, cover the plants with a mulch of straw so that the ground will not be frozen solid when you come to dig up the roots. Mark plants with a cane to make them easier to find. Roots left in the soil and lifted in spring can be stored in sand in the same way as beetroot (see p.137).

SWEDES

These plump, round roots are delicious roasted or mashed like potatoes, and provide welcome fresh crops in autumn and winter when the vegetable patch is pretty bare. These are slow-maturing plants, traditionally best suited to larger gardens where they can be left to grow. However, swedes can also be sown densely to produce "baby" roots, which can be eaten within a few weeks, leaves and all, or left a little longer for small, sweet roots, 5cm (2in) across.

	SPRING	SUMMER	AUTUMN	WINTER
SOW				
HARVEST				

TIME TO HARVEST: 20–24 WEEKS

SUITABLE FOR: BEDS

```
0          1m          2m          3m
```
12–15 plants

3M (10FT) ROWS
Plant 20–25cm (8–10in) apart

1 GETTING STARTED

Swedes need a long growing season compared to other crops and will take five or six months to mature fully. In the autumn before growing, dig in plenty of well-rotted organic matter, such as compost or manure. As brassicas, they need to be planted where no other brassicas have been grown in the past year.

'Brora' roots are fast-growing and have good disease-resistance. The yellow flesh is very tasty.

'Best of All' is a reliable variety, giving medium-sized, purple roots with yellow flesh.

'Tweed' has attractive, purple-topped roots and grows well in less fertile soil.

'Marian' produces deep purple roots that have an excellent flavour and good disease resistance.

Sow seed thinly along your rows before covering it over, watering it in, and then firming gently. Multiple rows should be spaced about 30cm (12in) apart.

Once seedlings begin to appear, gradually thin them out leaving the strongest to grow on. The plants should be spaced eventually around 20–25cm (8–10in) apart.

2 SOWING SEEDS

Because they develop a relatively long tap root, swedes are best sown direct into the ground rather than in modules or seed trays. In mid- to late spring, prepare the site for sowing by digging it over thoroughly to remove any weeds and large stones, then firm it gently and rake it level. Make a drill 2cm (¾in) deep and water it well. Sow your seeds along it, cover them over with a little more soil to level the soil surface, and then firm down gently.

TIP For baby swedes, sow seed densely then thin to 8–10cm (3–4in) apart.

3 GROWING ON

Swedes are exceptionally hardy crops, although very early sowings may need protection if there is a risk of frost. Cover them with a single or double layer of horticultural fleece, or a cloche or cold frame, to offer insulation and speed up growth. Ensure that the plants remain well watered under their protective covering.

Swedes are fully hardy but cover early sowings with garden fleece to protect them from frost, especially in colder regions.

4 PROTECTING PLANTS

Swedes are prone to the same pests and diseases as other members of the brassica family. Flea beetle can be damaging to plants during hot weather. To reduce the risk, cover over rows with fine, insect-proof mesh to prevent beetles getting to the plants.

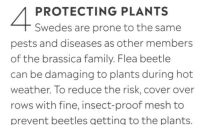

Cover plants with wire netting to deter pests such as pigeons. Use finer mesh if you need to protect against flea beetles and cabbage root fly.

5 ROUTINE CARE

Avoid a check in growth due to a lack of moisture by keeping your plants well irrigated, especially during dry spells. After watering apply a 6–7cm (2½–3in) deep mulch of organic matter to lock in soil moisture. This technique is especially useful on light soils.

Hand-weed or hoe between the plants regularly to prevent competing weeds from checking growth; take care not to damage the roots.

6 HARVESTING

In early to mid-autumn, roots will become large enough to harvest. Push a garden fork into the soil alongside the plants and lever the roots out gently. Swedes lifted in autumn can be stored in boxes of sand or kept in a shed or garage until required. If you don't have storage space, swedes can be left in the soil under a layer of straw all winter, but be aware that it is almost impossible to lift roots when the soil has frozen hard.

After lifting your swedes, clean them and cut the stems off before storing.

STEP-BY-STEP

POTATOES

Whether you prefer them chipped, roasted, baked, mashed, or new and slathered in butter, potatoes are a delicious must-grow crop in any garden. This popular vegetable is one of the easiest for beginner gardeners and can be grown in large containers and sacks if you don't have ample amounts of bed space. There is a huge selection of varieties to choose from, classed, in order of maturity, as first earlies, second earlies, early maincrops, maincrops, and late maincrops.

	SPRING	SUMMER	AUTUMN	WINTER
SOW				
HARVEST				
TIME TO HARVEST: 12-22 WEEKS				

SUITABLE FOR: BEDS AND CONTAINERS

4–8 plants

3M (10FT) ROWS
Plant 35–70cm (14–30in) apart

CONTAINERS
2 plants in each

1 START UNDER COVER

Potatoes bought for planting are called "seed potatoes", and are available to buy in mid- to late winter. Early types can be "chitted" before planting to give them a head start. Chitting means allowing the "eyes" to sprout before the tubers are planted out. Place your seed potatoes "rose-end" – the end with the most eyes – upwards, in an egg box or tray, and position it in a cool, well-lit place such as a windowsill until the sprouts appear.

Choose seed potatoes that are of good quality and certified as disease-free to maximize your chance of a good crop.

Stored in a well-lit, frost-free place, the tubers will begin to develop "chits" within a few weeks. They are then ready to plant out.

Place the tubers into the soil, ensuring that they are planted with the rose-end facing up.

Water the chitted tubers in well before covering them to help them establish quickly.

Cover the tubers with soil, leaving the surface raised up into a slight mound.

2 PLANTING OUT

Seed potatoes can be planted in the ground or in containers. The main season to plant outside is early spring for early varieties, and mid-spring for maincrops. Dig over and weed the soil, and work in some general purpose fertilizer. Dig a drill about 15cm (6in) deep and place your potatoes along the bottom, spaced 35–70cm (14–30in) apart. Cover over with 20cm (8in) of soil to create a slight mound.

TIP The closer the potatoes are planted together, the smaller the tubers will be.

3 CONTAINER-GROWING

Alternatively, potatoes can be planted in containers, such as specially designed potato "barrels" or large tubs or plastic sacks. Use a 50:50 mix of multipurpose compost and good garden soil, placing a 15cm (6in) layer of this in the base. Lay the potato tubers on top and then cover with a further 10cm (4in) of soil. Water them in well.

As long as you make drainage holes before planting, a large plastic barrel makes a great space-saving, growing container for potatoes.

Plastic sacks make good growing containers as they can be emptied and folded away once all the potatoes have been harvested.

4 ROUTINE CARE

Water plants well, and feed using an all-purpose granular fertilizer. Young plants need weeding but soon develop a smothering canopy of foliage. After flowering, green, tomato-like fruits, may appear – these are poisonous and should not be eaten. Check plants regularly for potato blight (see p.248).

5 EARTHING UP

Plants will need "earthing up" as they grow: draw the soil up around the stem to leave the top 10cm (4in) of the plant visible. This encourages the plant to produce greater yields, and prevents the developing tubers from becoming exposed to sunlight, which makes them green and inedible.

Potatoes are tender, and emerging shoots can be damaged by frosts. Cover plants with garden fleece when cold weather is predicted.

Earth up potatoes three or four times during summer. Containers should be earthed up until the compost reaches just below the rim.

6 HARVESTING

Begin harvesting early potatoes in early summer – generally they will be ready to lift once their flowers develop; leave maincrop types until late summer or early autumn. Lift soil-grown plants gently with a fork, taking care not to damage the tubers. Container-grown plants can either be tipped out in one go, or excavated to remove the tubers as you need them. Gently refirm the compost afterwards and water well.

Harvest potatoes on a dry day, if possible, and leave them to dry in the sun for a few hours.

POTATOES

1 'Accent' This yellow-skinned first early potato bears reliably high yields. It has moderately good disease resistance and the tubers suffer less slug damage than other varieties.

2 'Charlotte' A second early, this yellow-skinned salad potato is reliable and has a good flavour. Higher yielding than others of this type, individual tuber-size is also impressive.

3 'Red Duke of York' This versatile first early variety can be lifted and eaten young as a new potato, or allowed to mature for baking. It has red skin and creamy-white flesh.

4 'Belle de Fontenay' This early maincrop variety is renowned for being a great salad potato. The yield of knobbly tubers is good, and the flesh is yellow and waxy.

5 'Pink Fir Apple' An heirloom maincrop variety, it produces knobbly, red-skinned tubers that have a waxy texture and a good flavour. It is widely grown as salad potato.

6 'Jazzy' This second early variety produces a large crop of small waxy tubers with great flavour. A good salad potato, it can also be boiled, mashed, roasted, or steamed.

7 'Foremost' This early variety produces high yields of tasty, firm, white-fleshed tubers, with good scab resistance. They store well under cover if kept dry and well-ventilated.

8 'Yukon Gold' A second early, it has great flavour and can be used in a variety of different ways in the kitchen: boiled as a new potato, or baked, roast, or chipped.

9 'Ratte' A good alternative to 'Pink Fir Apple', the tubers mature earlier and have smoother skins, which makes them easier to prepare in the kitchen. It has a tasty salad-potato flavour.

OTHER VARIETIES
'Sarpo Axona'
'Anya'
'Maris Bard'
'Maris Piper'
'Lady Christl'
'Blue Danube'

GROW YOUR OWN VEGETABLES **ROOT CROPS**

ROOT CROPS

The secret to tender, succulent roots is a steady moisture supply through all stages of plant growth – that way, woodiness is deterred. An open, organic-rich soil is ideal because it also ensures that long taproots can develop unhindered. Crop rotations help to prevent a build-up of soil diseases, and insect pests can easily be thwarted by growing crops under a fine mesh.

Q My beetroot and turnip drills put up flower spikes before any roots formed. Why?

This phenomenon, known as bolting, is a nuisance because you are left with very little harvestable root. Flowering is natural for all root vegetables, the vast majority of which are biennial, meaning they bloom in their second year. However, stresses on the plant can trigger premature flowering. Keeping roots moist reduces the risk of bolting, as does thinning out at the seedling stage to reduce competition. Aim for at least 8cm (5in) between plants, more on light soils.

Q Why did my early trays of radish take ages to grow in my cool greenhouse? They were also tough to eat.

Their slow growth may have been due to cool temperatures or dryness. These roots are some of the quickest vegetables to mature, with summer varieties being harvestable in as little as five weeks after sowing. This rapid growth, which needs ample warmth and moisture, results in very tender roots. When root crops grow slowly they're more likely to become tough and woody. This can be compounded if the crop isn't harvested as soon as it's ready.

Q My carrots had lovely, lush foliage but their roots were tiny. How can I prevent that happening the next time?

While root crops benefit from adequate nutrition, they can respond by giving miserly yields should watering and feeding be incorrect. Excess fertilizer, especially high-nitrogen formulations such as chicken pellets or other animal manures, will encourage lush foliage. Warmth and moisture speed up growth further, and often the result is generous tops but weak roots. In future, ensure feeds are correct by following the manufacturer's dosage recommendations (keep in mind that clay soils are more fertile than sandy ones).

Q On digging up my winter parsnips, I found that many of the roots had forked – why would this happen?

Parsnips, like other tap-rooted crops, prefer to be sown directly into the earth, rather than into pots then transplanted. A stony or compacted soil can cause problems, however, because if a developing tap root hits a physical barrier it often results in a split or "fork". Excess fertilizer can also cause this, with the feed scorching off the developing taproot tip. Consider sowing into raised beds with stone-free soil and follow fertilizer application guidelines carefully.

PEST AND DISEASE WATCH

Perfect roots are achievable if tunnelling pests are avoided via crop rotations and physical barriers.

- Seedlings of radish and turnip can become peppered with holes due to flea beetles (see p.240).
- If rows of seedlings disappear overnight, suspect slug damage (see p.242).
- Potato foliage can blacken and collapse – if the whole plant wilts, then black leg (see p.248) is the culprit. If blotches appear regularly yet rapidly, late blight (see p.248) will be to blame.
- If tiny maggots have tunnelled into the roots of swedes, turnips, or radishes, cabbage root fly (see p.242) has infested your crop.
- Carrot roots riddled with tiny, rusty orange holes suggests damage by carrot root fly larvae (see p.240).
- Parsnip roots stained with orange wounds implies canker infection (see p.246).
- Neat drills tunnelled into potato tubers and carrot roots implies cutworm damage (see p.242).
- Potato tubers covered in corky skin lesions are often infected by common scab (see p.246).

ONIONS

No vegetable garden is complete without onions and there are many to choose from, including red-, white-, and brown-skinned varieties. This traditional crop takes a long time to mature. Sizeable bulbs can be achieved by sowing seeds under cover early in the year. However, an easier method is to raise plants from "sets", small onion bulbs, which are planted in spring or autumn. Overwintered crops of hardy, often Japanese, varieties offer a useful early harvest.

	SPRING	SUMMER	AUTUMN	WINTER
SOW				
HARVEST				
TIME TO HARVEST: 20–24 WEEKS				

SUITABLE FOR: BEDS

0   1m   2m   3m

30 plants

3M (10FT) ROWS
Sow, plant, or thin to 10cm (4in) apart

1 SOWING UNDER COVER

For larger bulbs, sow seeds under cover from midwinter to early spring. Fill module trays with seed compost, firm gently, and water well. Make a hole in each cell 1cm (½in) deep and sow two seeds in each. The seeds require additional gentle heat and should be kept moist. Germination will take a week or two. Thin the seedlings to leave one stronger seedling in each module.

TIP For smaller, earlier bulbs, sow three or four seeds per cell and don't thin them.

Sowing seeds in modules removes the need to prick the seedlings out as they develop.

Thin seedlings once large enough to handle. They should pull easily from the compost.

Harden seedlings off and plant out in spring when "sets" are also planted out.

Spring sowings can bolt in cold weather so choose a bolt-resistant variety. Don't sow too early in the year, when a cold snap may occur.

Thin out the seedlings as they develop until they reach their final spacing, leaving only the strongest. Use the thinnings in your salads.

2 SOWING OUTSIDE

This method of raising onions is now less common since the introduction of "sets", which offer the crop a useful head start. Sow seeds in spring for early autumn crops, or in late summer for Japanese overwintering varieties. Dig over the soil to remove weeds, firm it down and rake the surface level. Prepare a drill 2cm (¾in) deep. Water the base well and then sow thinly along it. Cover and water in and, once the seedlings have emerged, thin them out to leave one every 10cm (4in).

3 PLANTING SETS

Sets are very small onion bulbs that are planted in either autumn or spring. Each one bulks up in size to produce a larger bulb. Autumn-planted sets of winter-hardy varieties often mature to produce larger bulbs than those planted in the spring. Plant the sets 10cm (4in) apart into prepared soil using a trowel, positioning the tip at soil level.

The space between sets will determine the final size of your onions – plant them further apart with a trowel if you want larger onions.

Firm the soil gently around the sets, leaving the tips showing above the soil surface. Water them in lightly to help settle the sets in.

4 ROUTINE CARE

Onions are very sensitive to plant competition so ensure you weed regularly between your bulbs. Keep the soil evenly moist, especially if you want good-sized bulbs. Autumn sowings and plantings benefit from an application of high-nitrogen fertilizer in late winter.

5 HARVESTING

Harvest onions when they reach full size and the stems have collapsed and bent over. On a dry day, partly lift them out of the soil using a fork gently. Leave them on the ground for a week or so to dry out; dry them indoors on racks if it is wet.

It is important to keep crops well weeded, especially while they are young. Weed around them by hand to avoid damaging the bulbs.

Onion bulbs are ready to harvest once the stems and leaves have naturally died back. Lift on a dry day to prevent the bulbs rotting.

DRYING THE BULBS

Lay the onions out on a wire rack to dry. Ensure that this is kept off the ground so that air can circulate around the bulbs. Leave them in a light, dry place such as a greenhouse or on a windowsill. Once the outer skins rustle you can either plait your bulbs and hang them up, or store them in net bags until needed.

ONIONS

1 'Sturon' This popular brown-skinned onion produces mid-sized bulbs with flavoursome, juicy flesh. The bulbs are resistant to bolting and keep well after harvesting.

2 'Ailsa Craig' A reliable variety, this onion develops large, globe-shaped bulbs with a mild flavour. Use them fresh, as the bulbs don't store well. Plants can be raised from seed or "sets".

3 'Senshyu' This hardy Japanese variety can be planted in autumn to harvest in early summer. It is a reliable onion and gives a good harvest of tasty, flat-bottomed bulbs.

4 'Centurion' Plant this variety in spring for an early crop of rounded, brown-skinned bulbs in summer that store well for short periods. The flesh is crisp with a good flavour.

5 'Hi Keeper' This is a Japanese variety to plant in autumn and overwinter outside, ready to harvest in early summer. It can also be sown in spring to harvest mid- to late summer.

6 'Red Baron' This variety gives a reliable crop of small to medium-sized, red-skinned bulbs in summer. It has a stronger flavour than many other red onions and stores well.

7 'Setton' Producing large, brown-skinned bulbs in late summer, these onions have a good flavour and store well. It is a reliable new variety that crops heavily. It is mainly sold as "sets".

8 'Shakespeare' Plant this variety in autumn ready to harvest the following summer. It produces brown-skinned, mid-sized bulbs that are excellent for storing. It has good flavour.

9 'Golden Bear' This variety produces large brown-skinned bulbs that mature in midsummer. It gives a good crop that stores well, and is resistant to onion white rot disease (see p.244).

OTHER VARIETIES
'Bedfordshire Champion'
'Hercules'
'Hytech'
'Marco'
'Stuttgarter Giant'

SHALLOTS

These small bulbs couldn't be easier to grow – simply plant sets during autumn or spring and each will divide up, producing a cluster of new bulbs. If their skins are properly dried, storage life is extremely long, giving you useful bulbs with an intense flavour for many months of the year. Shallots are expensive to buy and delicious used whole in casseroles, where they melt in the mouth. When they are roasted with meat or vegetables, they take on a sweet, caramelized flavour.

	SPRING	SUMMER	AUTUMN	WINTER
SOW				
HARVEST				
TIME TO HARVEST: 20–36 WEEKS				

SUITABLE FOR: BEDS

0   1m   2m   3m

15 plants

3M (10FT) ROWS
Thin and plant out to 20cm (8in) apart

1 GETTING STARTED

Shallots are most commonly grown from "sets" – small bulbs that, when planted, bulk up by splitting into numerous smaller bulbs. Alternatively, shallots can be grown from seed, either sown under cover in winter, or sown direct in mid- to late spring. Make sure that you give them rich, well-drained soil.

'Longor' bulbs have pinkish flesh and good flavour. They are uniform in size and shape.

'Red Sun' is a high-yielding variety with red skins and red-flushed, crisp flesh.

'Golden Gourmet' is a mild-tasting variety and the large, yellow bulbs can be eaten raw.

'Mikor' bulbs have brownish skin and pink flesh. The large bulbs are good for cooking.

2 SOWING UNDER COVER

Fill a module tray with seed compost, water well, and leave it to drain. Sow the seeds in small clusters and cover them with 1cm (½in) of compost. Water lightly and place the tray in a propagator; germination will take a week or two.

Once the seedlings emerge, they will need thinning to leave the strongest seedling per cell.

3 PLANTING SETS

Plant your sets, either in late autumn or spring, directly outside in an open, sunny site that has been dug over to remove weeds. Push them into the soil, leaving the tip of each bulb protruding just above the surface. Plant them at their eventual spacing – leaving 20cm (8in) between sets in each direction.

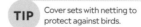
TIP Cover sets with netting to protect against birds.

Buy certified, virus-free sets to boost your chance of growing a prolific, healthy crop.

4 SOW AND PLANT OUT

Seed can be sown direct once the soil has warmed up at the end of spring. Dig in plenty of well-rotted manure or compost. Create a drill about 2.5cm (1in) deep and sow seed thinly along it. Cover with soil and water in. If you have seedlings that have been indoor-grown from seed, harden them off and plant them out 20 x 20cm (8 x 8in) apart.

Sprinkle the seed thinly along each drill – sow plenty, as seedlings will be thinned out once they are established.

Thin the seedlings, pulling the weakest ones out gently by hand, leaving approximately 2cm (¾in) between them.

If your seedlings need transplanting to their final position, dig them up gently and re-plant them 20cm (8in) apart.

5 ROUTINE CARE

Keep plants well watered and well weeded. To boost yields, overwintered shallots should have a granular high-nitrogen fertilizer sprinkled among the plants during spring – chicken pellets are ideal. There is no need to feed spring-planted shallots.

Weed the seedlings by hand or with an onion hoe. Keeping them well ventilated will prevent diseases such as downy mildew (see p.244).

6 HARVESTING

Leaves will turn yellow and wither in mid- to late summer – a sign that the bulbs are nearly mature. Stop watering at this point to encourage the bulbs to dry and set strong skins for long storage. Lift gently with a fork, taking care not to damage the individual bulbs.

Leave the bulbs to dry on the soil surface for a few days after lifting and then carefully split into individual bulbs before you store them.

DRYING THE BULBS

To store well, shallots should be dried fully on a raised rack in a greenhouse or a covered area for at least two weeks. After this, cut the stem off each bulb to leave a 1cm (½in) stump, rub off the loose outer skin, and store them in a net bag or cardboard box in a cool, dry, frost-free place until required.

SPRING ONIONS

Spring onions are ideally suited to small-space growing on plots and in containers so make sure you reserve space for a row or two. These small plants are suprisingly productive and extremely hardy, allowing you to extend the season with early and late sowings. Spring onions either form a small bulb underground, or grow like a miniature leek, producing cylindrical, non-bulbing stems. You can also choose from red-stemmed, pickling, and Japanese varieties.

	SPRING	SUMMER	AUTUMN	WINTER
SOW				
HARVEST				

TIME TO HARVEST: 10 WEEKS

SUITABLE FOR: BEDS AND CONTAINERS

0   1m   2m   3m

150 plants

3M (10FT) ROWS
Plant out 2cm (¾in) apart

0   40cm

CONTAINERS
40 plants in each

1 GETTING STARTED

Spring onions are grown from seed, either sown directly in the soil or into large containers during spring and summer. Early and late crops can also be raised under cover; sown directly into greenhouse borders, or into large containers. Small crops can also be sown on warm windowsills in late winter.

'Guardsman' has long, well-blanched stems and dark green leaves. It is a vigorous variety.

'North Holland Blood Red' produces striking red stems that deepen in colour with age.

'White Lisbon' is the most commonly grown spring onion and is good for container growing.

'Ishikura' is an oriental bunching onion. Stems can be harvested pencil-thin or carrot-thick.

Sow seed under cover from early spring to autumn. A propagator helps to protect seeds and boost germination.

For direct sowing under cover fill large containers with seed compost, water well, and sow seed thinly 1cm (½in) deep.

Seedlings will need to be thinned when they reach about 8cm (3in) tall – thin to leave 2cm (¾in) between each seedling.

2 SOWING UNDER COVER

Because certain varieties are hardy, early- and late-season sowings can be made under cover to extend the harvesting period. Fill large containers, 30cm (12in) wide, with seed compost, firm gently, water well, and allow to drain. Mark out drills 1cm (½in) deep and 10cm (4in) apart using a trowel or short length of bamboo cane. Sow seeds 1cm (½in) apart along the base, cover over with more compost, and water in lightly. As the seedlings emerge, thin them out to leave one strong plant every 2cm (¾in). Protect the young crop against slug damage with a light sprinkling of pellets.

3 SOWING OUTSIDE

If sowing spring onions outside, prepare the soil thoroughly by digging it over to remove weeds and any crop debris, firm it gently, and rake it level. Mark out drills 1cm (½in) deep and 10cm (4in) apart. Water the base of the drill well and then sow seeds roughly 1cm (½in) apart along its length. Cover them over with soil and water in lightly.

A late summer or early autumn sowing of a winter hardy variety will give crops in spring. Cover plants with fleece during harsh weather.

Once seedlings are 8cm (3in) tall thin them out to leave one every 2cm (¾in). These thinnings can be used in salads in the same way as chives.

4 UNDER COVER CROPS

Crops can be grown under cover in large containers to give an early or late harvest. Water them well and feed them with a dilute general-purpose liquid fertilizer as they mature. Keep the plants well-ventilated to deter fungal diseases, such botrytis (see p.246).

5 ROUTINE CARE

Keep crops well-watered, as dry conditions can cause plants to become stunted. Spring onions are very sensitive to weed competition, so hoe between the rows and hand-weed regularly. In cold areas, protect winter crops using garden fleece or a cloche.

Watering is crucial both indoors and out, while spring onion plants are young – drought can stunt the development of seedlings.

Keep plants well weeded – weeds will compete with the young plants for water and nutrients, and may encourage disease.

6 HARVESTING

Harvest individual plants when their stems are pencil-thick, gently lifting them with a hand fork and re-firming the soil so that other plants in the row can continue to grow. Spring onions don't store well, so only lift them as and when they are needed.

 TIP Spring onions prefer an open, sunny site; they do not do well in shade.

Spring onions reach a harvestable size after about ten weeks. Re-sow for a constant supply.

LEEKS

These mildly flavoured onion relatives are an invaluable alternative to brassicas during winter. Rather than producing bulbs, the long white stems or "shanks" of leeks are blanched by earthing up soil around them as they grow. Plant breeders are constantly improving their disease resistance and length of harvest, so choose from these new varieties where possible. Some varieties can be closely planted, giving rise to tender, pure white stems on baby leeks.

	SPRING	SUMMER	AUTUMN	WINTER
SOW				
HARVEST				

TIME TO HARVEST: 30–32 WEEKS

SUITABLE FOR: BEDS AND CONTAINERS

0   1m   2m   3m

11–15 plants

3M (10FT) ROWS
Plant out 20–30cm (8–12in) apart

0   30cm

CONTAINERS
5 plants in each

1 GETTING STARTED

Leeks are one member of the onion family that doesn't seem to mind root disturbance, so you can sow them in clusters with a view to lifting the young plants "bare-root", and planting them in their final positions. This allows you to plant the final growing space with another quick crop until your leeks are ready to be transplanted.

'Musselburgh' is a well-established variety that reliably gives short, flavourful stems.

'Oarsman' has white stems, dark foliage, and good resistance to rust and bolting.

'Toledo' leeks are late to crop and renowned for their uniform shape and size and good flavour.

'Swiss Giant Zermatt' has a mild flavour and can be pulled as "baby" leeks or left to mature.

Seeds can be sown under cover in midwinter as long as they are given enough heat – ensure they are kept at a minimum of 10°C (50°F).

Biodegradable module pots allow you to transplant seedlings straight into their planting holes without risking damage to the roots.

2 SOWING SEEDS

To sow under cover fill a tall, 15cm (6in) diameter pot with seed compost, firm gently, and water well. Allow to drain and then sow your seeds thinly on top. Cover with another 1cm (½in) layer of compost, water in lightly, and place in a propagator. Alternatively, sow seed in biodegradable module trays rather than pots. Seed can also be sown direct once the soil is suitably warm and workable in spring. Prepare a seedbed and then create a short drill 2cm (¾in) deep. Water the base well and then sow your seeds thinly. Cover with a little more soil to level, firm gently, and water in lightly.

3 TRANSPLANTING

Once seedlings are 20–30cm (8–12in) tall and 3–4mm-thick, they can be transplanted or planted out. Prepare the site then use a large dibber to create holes 2–3cm (¾–1¼in) wide, 15cm (6in) deep and between 20–30cm (8–12in) apart. Lift your leeks gently, trim the roots to about 2.5cm (1in) long, and then drop one plant into each hole.

After about eight weeks, carefully lift the seedlings from their seedbed, or separate them if they are pot grown.

Use a clean pair of scissors to trim the roots to 2.5cm (1in) before you transplant them; their roots will continue to develop.

Drop the seedlings into their deep holes, ready for watering. For "baby" leeks with thin stems, space plants 10cm (4in) apart.

4 WATERING

When the seedlings are standing in their holes, pour water around them, allowing it to drag some of the surrounding soil back around the plants. Planting deeply like this helps to blanch the stems. Keep plants well watered during the summer months.

5 ROUTINE CARE

Crops can be vulnerable to leek moth and onion fly (see p.240), so deter these pests by covering plants with insect-proof mesh. Leek yield can suffer if weeds are allowed to develop, so keep plants well weeded. Earth up soil around the stems to blanch them.

Water transplanted leeks in thoroughly. There's no need to refill the planting holes with soil. The plants will produce long white, tender stems.

Mound up soil around the developing plants to block out the light, blanching the stems. This will also help to keep the plants stable.

6 HARVESTING

Lift leeks using a fork. They will stand in the ground for a while but if you need the space for other crops, "heel" the leeks in: dig another hole and stand them in it, covering the roots with soil. In wintry weather, place leeks in a bucket of soil in a shed or garage.

 TIP Prevent leek rust from disrupting your crops by choosing a resistant variety.

Leeks do not store well so use them as soon as possible once they are out of the ground.

GARLIC

One of the most versatile vegetables in every type of cuisine, garlic is usually pretty easy to grow, even in containers. Plant out individual cloves in a sunny position between mid-autumn and early spring, when beds are often empty, and you can look forward to harvesting mature bulbs from early- to midsummer. Once lifted, these can be used while fresh, when they have a deliciously sweet flavour, or dried to use for many months to come.

	SPRING	SUMMER	AUTUMN	WINTER
SOW				
HARVEST				

TIME TO HARVEST: 20-36 WEEKS

SUITABLE FOR: BEDS AND CONTAINERS

0   1m   2m   3m
18-22 plants

3M (10FT) ROWS
Plant 15-18cm (6-7in) apart

0   40cm

CONTAINERS
5 plants in each

1 GETTING STARTED

There are two types of garlic: "hardneck", which develop flower spikes, and "softneck", which do not, and subsequently have a longer storage life. Whichever type you choose, plant the cloves in light, well-drained soil. If yours is heavy, dig in bulky, well-rotted organic matter, such as composted bark.

'Solent Wight' is a softneck-type that produces large, white, flavoursome bulbs.

'Early Wight' is a hardneck-type with early-maturing, easy-peel, chunky cloves.

'Elephant' is not a true garlic, but the large cloves are flavourful and ideal for roasting.

'Picardy Wight' can be grown in cool, wet conditions and produces strong-flavoured bulbs.

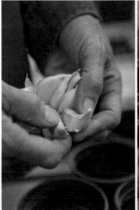

Final bulb size is directly related to initial clove size, so plant the largest and dispose of any that are very small.

Push the cloves into the compost leaving the tip showing above the surface. Firm around them and water in well.

Cloves will sprout after seven to ten days. Once the roots fill the pot, plant them on outside, spaced 15-18cm (6-7in) apart.

2 PLANTING INDOORS

If planting under cover, do so in early spring. Break the garlic bulb, or "head", into individual cloves, fill pots with compost, and plant one clove per pot. Water in well and allow to drain. Place the pots somewhere warm and bright; 10°C (50°F) is sufficient because too much heat causes sap-filled growth that is prone to disease. If you have a cold frame or sheltered spot outside, plants can be grown on here once their shoots reach 10cm (4in) tall.

TIP Cut off and eat the immature spike, or "scape", of hardneck varieties.

3 PLANTING OUTSIDE

Garlic cloves can be planted directly in the ground, any time between autumn or spring. Choose a sunny, sheltered spot and dig it over to remove any weeds. Work in a high-nitrogen granular fertilizer, gently firm the soil and rake it level. Plant the cloves with their tips facing up, deeper than those planted under cover in pots.

Space bulbs 15–18cm (6–7in) apart each way; plant cloves into the ground, using a trowel with 2cm (¾in) of soil above their tips. Water in well.

4 ROUTINE CARE

Keep young plants well watered while they develop a strong root system. Once established, garlic is quite drought-tolerant; too much water can impair its storage qualities, so only irrigate if there are prolonged dry periods. Keep crops well weeded.

Weed competition can affect yields, so keep plants well weeded with regular hoeing or hand-weeding between the plants.

5 HARVESTING

Lift as soon as the top third of the foliage has turned yellow and begun to die – leaving plants in the soil for too long can cause them to re-sprout, which shortens their storage life. Gently ease them out of the soil with a fork, taking care not to damage the bulbs.

Garlic bulbs can be harvested during summer. Those planted in the previous autumn will be ready sooner than those planted in spring.

DRYING THE BULBS

To store well, garlic bulbs must be completely dry. Lay them out on racks in a sunny, dry spot, or under cover if it is wet, for at least a fortnight, until the skins become crisp. Then hang them up in a cool, dry, well-ventilated place, either individually or by plaiting the stems together. Garlic can be stored this way for up to ten months.

ALLIUMS

These bulbous vegetables require a long growing season. Problems are relatively uncommon, and these can be kept to a minimum by rotating crops and providing adequate air flow. Sunshine helps to reduce the risk of diseases and ensures that skins set for long-term storage, while growing under insect-proof mesh will deter insect pests..

Q My onions this year were absolutely huge. Is it possible to grow smaller bulbs?

Onions will become large if given a long growing season, ample root space, and a steady moisture supply. Luckily, plants respond well to adjustments in their spacing, with wider plantings giving bigger bulbs and vice versa. By planting sets closely together (approximately 12–15cm/5–6in apart) you can still gain a good yield, while forcing smaller bulbs to form. You can also prise larger onions out of the soil with a garden fork when they reach your preferred size.

Q What is damaging my leeks? They have tunnels in the shanks that then rot.

The damage described implies attack by either leek moth or onion leaf miner, two relatively new pests to the UK. You can distinguish between them because leek moth larvae are caterpillars with visible legs, while onion leaf miner grubs are legless. Moth caterpillars often feed on the outer tissues initially and then tunnel into stems which causes secondary rots. Leaf miners tunnel into stems rapidly: their pupating grubs, resembling grains of wheat, are often found inside. Control both by rotating crops and covering rows permanently with insect-proof mesh.

Q How do I get a sizeable harvest from my leeks? I've been disappointed in the past.

Leeks require a long time to bulk up, often remaining in the ground for eight to ten months before harvest. Sow in pots under cover in March or April, then transplant out seedlings once they are 3–4mm ($1/2$in) thick (larger seedlings give rise to bigger leeks). Use a dibber to make holes 20cm (8in) deep, dropping a transplant into each. Gradually draw earth up around the developing stems to encourage blanching. Try vigorous F1 hybrid varieties – these early season leeks generally produce a longer shank than later types.

Q I'm hoping to store my onions well into the spring. How do I do this?

The key to long storage is to choose healthy, unblemished bulbs that have set strong outer skins. Avoid over-feeding plants with high-nitrogen fertilizer, and position plants in an open, sunny spot. Take care when prising bulbs out of the earth, gently rubbing off surplus soil and placing only top-grade bulbs on a tray in a sunny, dry spot (eat damaged bulbs as a priority – they won't store). Once the outer skins have become papery, rub off loose material, weave into ropes, then hang in a dry, airy place.

PEST AND DISEASE WATCH

Bulbs can be vulnerable to rots and fungi, and various pest species demand vigilance on the plot.

- Bulbs decaying at their base while in growth can be confirmed as onion white rot (see p.244) if white, fluffy mould is visible.
- A grey, fuzzy mould on the leaves of onions and shallots implies downy mildew infection (see p.244). Foliage yellows and withers, reducing the yield.
- Numerous orange pinprick pustules on the foliage of leeks or garlic signifies rust infection (see p.244), especially common in shady or humid conditions.
- Onion fly larvae (see p.240) will tunnel into the base of onions and leeks, causing damage, and encouraging secondary rots to form.
- .Wireworms (see p.240), the larvae of click beetles, are found occasionally tunnelling into onion bulbs.
- Aphids (see p.242) quickly increase into large colonies, smothering foliage in black insects.
- Onion, shallot, or garlic bulbs collapsing and rotting where the leaves meet the bulb indicates onion neck rot (see p.244).

SWEETCORN

Boiled and slathered in melted butter or grilled on a barbecue, sweetcorn is a delicious treat in late summer and early autumn. Pick and eat the sugary, tender cobs as soon as possible, as they are at their sweetest immediately after harvest. The flowers are pollinated by the wind, not insects, so grow them closely in blocks or groups. This is a productive crop, good for smaller plots, giving up to 20 tasty cobs from a one-metre-square block of plants.

	SPRING	SUMMER	AUTUMN	WINTER
SOW				
HARVEST				

TIME TO HARVEST: 16–24 WEEKS

SUITABLE FOR: BEDS AND CONTAINERS

11 plants

3M (10FT) ROWS
Plant in blocks, 30cm (12in) apart

CONTAINERS
4 plants in each

Cardboard "growing tubes" are ideal as they are deep enough for sweetcorn's long roots. Seedlings can be planted out in the tubes.

The seedlings will emerge within a few weeks. They prefer rich, well-drained soil, so ensure that you dig in plenty of organic matter before planting out.

1 SOWING UNDER COVER

Fill growing tubes or pots with seed compost, water well, and allow to drain. Sow one seed per cell or pot, 2cm (¾in) deep, water in lightly, and place in a heated propagator. Once the plants reach 10cm (4in) high, begin to harden them off. At the same time, prepare the ground by warming it with a cloche or cold frame. It is important to plant the seedlings out in a grid formation, 30 x 30cm (12 x 12in) apart.

TIP Keep different varieties separate or their flavour may be impaired.

Use cloches or cold frames to warm the soil. Put them in place about two weeks before sowing.

Sow two seeds per hole to maximize your chance of success, then thin to leave the stronger seedling.

Plant sweetcorn in blocks so the wind can blow the pollen from flower to flower.

2 SOWING OUTSIDE

If you don't have space to raise seed under cover, they can be sown directly into their final positions. The soil needs to be at least 10°C (50°F) before sowing – but you can warm it up more quickly by covering the area with cloches or cold frames. Water the soil thoroughly and sow the seed in pairs into individual holes, 2cm (¾in) deep, spaced 30cm (12in) apart in a grid pattern. Keep the cloches in place until the seeds germinate in about two weeks.

3 ROUTINE CARE

Sweetcorn should be kept well-watered throughout summer, especially when the plants are in flower and the cobs are developing. It is possible to underplant sweetcorn with low-growing crops like squash, but this will mean additional watering. Protect seedlings from slugs and snails and weed young plants regularly until they establish.

Weeding is important in the initial stages but as plants become established they are increasingly able to compete with weeds.

Water at the base of plants so it soaks down to the roots. Plants are especially responsive to watering once the cobs start to fill in midsummer.

4 PROVIDING SUPPORT

These tall plants reach up to 2m (6ft) and may need support, especially in more exposed gardens. Earth up soil around the base of the stems to stabilize them and insert canes around the edge of the blocks, joining them with string to form a flexible frame.

5 CHECKING COBS

In order to enjoy the cobs at their sweetest it is important to check they are ripe before harvesting. A good indication is when the tassels emerging from the cobs begin to turn brown. Gently peel back the outer leaves of the cobs to check the maturity of the kernels.

Earth up soil at the base of plants as they grow. This will support the stems and prevent the roots being loosened by wind rock.

Gently peel back the cob's outer leaves to check for ripeness. If the kernels are white or pale, give them a few more days to turn yellow.

6 HARVESTING

The cobs should be picked as soon as they are mature – they turn starchy and lose sweetness if left on the plant for too long. Twist off the cobs when they are ready and eat them as soon as possible; the sugar levels can start falling almost immediately. Picked cobs keep best with their outer leaves still in place, and can be kept in a fridge for a few days until needed. If you have a glut of cobs, they can be frozen.

Firmly twist the ripe cobs to release them from the plant stem. You can expect each plant to produce two cobs.

SWEETCORN

1 'Honey Bantam' An heirloom variety with creamy yellow-coloured, delicious, sweet kernels. It crops in two-and-a-half months.

2 'Minipop' This variety is grown for its baby cobs, picked at finger-size. It is planted more closely than conventional varieties; the plants may bear more than one stem, giving a larger crop.

3 'Lark' Cropping from late summer onwards, this variety bears tender, thin-skinned kernels that can be eaten cooked or raw. It is reliable and a good choice for cooler areas.

4 'Sundance' This variety produces large cobs, 20cm (8in) long, packed with sweet-tasting kernels. It is a reliable early-maturing variety with shorter stems, suitable for cooler regions.

5 'Double Red' A variety that produces surprising red and white kernels, this is one of the few red sweetcorns that ripen in a European climate.

6 'Northern Extra Sweet' This variety crops especially early, so it is ideal for areas with shorter summers. The plump kernels are sweet and tender, and are packed into cobs 20cm (8in) long.

7 'Mirai 003' Producing smallish cobs, 15cm (6in) long, filled with especially sweet and tender kernels that can be eaten cooked or raw, this variety crops well even on poorer soil.

8 'Swift' This is an early variety that produces large cobs filled with sweet-tasting, thin-skinned kernels. It is a reliable variety with sturdy stems, and crops well in cooler regions.

9 'Incredible' This maincrop sweetcorn has exceptional flavour. The cobs are around 20cm (8in) long with bright golden kernels. It has good rust tolerance.

OTHER VARIETIES
'Bodacious'
'Early Xtra Sweet'
'Extra Tender Sweet'
'Sparrow'
'Conqueror'

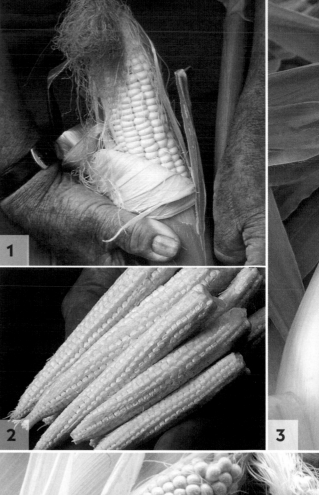

KOHL RABI

This unusual-looking vegetable is a type of brassica, and is closely related to more familiar crops such as cabbages and Brussels sprouts. However, while these are grown for their leaves, kohl rabi is prized for its mild-tasting "bulbs" – which are actually swollen stems. The crop is increasingly popular with gardeners because it is easy to grow and quick-maturing, and can be planted alongside slower crops when space is limited. It will also crop in containers.

	SPRING	SUMMER	AUTUMN	WINTER
SOW				
HARVEST				

TIME TO HARVEST: 6–12 WEEKS

SUITABLE FOR: BEDS AND CONTAINERS

3M (10FT) ROWS
Plant 25cm (10in) apart
12 plants

CONTAINERS
3 plants in each

1 GETTING STARTED

Kohl rabi is raised from seed, which can be started off under cover in spring to give early crops a head start. Later crops can be sown directly where they will mature, and will be ready to harvest in a few weeks. As a brassica, kohl rabi is prone to club root disease, which can reduce yields (see p.244).

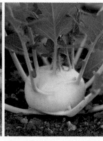

'Purple Vienna' is a versatile, heirloom variety with purple skin and a mild, nutty flavour.

'Olivia' is a hybrid with upright leaves and a good tolerance of powdery mildew.

'Superschmelz' bulbs are very large and sweet-tasting and can reach up to 20cm (8in) across.

'Kolibri' produces purple-skinned bulbs with sweet, juicy flesh. Good for a late harvest.

Sow seeds under cover until around mid-spring, after which they can be sown directly outside. Sow into modules or small pots.

Kohl rabi can be prone to bolting if exposed to sudden drops in temperature, so it's important to harden off plants gradually before transplanting to their final position.

2 SOWING UNDER COVER

Early sowings can be made under cover, ready to transplant outside later. Fill module trays with seed compost, firm, water well, and allow to drain. Make a 1cm (½in) deep hole in each cell using a dibber or pencil and place two seeds in each. Keep trays in a well-lit spot until seedlings emerge, then thin them to leave the stronger seedling. While the seedlings are hardening off, use a cloche to warm the soil where they are going to be planted.

TIP Sow the seed successionally so that you don't end up with a glut.

3 SOWING OUTSIDE

During the summer months mark out drills 2cm (¾in) deep using the back of a hoe or rake, water the base well, and then sow a pinch of seed every 25cm (10in). Cover the seed over with soil and lightly water in. Germination takes a week or two; once the seedlings emerge, protect them from slugs with a light sprinkling of organic pellets.

Being fairly robust, kohl rabi can be sown direct from mid-spring. Purple-skinned varieties may be more cold-tolerant than green-skinned types.

Once the seedlings emerge, thin them out to leave the strongest per station, at a final spacing of 25cm (10in) between plants.

4 ROUTINE CARE

Although kohl rabi is a fairly drought-tolerant crop, keeping the soil constantly moist will produce the most tender roots: growth checks result in woodier harvests. You may need to cover the plants with fine mesh to deter pigeons and cabbage white butterflies.

Kohl rabi are brassicas and suffer from brassica pests such as cabbage white butterfly caterpillars (see p.240). Net as a precaution.

5 WEEDING

Keeping plants weed-free is beneficial for many reasons: it will discourage competition for moisture, as well as keep your plot tidy and discourage the spread of disease. Pull out weeds next to the plants by hand and hoe between the rows.

Hand-weed next to your plants to prevent damage to the stems. Do this on a warm day so that weed seedlings shrivel fast.

6 HARVESTING

Although baby crops will be ready to harvest in around six weeks, the swollen stems will generally take around 12 weeks to develop fully. Kohl rabi can be harvested when they are between golf-ball and tennis-ball size – this is when they are most tender. Cut the bulb off whole, just above the root. You can store kohl rabi at the end of the season. Simply trim off the leaves and store in sand as for beetroot (see p.137).

Cut the bulbs as soon as they mature – left too long, the quality deteriorates.

FLORENCE FENNEL

The green stems of Florence fennel form a tight, crunchy "bulb" at their base, which has a mild aniseed taste – a unique flavour from the vegetable patch. Florence fennel is a star ingredient in a variety of dishes including fish recipes, stir-fries, and soups. Moisture is the key to successful crops: ideally, sow in summer and then water and mulch the plants well to keep them growing steadily. This highly ornamental vegetable is happy in small spaces.

	SPRING	SUMMER	AUTUMN	WINTER
SOW				
HARVEST				
TIME TO HARVEST: 12–22 WEEKS				

SUITABLE FOR: BEDS AND CONTAINERS

11 plants

3M (10FT) ROWS
Plant 30cm (8in) apart

CONTAINERS
3 plants in each

1 GETTING STARTED

Don't be tempted to sow too early in the year as the plants may bolt: late spring should be the earliest. Florence fennel can be grown in containers filled with multipurpose compost but these must be large enough to provide constant moisture. Choose a container with a minimum diameter of 40cm (16in) for three plants.

'Zefa Fino' produces large rounded bulbs that are slightly flattened. They have good flavour.

'Perfection' bears large bulbs with an excellent flavour and good bolt-resistance.

'Finale' bulbs are large and flattened in shape, with good bolt-resistance and excellent flavour.

'Sirio' produces large, rounded, slightly flattened white bulbs with an aromatic scent.

Florence fennel seed should be sown under cover from late spring onwards. Ensure that you keep the soil moist at all times.

Grow your seedlings on in a well-lit spot, hardening them off gradually before planting them in their final positions outside.

2 SOWING UNDER COVER

Sow this early crop under cover, into modules or small pots of moist seed compost. Seed can be unreliable, so sow three seeds 1cm (½in) deep in each module or pot. As the seedlings emerge, thin them out to leave the strongest. As soon as the roots of your module- or pot-raised plants begin to fill their containers, start to harden the plants off. Place them outdoors during the day and bring them back in at night for seven to ten days.

TIP A bolt-resistant variety deters premature flowering, especially on light soils.

3 SOWING OUTSIDE

Seed can be sown directly in early summer. Prepare the soil by digging it over to remove any weeds, firm it gently, and rake it level. Create drills 2.5cm (1in) deep, 30cm (12in) apart, and water thoroughly. Sow seed in clusters of three or four, cover with soil, firm gently, and water in lightly. Thin to leave the strongest seedling per cluster.

Sow clusters of seeds every 30cm (12in). Cover the soil with newspaper to prevent it drying out: check daily and remove once seedlings appear.

Transplant indoor-sown seedlings 30 x 30cm (12 x 12in) apart in midsummer. Enrich the soil well before planting and water plants in well.

4 ROUTINE CARE

Keep the plants well watered at all stages of growth. A dilute general-purpose liquid feed can be applied to containers or to light soil. Keep plants well weeded; they are fairly upright in habit and cannot smother adjacent weeds.

5 TRIMMING STEMS

If you want the plants to develop to their full size, water them regularly, especially during dry spells. If smaller sideshoots begin to develop around the base of the bulb, these can reduce its eventual size. Trim them off carefully with a sharp knife.

Plants need constant moisture to develop good-sized bulbs. In warm, moist conditions the plants can develop rapidly.

Mulch regularly around the plants to help conserve moisture. This will also help to prevent weeds growing close to the roots.

6 HARVESTING

You can harvest Florence fennel at all stages of growth. The leaves can be cut in moderation at any time and used as a flavouring. Baby bulbs with a diameter of roughly 5cm (2in) can be ready in as little as six weeks, while full-sized mature plants with bulbs approximately 15cm (6in) across, will have been growing for between three and four months. Harvest the bulbs whole by cutting or lifting them.

Lift plants whole or cut them off at the base with a knife if they prove stubborn to lift.

CELERY

Old fashioned "trenching" celery has always been challenging to grow, but the introduction of self-blanching varieties has made this crop more manageable for novice gardeners. The blanched, tender stems are a key addition to summer salads, and add flavour to soups and casseroles. Celery needs to be planted closely to exclude the light and blanch the stems, which makes this a highly productive crop for small spaces. The plants are hardy and will stand well into the autumn.

	SPRING	SUMMER	AUTUMN	WINTER
SOW				
HARVEST				

TIME TO HARVEST: 18 WEEKS

SUITABLE FOR: BEDS

```
0          1m         2m         3m
```

15 plants

3M (10FT) ROWS
Plant in a block, spacing them 20cm (8in) apart

1 GETTING STARTED

Celery requires a long growing season so seed is best started off under cover in early to mid-spring. If you don't have a suitable growing environment you can purchase plug plants later in the spring. Celery needs rich, well-drained soil but isn't really suitable for containers as it would need watering so frequently.

'Tango' is an excellent self-blanching variety. Its tasty, long white stems resist bolting.

'Celebrity' stems are self-blanching with a good flavour and succulent texture.

'Green Utah' is a self-blanching type that produces tall, green, slightly variable stems.

'Victoria' produces fleshy, mid-green stems that are vigorous, tall, and self-blanching.

To encourage germination, seed should be kept moist and placed in a heated propagator for a couple of weeks, until it germinates.

Celery seedlings sown in early to mid-spring should be strong enough to transplant between late spring and early summer.

2 SOWING UNDER COVER

Fill pots or seed trays with seed compost, water well, and allow to drain. Sow the seeds thinly over the surface but don't cover them with compost: they need light to germinate. Germination can be slow, so place the trays in a heated propagator set at 15°C (59°F). As soon as seedlings emerge and are large enough to handle, prick them out into individual module trays. Don't let them get too big before transplanting, as the roots will become congested. Water the plants in well and grow them on in a warm position under cover. A growth check caused by cold weather can reduce yields considerably.

3 PLANTING OUT

When plants are about 15cm (6in) tall, harden them off ready for the move outside. Celery requires moist soil; to improve moisture retention, prepare the site before planting by digging in plenty of well-rotted organic matter, such as manure or garden compost. Just prior to planting, work in a granular general-purpose fertilizer.

Place plants outdoors during the day and bring them back under cover at night for a fortnight. As they harden off, prepare the soil for planting.

Plant out in blocks, 20cm (8in) apart in each direction. This dense planting will encourage the celery to blanch. Water the plants in well.

4 ROUTINE CARE

Keep plants well watered during the growing season – plants bulk up during some of the hottest and driest months of the year and a lack of water can result in stringy, pungent stems. Prevent slugs attacking your plants with a thin scattering of organic pellets.

Keep the plants well weeded. Remove any weeds that grow in and around the blocks of plants by hand to avoid damaging the stems.

5 BLANCHING STEMS

If densely planted, the stems partially shade each other from the sunlight, causing them to become blanched. Plants on the outside of the bed are less shaded and will develop green stems; blanch these by wrapping cardboard around their stems.

Applying an organic mulch 5–6cm (2–2½in) deep around your plants can help to lock in soil moisture. It will also keep down weeds.

6 HARVESTING

You can begin harvesting celery in late summer, as soon as it is large enough. Water the plant well and then dig it up whole – stems can be broken off as needed. As nights become cooler, cover plants with fleece or a blanket and harvest before harsh frosts.

 TIP Wash celery well before use – soil can accumulate between the stems.

Harvest plants whole with roots intact. They last better this way; cut stems turn brown.

CELERIAC

This unusual vegetable has enjoyed something of a renaissance in recent years and has now graduated to almost gourmet status. What it lacks in looks, celeriac more than makes up for in flavour – a nutty, celery-like taste that is pleasantly mild. Roots can be grated raw, boiled and mashed, sliced and braised in milk and butter, or added to soups, roasts and casseroles. The long storage life of this crop makes it a great winter staple.

	SPRING	SUMMER	AUTUMN	WINTER
SOW				
HARVEST				
TIME TO HARVEST: 30 WEEKS				

SUITABLE FOR: BEDS

```
0          1m          2m          3m

     🌰🌰🌰🌰🌰🌰🌰🌰🌰🌰🌰
              11 plants
```

3M (10FT) ROWS
Plant 30cm (12in) apart

1 GETTING STARTED

Like its celery relative, celeriac prefers an open site and rich, well-drained soil, so dig in well-rotted organic matter in the season before planting. Celeriac can occasionally bolt, so choose resistant varieties. Plant out strong seedlings in late spring after the risk of frost has passed and keep young plants well watered.

'Monarch' bears strong yields of high quality white roots with good flavour that store well.

'Brilliant' is an early variety with smooth roots and flesh that does not discolour.

'Prinz' is an exceptional variety, known for its flavour, bolt-resistance, and storage qualities.

'Mars' bears large, high-growing roots, that have dense, flavourful flesh and keep well.

Plants need a long season to mature fully so sow seed under cover in early to mid-spring for autumn–winter crops.

After sowing, place the module trays in a propagator and ensure that they have a minimum temperature of 10°C (50°F).

Celeriac can be slow to emerge, but once the seedlings are large enough to handle, thin to leave one stronger one per module.

2 SOWING SEEDS

For large roots it is best to sow celeriac seed under cover to extend the growing season. Fill module trays with seed compost, firm gently, water well, and allow to drain. Make a hole in each cell 1cm (½in) deep and sow two seeds into it. Cover with compost and water lightly, then place in a propagator. Keep the compost moist to ensure germination. Grow on under cover and, once the seedlings' roots fill their modules, begin to harden them off.

TIP Plant out in late spring so celeriac can establish before the warmth of summer.

3 PLANTING OUT

Celeriac can be planted out into large containers of multipurpose compost but a far easier option is to grow the plants in the ground. Dig over the soil to remove any weeds – and add some well-rotted organic matter, such as garden compost, before planting. Firm gently and plant seedlings 30 x 30cm (12 x 12in) apart. Water them in well.

Harden off the seedlings by placing them outside during the day and under cover at night for a week to ten days.

The swollen stems will need plenty of space to develop, so ensure that seedlings are planted at least 30cm (12in) apart.

Keep the plants well watered. Celeriac is native to boggy areas, so these conditions need to be replicated in the garden.

4 FEEDING

To produce good-sized roots it is important to keep celeriac evenly watered at all stages of growth. Its food requirements are fairly low, so there is no need to apply heavy doses of fertilizer. A half-strength, general-purpose liquid feed every fortnight will be sufficient.

5 ROUTINE CARE

As plants develop, remove the outer leaves gradually so that the crown is exposed. Celeriac is relatively free from pests or diseases, but celery leaf miner may be a problem; it causes dry, blotchy patches on leaves. Pick off affected leaves and dispose of them.

Plants can be mulched by applying a 6–7cm (2½–3in) layer of compost, but do not let this bury the exposed crown.

Plants will form small offshoots that compete with the main crown and impede its growth. Carefully remove these as you spot them.

6 HARVESTING

Celeriac roots can be lifted from autumn onwards. It is best to lift the roots as and when you need them, although they also store well in boxes of damp sand. Gently insert a fork under each individual plant when harvesting, and tease the root out of the soil. During the winter cover the crowns with a straw mulch to protect them. Don't try to lift the roots when the ground is frozen hard.

Take care not to damage the root when levering it out. Keep the fork 10–15cm (4–6in) away.

OTHER CROPS

This diverse collection reveals the varied needs of different vegetables. Sweetcorn thrives in full sun, but a shadier, moister position is preferred for celery or celeriac. Florence fennel, too, enjoys a long growing season, whereas kohl rabi is best harvested young to ensure tender "roots". Pests and diseases are infrequent, but some can be destructive if not controlled promptly.

Q My sweetcorn patch has been trampled overnight and half the cobs have been eaten – what would do that?

The most likely culprit for this devastation is badgers. These nocturnal mammals love gorging on the mature cobs and also the plants themselves, eating the stems like sugarcane. With their determined nature, one night-time visitor can quickly destroy a bed, and controlling them is tricky because of their strength. Establish where they enter and exit your garden (they usually have a favoured route) and block this with builder's rubble or reinforced chicken wire.

Q I've grown kohlrabi for the first time this year but the harvest was disappointingly woody and tough – what did I do wrong?

The secret to tender harvests of these brassicas is encourage fast growth by supplying plants with ample moisture and adequate warmth. Cold temperatures inhibit growth, which is why early sowing can cause woodiness. Delay sowing and use heat-boosting cloches. If the problem occurs during summer then lack of water is often to blame. Work ample organic matter into your soil, mulching and irrigating rows well.

Q I planted out celeriac in a sunny spot in early June – why was the yield so miserly?

Celeriac, grown for its deliciously nutty "bulbs" (actually swollen stems) is a crop that revels in cool, moist conditions rather than sunshine. A long growing season is also essential for this slow-to-bulk-up crop. Next year, sow under cover in February, transplanting the resulting seedlings in April. Choose a spot that doesn't get baked by the sun, adding generous quantities of well-rotted farmyard manure or other organic matter into the soil prior to planting. Irrigate weekly to keep the earth reliably moist until they are ready to harvest in October.

Q My celery always seems to have a strong, unpalatable flavour. How can I adjust this?

Celery requires close spacings (a grid of 20cm x 20cm/8in x 8in) to blanch the developing stems by excluding sunlight. Unblanched plants on the outside of the bed can be stunted, green, and bitter. To prevent this, you can also encircle beds with black sheeting to limit light penetration. A lack of moisture can concentrate flavour, so keep crops constantly well watered, adding organic matter to sandy or flinty soils. Growing a vigorous self-blanching F1 hybrid (for example, 'Granada') will also improve quality.

PEST AND DISEASE WATCH

This varied group are relatively free from pests and diseases, though a few may attempt to gain a foothold.

- Slugs and snails (see p.242) can quickly devour seedlings and transplants.
- Kohlrabi can be targeted by the usual brassica pests: Cabbage caterpillars (see p.240) can strip foliage bare. Seedlings peppered with tiny holes indicates flea beetle damage (see p.240). If plants suddenly wilt, suspect clubroot (see p.244), or check for cabbage rootfly larvae (see p.242). Grey blisters on foliage implies mealy cabbage aphid damage (see p.240).
- In warm, wet summers, sweetcorn can succumb to smut – a fungal disease that causes kernels to distort and release masses of black spores. Dispose of affected plants promptly.
- Celery and celeriac can suffer from leaf miner, which causes brown-yellow irregular markings on the foliage. Pick off damage promptly.
- Sclerotinia (see p.246) causes a white, fuzzy growth around the base of celery (and occasionally celeriac).

STEP-BY-STEP
ASPARAGUS

Asparagus is regarded as a luxury crop, available for just ten weeks of the year and offering a brief, uniquely delicious harvest from spring to early summer. Asparagus is easy to grow but is a long-term investment in that it takes time to establish and then occupies the space permanently. Be patient and you will be rewarded for the next 20 years with an annual supply of succulent freshly-picked shoots, or "spears", that will be superior to any you can buy.

	SPRING	SUMMER	AUTUMN	WINTER
PLANT				
HARVEST				

PLANTING TO HARVEST: 2–3 YEARS

SUITABLE FOR: BEDS

0   1m   2m   3m

7–8 plants

3M (10FT) ROWS
Plant out 40cm (16in) apart

1 GETTING STARTED

Asparagus can be raised cheaply from seed in spring if you want lots of plants and are happy to wait for them to grow large enough to crop. The quicker option is to buy asparagus as young plants, either bare-root to plant out from late winter, or as pot-grown specimens, which you can plant at any time if you keep them well watered.

'Gijnlim' is an early-cropping variety that gives a reliable harvest of thick green spears.

'Ariane' produces early, large, purple-tipped spears. It can be bought as seed.

'Jersey Knight' gives a good crop of thick, flavoursome stems. It is a modern variety.

'Purple Pacific' bears attractive purple-flushed spears that are sweeter than many green types.

Asparagus plants grow in the same position for up to 20 years, so prepare the soil well before planting and remove all perennial weeds.

Mounding the soil at the base of the planting holes helps ensure good drainage. This isn't needed if your soil is light and sandy; the holes can be flat.

2 PLANTING OUT

Bare-root asparagus plants are known as "crowns", and should be planted as soon they are available in spring or autumn. Before planting, prepare a hole or trench 30cm (12in) wide, 10cm (4in) deep, and mound up the base so it slightly lower than the soil surface. Spread the "crowns" out on top of the mound so that the central growing point is at soil level, with the roots below. Fill the hole with soil, firm it in gently, and water the plants in well.

TIP Avoid berry-bearing female plants, which give a smaller crop than males.

3 GROWING ON

Mulch new plants with well-rotted organic matter, such as garden compost, after planting and apply granular general-purpose fertilizer. Keep plants well-watered and weeded during their first year. The plants take time to establish and should not be harvested during their first year and only lightly in their second.

Ferny asparagus growth makes an attractive backdrop in the garden. If space is limited, plant it at the back of your ornamental borders.

4 ROUTINE CARE

Established plants are drought-tolerant and only need watering in very dry spells. Mulch plants in autumn with organic matter, and apply granular general-purpose fertilizer in spring and again after harvesting. The tall foliage may need support on windy sites.

5 HARVESTING

When fully established after three years, plants can be harvested each spring for about ten weeks. Cut all spears, thick and thin, as this encourages more to develop. When they are about 20cm (8in) tall slice them off just below soil level using a sharp knife.

Mulching plants with organic matter helps retain moisture and suppresses weeds. The mulch also releases nutrients to your plants.

Check plants every few days to cut the young spears at their best. They grow very quickly and soon become tough and inedible.

OVERWINTERING PLANTS

After harvesting the shoots for ten weeks, stop cutting and allow the plants to develop their "fern"– a tall, feathery top growth. Allow them to grow on all summer, giving the plants time to bulk up and recover. The "fern" will turn yellow and die back in autumn, at which point it should be cut off at the base.

GLOBE ARTICHOKES

Attractive and delicious to eat, these eye-catching perennial plants produce a mass of architectural foliage before bearing delicately flavoured, thistle-like flowerheads. This makes them just as suitable for the flower garden as the vegetable patch. Quality not quantity is what matters here, as each plant only bears a few heads. The artichoke "scales" can be braised and dipped individually into hollandaise sauce before the heart is eaten as a tender treat.

	SPRING	SUMMER	AUTUMN	WINTER
PLANT				
HARVEST				

PLANTING TO HARVEST: 64–68 WEEKS

SUITABLE FOR: BEDS

0   1m   2m   3m

2 plants

3M (10FT) ROWS
Plant 1.5m (5ft) apart

1 GETTING STARTED

Globe artichoke plants can be grown from seeds or "offsets" of existing plants (see step 3). Although the simplest method is to buy pot-raised seedlings from garden centres or nurseries, there is often only a small selection of varieties. Buying seeds online offers the greatest choice, so don't rule out the other methods shown here.

'Gros Vert de Laon' is best propagated from offsets to give flavourful, attractive round heads.

'Green Globe Improved' is a reliable, vigorous plant that bears firm, tasty heads.

'Purple Globe' yields small dark heads that are very tasty, but can be variable in quality.

'Purple de Provence' is an early-cropping variety with delicious purple heads.

For larger quantities of plants, sow into seed trays. Sow the seeds at a depth of 2cm (¾in), spacing them 2cm (¾in) apart.

Once the seedlings have their first true leaves they can be pricked out and potted on. Plant each seedling in its own pot so that it has sufficient space.

2 SOWING SEEDS

Raising globe artichokes from seed in early to mid-spring will provide plants that will crop in their second year. You should remove any heads that develop in this first growing season. Fill a 9cm (3½in) diameter pot with seed compost, water it well, and allow it to drain. Make holes 2cm (¾in) apart and 2cm (¾in) deep using a pencil or dibber, and then drop a seed into each. Cover over with more compost, water lightly, and place in a heated propagator.

TIP Dig in plenty of well-rotted manure and apply fertilizer before planting.

3 PLANTING OUT

Harden off seed-raised plants in late spring. Offsets can also be propagated at this time: gently lift an established plant, cut off a section that is complete with roots and leaves using a sharp knife, and transplant it immediately to its new position. Space both offsets and seed-raised plants about 1.5m (5ft) apart.

Harden off globe artichoke seedlings by placing them outside for seven to ten days, bringing them back under cover overnight.

4 ROUTINE CARE

Keep plants well watered until established, so that they develop a strong root system. Ultimately plants become extremely drought-tolerant and won't require additional irrigation, but these first two months are an exception. Remove any weeds that appear.

5 HARVESTING

The largest bud will be at the tip of the spike; smaller ones often develop later on any sideshoots. Harvest each artichoke once it is a good size but before the scales begin to open and the purple flowers appear. Use a knife or secateurs to cut the tough stalks.

Blackfly may be a problem, and will swarm over flower buds and stems. Wash them off by hand or apply an organic insecticide.

Harvest globe artichokes whole, while they are still young and tight. You may get a secondary crop after the main head has been cut.

OVERWINTERING PLANTS

After harvesting, cut the old stems back to ground level. The plants are quite hardy but severe winters can kill them, especially if the soil is wet. Lay the cut leaves on the soil and apply a thick mulch of garden compost or straw on top of them. This will protect the plant through the winter and can be dug into the soil in spring.

JERUSALEM ARTICHOKES

Towering above other vegetables, this perennial relative of the summer sunflower often bears attractive, bright yellow flowers. They are grown for their delicious knobbly tubers, which are harvested in autumn. Jerusalem artichokes are expensive to buy yet easy to grow, and can form a sizeable clump in a season. Although they are unsuitable for containers, they are ideal for a corner of your plot, but may need to be confined as they can become invasive.

	SPRING	SUMMER	AUTUMN	WINTER
PLANT				
HARVEST				
TIME TO HARVEST: 30–36 WEEKS				

SUITABLE FOR: BEDS

0   1m   2m   3m

11 plants

3M (10FT) ROWS
Plant 30cm (12in) apart in a grid pattern

1 PLANTING TUBERS

Jerusalem artichokes are planted as bare tubers, which can either be bought from seed suppliers – or from the supermarket if you don't want a named variety. Before planting in early spring, prepare the site by digging it over to remove weeds. Plant each tuber 15cm (6in) deep and space them 30cm (12in) apart each way. Large tubers can be cut into two or three sections, as long as each one has a distinct growing bud. Cover with soil and water the tubers in.

Plant the tubers into individual holes with the growing point, which is usually swollen and slightly pointed, facing upwards.

Tubers can be started off in pots if your soil is too wet to work in early spring. Keep them outside and plant out as soon as conditions allow.

The new shoots grow quickly in spring but may need slug protection with a sprinkling of organic pellets. Mature growth is less vulnerable.

Developing plants form dense clumps and may compete for moisture. Water regularly until they reach their full height of around 3m (10ft).

2 PLANTING OUT

Shoots will appear after a few weeks. Once these are 20–30cm (8–12in) high, earth up soil around the plant to help support the growing stems. Keep plants well watered, especially during dry periods, otherwise tubers will become knobbly and small. On lighter soils, apply a thick mulch to help retain moisture. Weed young plants until they are growing strongly; they will then out-compete most neighbouring plants.

TIP If your garden is exposed, use this crop as a productive summer windbreak.

3 PROVIDING SUPPORT

Jerusalem artichoke stems are sturdy but may need support as they reach full height. Insert tall canes around the edge of the clump or bed, about 1.8m (6ft) high, and tie string around them to form a flexible frame. This will also help keep plants tidy. Use secateurs to cut back any stems that are damaged by the wind.

Larger clumps may withstand the wind but it's worth providing support as a precaution. Damaged plants will still crop, but less freely.

4 ROUTINE CARE

If the plants are on an exposed site, cut back the tall stems to 1.5m (5ft) high in late summer to prevent them rocking in the wind and loosening the tubers. This will delay or even prevent flowering, so consider leaving them unpruned on sheltered sites.

The flowers are attractive, and if your plants are in a sheltered position, they will entice beneficial bees and butterflies.

5 CUTTING BACK

As their leaves begin to turn yellow in autumn, the plants start to take nutrients down the stems to store in the tubers; this is a sign that they are nearly ready to harvest. Once the leaves begin to yellow or fall, cut the stems back to under 30cm (12in) in height.

Once they have been cut back, the stems will act as a marker, showing you where to dig for tubers during the winter months.

6 HARVESTING

Jerusalem artichoke tubers should be lifted as required. Since they have relatively thin skins and will not store well, they are best left in the soil and dug up as needed. Any tubers left in the ground will re-grow the following year. If you plan on growing a different crop in the same position, dig over the site thoroughly at the end of winter to make sure you remove any tubers that are lying deep in the soil.

Harvest the tubers fresh through the winter months – they are cold-hardy and their flavour actually improves after frost.

RHUBARB

Often thought of as a fruit because it is used in desserts, this crop is actually a vegetable, and is one of the easiest to grow. Its giant leaves have their own architectural merit, but the pink-flushed stems are what rhubarb is really about. The earliest stems are often "forced" to make them especially tender. Traditionally used for delicious jams, chutneys, and crumbles, rhubarb has become a two-season crop thanks to the development of new autumn-cropping varieties.

	SPRING	SUMMER	AUTUMN	WINTER
PLANT				
HARVEST				
PLANTING TO HARVEST: 16–25 MONTHS				

SUITABLE FOR: BEDS

0   1m   2m   3m

3 plants

3M (10FT) ROWS
Plant at least 1m (3ft) apart

1 GETTING STARTED

Rhubarb is best bought as a young plant and grown on. It can also be raised from seed, but the quality of seedlings can be variable. Plants are available bare-root to plant between autumn and early spring. Pot-grown plants can be planted at any time providing they are kept well-watered afterwards.

'Champagne' produces long, red-tinged stems that have a sweet, sharp flavour, ideal for cooking.

'Timperley Early' is an early variety that is good for forcing. It has thick, juicy red stems.

'Victoria' gives a later, sweet-tasting harvest, and is a good choice to grow in cooler regions.

'Cawood Delight' gives a smaller crop of richly-flavoured and coloured stems.

Plant pot-grown plants at the same depth as they were in their pots. Bare-root plants should be planted with the crown level with the soil.

Bare-root plants are particularly susceptible to drying out during dry spells, even in autumn and spring. Keep moist and mulch as a precaution.

2 PLANTING

Before planting, prepare the site thoroughly by digging in plenty of well-rotted organic matter, such as garden compost or manure, especially if your soil is light. Rhubarb is a long-lived crop, so also take care to remove any perennial weeds (see p.236). Dig a hole large enough for the roots, then plant, firm in gently, and water well. Plants should be kept well-watered and weeded during their first year, until fully established.

TIP Rhubarb will tolerate light shade, so make use of these areas.

3 ROUTINE CARE

Mulch plants in spring with well-rotted organic matter but avoid piling it around the crown, as this can encourage decay. Older, congested plants can be divided in late autumn to promote healthy new growth. Lift the plant with as much root as possible, split it into sections with a spade, and replant one or two vigorous outer clumps.

Mulching around plants with straw helps to retain moisture. It also lifts them away from the soil and keeps them clean during watering.

4 FORCING STEMS

Rhubarb can be "forced" to give an earlier harvest by placing a "forcing pot" or an upturned dustbin over the plant before it emerges. The new stems then grow up into the dark forcer, making them sweet and tender. Remove the forcer after two weeks of harvesting.

Forced stems are blanched in the darkness within the forcer. Only force the earliest stems and allow later ones to develop normally.

5 HARVESTING

New plants can be harvested after their first year. Harvest by sliding your thumb down the curved centre of a stem until you reach the base, then gently twist to remove. Harvest spring rhubarb until midsummer and later varieties until mid-autumn.

Harvest the stems while young and tender by gently twisting them off at the base. Discard the leaves and only use the stems.

GROWING ON

Plants need time to recover after you harvest them, so leave all bar autumn-cropping varieties to grow freely from midsummer onwards. Cut out any stems that develop flowers and remove any yellowing leaves as they occur. In late autumn, cut the plant to the base and mulch well with organic matter. The spent growth is safe to compost.

Crops that stay in the ground year on year can attain a sizeable root system that supports impressive growth. Careful positioning is needed primarily because of their size, but also because these perennials can provide you with harvests for a decade or more if established well. Most enjoy full sun, although rhubarb will grow in part shade.

Q Why is my established asparagus bed producing weak, distorted spears?

A well tended asparagus bed will deliver high-quality spears for 15 years or more, but crowns can become exhausted. Spring mulching and feeding is key. Also, your asparagus should not be harvested for more than 10 weeks each year, so make a note of the date of first cut and stick to that timeframe. Distortion can be due to frost damage early in the season, or slug damage. Apply organic pellets in early spring, and biological control nematodes as the season warms up.

Q My first Jerusalem artichokes were delicious, but I had trouble digesting them – any tips?

Jerusalem artichokes are known to induce wind due to their tubers containing the carbohydrate inulin, which causes bacteria in the lower intestine to produce excess gas. By eating small portions (one medium-sized tuber per day) you can adapt your gut's bacteria to cope with the inulin. Soaking thin slices of the tuber in lemon juice can help by converting inulin into digestible fructose. Pickling and fermenting the crop also makes it easier to digest because the bacteria within the ferment partly break down the inulin.

Q I've been told that I need to propagate my rhubarb periodically to keep it productive – what exactly should I do?

This vigorous, clump-forming plant will happily produce its thick, succulent stems for two to three years without intervention, but if you notice stems becoming weaker over time, or flower spikes developing in summer, this can indicate root congestion. Lift and divide your crowns in late autumn. Excavate the fleshy root system, slicing it into sections containing at least three buds. Discard old, woody central divisions, and replant the remainder into soil improved with well-rotted farmyard manure.

Q The mature asparagus bed on our allotment plot is riddled with nettles and ground elder. Should we scrap it and start again?

If the asparagus spears are healthy and of good quality, it's worth trying to renovate this neglected bed. On light, sandy soils it's possible to dig out ground elder, but proceed slowly, taking care not to inadvertently damage the fleshy asparagus "crowns" (roots). Perennial nettle roots will also need careful forking out, and the annual species will self-seed prolifically. Once any perennial weeds are removed, hoe the bed regularly and mulch each spring to make hand-weeding easier.

PEST AND DISEASE WATCH

These botanically unrelated plants suffer from few pests and diseases but be mindful of the following:

- Slugs and snails (see p.242) may target the growing shoots of Jerusalem artichokes and asparagus.
- Globe artichokes are prone to attack from aphids (see p.242). Check for colonies of black insects on growing points and control before they escalate.
- Root aphids (see p.242) stunt the aerial growth of globe artichokes, and a mass of white, powdery insects is seen on the roots.
- In long, hot summers red spider mites (see p.242) can populate globe artichoke foliage.
- Powdery mildew (see p.246) can strike globe artichokes, especially if drought-stressed. A white fungal coating eventually causes leaf browning.
- Small red insects with black, yellow, or white spots on asparagus spears are the adult stage of asparagus beetle (see p.242). Colonies of black eggs are seen on shoots; black grub-like larvae feed on the fern.
- Rhubarb can suffer from crown rotting if waterlogged. Dispose of rotted crowns and improve drainage.

PERENNIAL HERBS

Perennial herbs range from low creeping plants to large shrubs, and can be planted all around the garden or given their own dedicated bed, window box, or collection of pots. Most grow well and look attractive in containers, with the advantage that they can be kept within easy reach of the kitchen for handy picking. Evergreen rosemary, sage, and thyme are essential ingredients in many recipes and can be enjoyed fresh or dried all year round.

	SPRING	SUMMER	AUTUMN	WINTER
PLANT				
HARVEST				
TIME TO HARVEST: 4–16 WEEKS				

SUITABLE FOR: BEDS AND CONTAINERS

3M (10FT) ROWS
Plant out 30cm (12in) apart
11 plants

CONTAINERS
3–8 plants in each

1 RAISING NEW PLANTS

Perennial herbs are widely sold but if you want several plants they are easy to propagate yourself. For lots of new plants, sow seeds into pots or trays, following the instructions given on the packet (once established, fennel and chives will seed themselves freely). Many creeping herbs can be propagated easily as the spreading stems often have roots that can be cut off, potted up and grown on as new plants. Established clumps of herbs, such as mint, can also be lifted and split in spring or autumn.

Sowing plants from seed is ideal if you want lots of the same herb, as edging, for example.

Rooted stems provide a quick and easy way to propagate your own herbs. Just pot them up.

New herb plants may be large enough to divide when you buy them. Split them into clumps.

Herb planters are ideal for growing a mixture of plants. Plant up the side pockets first.

Choose a variety of plants that creep or grow upright to make best use of the space.

Fill with compost to within 5cm (2in) of the rim of the pot to make watering easier.

2 PLANTING A CONTAINER

Most perennial herbs grow well in containers, and smaller plants can be planted together in the same pot. Many are Mediterranean plants that require good drainage and sunshine. Plant them using a 50:50 mix of sharp grit and soil-based compost. Give them a sunny position and keep plants well watered. Feed only occasionally to avoid encouraging soft, flavourless growth.

TIP Some perennial herbs can be short-lived, especially in cool, wet regions.

3 PLANTING IN BEDS

Most herbs prefer well-drained soil; dig in some horticultural grit if yours is heavy, and choose a sunny site. Herbs rarely require additional feeding, and improving the soil with compost or fertilizer can encourage sappy growth. Mint is a spreading herb, and can be invasive, so is best planted into a large container sunk into the soil.

Dig planting holes and plant your herbs at the same depth as they were in their pots.

Tease any impacted roots away from the root ball to encourage them to grow out into the surrounding soil.

Water plants well until they have established fully. Pinching out the tips occasionally will help encourage bushy new shoots.

4 ROUTINE CARE

Most herbs need little care once established. Stake taller plants as they grow and weed low-growing herbs so they don't become smothered. You can cut back mint and marjoram in summer to encourage new growth. Alternatively, leave them to flower to attract beneficial insects to your plot.

5 HARVESTING

Once well established, perennial herbs can be harvested as and when required. Pinching out the growing points of mint, thyme, sage, rosemary and marjoram provides you with the most tender foliage, and will also encourage plants to bush out. Individual chive leaves can be cut when needed.

Water young plants well – once established many herbs, such as sage, rosemary and marjoram, are relatively drought-tolerant.

Harvest leaves and shoots using scissors or a sharp knife. Harvest plants regularly to encourage a constant fresh crop of new growth.

DRYING HERBS

Perennial herbs are ideal for drying to use throughout winter. In summer, cut and bunch the stems, and hang them up somewhere warm, dry, and well-ventilated. Shorter stems, such as thyme or marjoram, can be laid out on wire racks. Dry the growth over 24–48 hours, and store it away from the light in sealed containers.

PERENNIAL HERBS

1 **2** 3

6

1 Parsley The leaves of this popular and useful herb are excellent used in a variety of dishes; curly types (shown) have a milder flavour than flat-leaved types. This is a biennial herb that flowers and dies after two years. Sow seed each spring to ensure a constant supply.

2 Fennel Not to be confused with Florence fennel (see pp.172–173), almost every part of this herb has a culinary use. It is also highly decorative and does not look out of place in ornamental borders, if you don't have space for a herb bed.

3 Chives If you don't have a lot of space, this attractive herb makes an excellent container plant. A member of the onion family, chives have a mild onion-like flavour. The flowers and stems can be used in a range of dishes.

4 Rosemary Both highly ornamental and extremely versatile, this is a must-have shrubby herb for any garden. The aromatic leaves are excellent for use in stews, particularly with lamb. It needs a sunny site and well-drained soil to grow well, but can be short-lived.

5 Thyme There are upright and creeping forms of this staple herb, but the former are easier to harvest for culinary use. The flavourful leaves are excellent for use in a variety of dishes, either harvested fresh or dried. It is a good choice for pots.

6 Sage There are several varieties of this shrubby herb, including purple-leaved and variegated forms. It has many uses in the kitchen, and is easy to grow when given a sunny spot and well-drained soil. It can be short-lived in cooler areas.

7 Marjoram Closely related to oregano, this versatile, creeping herb can be used in a variety of dishes; the leaves have a spicy flavour and are often used in Mediterranean cuisine. The flavours are strongest when planted in a sunny position.

8 Mint This vigorous upright herb can be invasive when planted in borders, and is best contained to a large pot sunk into the soil. There are several varieties to grow, including peppermint and spearmint. All are easy to grow in most soils.

9 Bay A bay tree makes a great addition to the garden, and its evergreen leaves are used in many dishes. It is easy to grow but can become large, so keep plants well pruned.

GROW YOUR OWN VEGETABLES **PERENNIAL HERBS**

ANNUAL HERBS

Growing annual herbs from seed is easy and rewarding, and provides an exciting range of flavours to use in the kitchen. You can obtain a good crop in the smallest space – herbs don't need a dedicated bed and can be planted alongside your other crops, or in mixed beds or containers. Crops such as basil, dill, coriander, and parsley – which is grown as an annual – are ideal for cultivation in pots where the free-draining environment suits them perfectly.

	SPRING	SUMMER	AUTUMN	WINTER
SOW				
HARVEST				
TIME TO HARVEST: 10–14 WEEKS				

SUITABLE FOR: BEDS AND CONTAINERS – UNDER COVER OR OUTSIDE

15–30 plants

3M (10FT) ROWS
Plant 10_20cm (4–8in) apart

CONTAINERS
5–7 plants in each

1 GETTING STARTED

Annual herbs generally prefer sunny, well-drained soil, so if you are growing them directly in the ground, dig in some well-rotted organic matter and horticultural grit before planting. Give containers and windowboxes a warm, sunny spot – have them close to the kitchen for easy access during cooking.

Basil is great in pesto or with tomatoes. It is most often green, but purple varieties are available.

Parsley has both flat- and curly-leaved forms. It is useful in cooking and as a garnish.

Dill produces feathery leaves with a delicious mild aniseed flavor. It partners well with fish.

Coriander leaves and seeds have a distinctive flavour and are used in a variety of cuisines.

Sow seed under cover from early spring, but check individual seed packets as the timings vary for different varieties.

Once the seedlings emerge, prick them out to 5cm (2in) apart, so that they have more space to grow on.

Once seedlings are 15cm (6in) tall, harden them off. Transplant directly, or plant in containers, a windowbox, or hanging basket.

2 SOWING UNDER COVER

Fill pots or trays with compost, water well, and allow to drain. Sow your herb seeds thinly on top, cover with a 0.5cm (¼in) layer of compost, water lightly, and place in a propagator. Once seedlings are large enough to handle, thin them or prick out. When larger, ease the compost out and gently split it into clumps, each containing three or four seedlings. Plant each clump in a larger pot of compost, water in well, and grow on under cover.

TIP Pinch out the growing tips regularly to delay leafy herbs from flowering.

3 SOWING OUTSIDE

Alternatively, your herbs can be sown directly into garden soil. Choose a well-drained, sunny spot, and dig this over lightly to remove any weeds. Firm gently, and rake level, then create drills 1cm (½in) deep, water these well, and then sow seeds thinly along the base. Cover with more soil, firm gently, then lightly water in.

Herb seed can be sown directly in the ground from spring onwards, but check the seed packets as the timings vary between different herbs.

Once the young herb seedlings appear, carefully thin them out to 10–20cm (4–8in) apart, depending on the variety you have sown.

4 WATERING

Keep the herbs well watered, paying particular attention to those planted in containers, as these will dry out more quickly than those planted in the ground. Annual herbs generally don't need any extra feeding, but if leaves begin to look yellow, give them a dose of diluted liquid fertilizer.

5 ROUTINE CARE

Keep the plants well weeded. Basil will create a single stem initially but has a bushy habit and will branch out naturally. You can speed up this process by pinching off the growing tip. Parsley, coriander, and dill form a rosette of leaves. Protect against slugs with a scattering of organic pellets.

Keeping your herbs well watered will encourage rapid, tender growth, which is ideal for eating raw or cooked..

Keep plants well weeded to reduce competition for nutrients, light, and water. Pull out weeds by hand when young.

6 HARVESTING

Leaves can be harvested as soon as they are large enough, although it's important not to over-crop the plants or this will impede their growth; take just a few leaves from each plant at any one time. Herbs such as basil and coriander are particularly fast-growing, so you may want to make two or three sowings throughout the spring and summer to ensure a succession of fresh, tender leaves.

Treat plants as cut-and-come-again crops, snipping the leaves for use as you need them.

VEGETABLE CROP PLANNER

Use this table to check when to sow and harvest your vegetable crops. The precise timings will vary slightly for each region, so adjust them to suit your own site and conditions. Sow most seeds under cover until the risk of frosts has passed.

CROPS		SPRING			SUMMER			AUTUMN			WINTER		
		EARLY	MID	LATE	EARLY	MID	LATE	EARLY	MID	LATE	EARLY	MID	LATE
TOMATOES	SOW	■											■
	HARVEST					■	■	■					
PEPPERS	SOW	■											■
	HARVEST					■	■	■					
CHILLIES	SOW	■											■
	HARVEST					■	■	■					
AUBERGINES	SOW	■											■
	HARVEST					■	■	■					
PEAS	SOW	■	■							■			
	HARVEST			■	■	■	■						
RUNNER BEANS	SOW		■	■									
	HARVEST					■	■	■					
FRENCH BEANS	SOW			■	■								
	HARVEST					■	■	■					
BROAD BEANS	SOW	■	■								■		
	HARVEST			■	■	■							
CUCUMBERS	SOW	■	■										
	HARVEST					■	■	■					
COURGETTES	SOW		■	■									
	HARVEST					■	■	■					
SUMMER SQUASHES	SOW		■	■									
	HARVEST					■	■	■					
WINTER SQUASHES	SOW		■	■									
	HARVEST						■	■	■				
PUMPKINS	SOW		■	■									
	HARVEST						■	■	■				
SUMMER/AUTUMN CABBAGES	SOW	■	■										
	HARVEST				■	■	■	■	■				
WINTER/SPRING CABBAGES	SOW				■	■							
	HARVEST	■	■							■	■	■	■
CAULIFLOWERS	SOW	■	■	■						■			
	HARVEST	■			■	■	■						
CALABRESE	SOW	■	■										
	HARVEST					■	■	■					
SPROUTING BROCCOLI	SOW	■	■										
	HARVEST	■	■								■	■	■
BRUSSELS SPROUTS	SOW	■	■										
	HARVEST								■	■	■	■	
KALE	SOW	■	■										
	HARVEST							■	■	■	■	■	■
LETTUCES	SOW	■	■	■	■	■							
	HARVEST			■	■	■	■	■	■				
CUT-AND-COME-AGAIN SALAD	SOW	■	■	■	■	■							
	HARVEST		■	■	■	■	■	■	■	■			
MICROGREENS	SOW	■	■	■	■	■	■	■	■	■	■	■	■
	HARVEST	■	■	■	■	■	■	■	■	■	■	■	■
ORIENTAL GREENS	SOW		■	■	■	■							
	HARVEST				■	■	■	■	■				

CROPS		SPRING			SUMMER			AUTUMN			WINTER		
		EARLY	MID	LATE	EARLY	MID	LATE	EARLY	MID	LATE	EARLY	MID	LATE
SPINACH	SOW		●	●	●	●	●	●	●				
	HARVEST				●	●	●	●	●				
SWISS CHARD	SOW		●	●	●	●	●						
	HARVEST	●	●	●	●	●	●	●	●	●	●	●	●
CHICORY	SOW		●	●	●								
	HARVEST					●	●	●	●		●	●	
ENDIVE	SOW		●	●	●	●	●						
	HARVEST				●	●	●	●	●				
WATERCRESS	SOW				●	●							
	HARVEST				●	●	●	●	●				
RADISHES	SOW	●	●	●	●	●	●	●	●				
	HARVEST			●	●	●	●	●	●	●	●	●	
BEETROOTS	SOW		●	●	●	●	●	●					
	HARVEST				●	●	●	●	●	●		●	●
CARROTS	SOW	●	●	●	●	●	●	●					
	HARVEST				●	●	●	●	●	●			●
TURNIPS	SOW		●	●	●	●	●						
	HARVEST				●	●	●	●	●	●			●
PARSNIPS	SOW	●	●										
	HARVEST	●	●										
SWEDES	SOW				●	●							
	HARVEST							●	●	●			
POTATOES	SOW	●	●	●									
	HARVEST				●	●	●	●	●				
ONIONS	SOW	●	●	●				●	●				
	HARVEST				●	●	●	●	●		●		
SHALLOTS	SOW	●	●										
	HARVEST				●	●	●	●	●	●			
SPRING ONIONS	SOW	●	●	●				●	●				
	HARVEST				●	●	●	●	●				
LEEKS	SOW	●	●	●									
	HARVEST	●	●	●				●	●	●	●	●	●
GARLIC	SOW	●									●	●	
	HARVEST				●	●							
SWEETCORN	SOW		●	●									
	HARVEST						●	●	●				
KOHL RABI	SOW		●	●	●	●							
	HARVEST			●	●	●	●	●	●	●			
FLORENCE FENNEL	SOW			●	●	●							
	HARVEST					●	●	●	●	●	●	●	
CELERY	SOW	●	●										
	HARVEST						●	●	●	●			
CELERIAC	SOW	●	●										
	HARVEST							●	●	●	●		
ASPARAGUS	PLANT	●	●										
	HARVEST		●	●	●	●							
GLOBE ARTICHOKES	PLANT	●	●	●				●	●				
	HARVEST				●	●	●	●					
JERUSALEM ARTICHOKES	PLANT	●	●										
	HARVEST								●	●	●	●	●
RHUBARB	PLANT	●	●										
	HARVEST			●	●	●	●	●					
ANNUAL HERBS	SOW		●	●	●	●							
	HARVEST				●	●	●	●	●				
PERENNIAL HERBS	PLANT		●	●	●	●							
	HARVEST	●	●	●	●	●	●	●	●	●	●	●	●

GROW YOUR OWN
FRUIT

STRAWBERRIES

This fruiting perennial is extremely popular, and deservedly so, with varieties that produce sweet home-grown fruit from late spring until the first frosts. Traditionally served fresh with cream, they are also delicious made into jam. Strawberries grow well in containers, window boxes, and hanging baskets, making them perfect for small spaces. They are easy to propagate from plantlets or "runners", and can be brought under cover successfully to give out-of-season crops.

	SPRING	SUMMER	AUTUMN	WINTER
SOW				
HARVEST				

TIME TO HARVEST: 2–4 WEEKS

SUITABLE FOR: BEDS, CONTAINERS, AND HANGING BASKETS

0   1m   2m   3m

11 plants

3M (10FT) ROWS
Plant 30cm (12in) apart, 45cm (18in) between rows

0   30cm

CONTAINERS
3 plants in each

1 GETTING STARTED

There are two main types of strawberries to consider. Summer-fruiting varieties are the tastiest, and crop in a single flush in early- to midsummer. "Everbearers" or "perpetual" strawberries produce their main harvest in summer, then give smaller subsequent flushes of fruit until the first frosts.

'Pegasus' is a summer-fruiting variety that freely produces large, sweet, glossy berries.

'Symphony' is a late-season, summer-fruiting variety, grown for its heavy crops.

'Florence' produces firm, well-flavoured fruits on compact plants that grow well in containers.

'Flamenco' is a perpetual variety that crops heavily from midsummer to autumn.

To plant bare-root strawberries, spread the roots out and work soil in between them. Ensure the crown of the plant sits on the soil surface.

Planting into a container will help you keep on top of weeds. Trail fruiting stems over the container's edge to keep the developing fruit clean of soil.

2 PLANTING

Strawberries are available to buy bare-root or pot-grown. They can be planted in spring, although planting in autumn gives them longer to establish before their first crop. Choose a sunny, sheltered spot, and if planting directly into the soil, fork it over to remove all weeds. Plant out leaving 30cm (12in) between plants, 45cm (18in) between rows. If you are planting into troughs, space plants 20cm (8in) apart; in containers and baskets, 10cm (4in).

TIP When planting into containers and baskets, use loam-based compost.

3 MULCHING

As plants growing in beds begin to flower, lay a mulch of straw or hay around them, so the developing fruits are held away from the soil. This keeps them clean and ensures good air movement, whilst also deterring slugs. Alternatively, use "collars" around individual plants or plant through weed-control fabric.

Straw was traditionally used to lift the fruits from the soil, hence straw-berry. It is cheap and easy to buy, and can be composted at the end of the season.

Ready-made strawberry collars are ideal if you only have a few plants, and can be used from year to year. You can easily make your own.

4 PROTECTING THE FRUIT

Birds will attack the fruit as soon as they start turning red; erect net tunnel cloches over rows or create small cages over single plants. Check netting regularly and keep it taut, so birds don't become entangled. Protect against slugs and snails by lightly spreading organic pellets around plants.

Support bird netting above the plants with canes to prevent them growing through it and exposing the fruit to attack from birds.

5 HARVESTING

Pick the individual strawberry fruits as soon as they turn completely red. Do this by pinching them off at the stalk, rather than pulling the fruit itself, which can cause bruising and make them liable to rot. The berries will keep fresh for a few days in a cool place, or can be frozen raw or cooked.

Pick the fruit when it is fully coloured but still firm to the touch. Leave the leafy calyx in place until you eat the fruit to prevent decay.

6 PROPAGATING PLANTS

After fruiting, summer varieties send out stems or "runners", with small plantlets along their length, which can be used to propagate new plants. Plunge small pots of compost near the plantlets and peg them into it. Keep them moist until autumn, when they will be well-rooted. Cut the joining stem and grow the new plant on.

Anchor the plantlet in place with a bent piece of thick wire, such as from an old clothes hanger.

RASPBERRIES

You could be forgiven for thinking that raspberries demand a lot of space – visit any allotment and you'll see row after row of canes. However, for the majority of people these will yield too much fruit. Raspberries are easy to grow: just a few canes on a small plot will produce a rewarding crop, and modern "dwarf" varieties are now available. By choosing summer- and autumn-fruiting varieties, you'll be able to enjoy sweet berries from midsummer right through to the first frosts.

	SPRING	SUMMER	AUTUMN	WINTER
SOW				
HARVEST				

TIME TO HARVEST: 6-8 WEEKS

SUITABLE FOR: BEDS AND CONTAINERS

0   1m   2m   3m

11 plants

3M (10FT) ROWS
Plant 30cm (12in) apart, with 1m (3ft) between rows

0   40cm

CONTAINERS
3 plants in each

1 GETTING STARTED

Summer-fruiting raspberries crop from mid- to late summer; autumn varieties fruit from late summer to mid-autumn, so plant both for the longest harvest. Summer raspberries should be planted against horizontal wires held 40cm (16in) and 80cm (32in) above the soil. Autumn-fruiting varieties can be grown free-standing.

'Polka' is a disease-resistant, nearly spine-free, variety that bears delicious, sweet berries.

'Cascade Delight' is a free-fruiting summer raspberry, with large, rich-tasting berries.

'Tulameen' fruits in summer over several weeks, and is a good choice for cooler areas.

'All Gold' crops in autumn, producing tasty yellow fruits that won't stain your fingers.

Plant new canes in evenly spaced rows and provide suitable support for summer-fruiting varieties. Water and mulch after planting.

New shoots develop in spring after which the original woody cane can be cut to the ground. This will encourge further new canes to develop.

2 PLANTING

New canes are best planted in late autumn, although planting in winter and early spring is also an option. Canes are generally sold bare-root or root-wrapped – lifted from the ground and bundled together loosely in compost. They prefer moist, free-draining soil, and will tolerate a little shade. Dig well-rotted organic matter into the soil in autumn, allowing it to settle for two weeks before planting. Space the canes 30cm (12in) apart in rows at least 1m (3ft) apart.

TIP Rasberries are easy to grow in large tubs, especially compact varieties.

3 ROUTINE CARE

Keep plants well watered during summer and apply a tomato feed to promote a good harvest. Mulch near the base of the canes with composted organic matter to help retain moisture. As soon as the fruit starts to ripen, protect it from birds. Cover plants with a cage or use netting, held taut using canes to prevent snaring birds.

Water the plants once or twice a week during summer, even daily on light soils during dry spells. Avoid splashing the stems, which spreads disease.

Birds soon attack summer raspberries but are less interested in autumn-fruiting varieties, which crop as other wild berries become abundant.

4 HARVESTING

The berries are ready as soon as they turn fully red or yellow, depending on the variety, and pull easily from the plant leaving the central "plug" behind. Avoid picking on rainy days as wet fruit does not store well. Check your plants daily to ensure you harvest them at the perfect point of ripeness.

Handle the berries carefully when picking as they are easily damaged. Squashed fruits quickly spoil so are best eaten straightaway.

5 SUMMER PRUNING

Summer-fruiting raspberries are pruned straight after the last fruits have been harvested, cutting the fruited canes to the base. Younger, unfruited stems, produced that summer, should be tied to the wires in their place. Keep only the strongest and tie them in 10cm (4in) apart, to fruit next year.

After pruning summer varieties, tie the new shoots onto horizontal wires. These will fruit the following year, then be replaced by new growth.

6 WINTER PRUNING

Autumn raspberries are pruned in winter by cutting all the canes down to the ground. Alternatively, to encourage a staggered harvest the following year, cut a few canes down by only half their height in winter. The half-height canes will then produce an earlier crop in early to midsummer. These fruited canes can then be pruned out completely after harvesting.

Cut autumn-fruiting canes closely to the ground. New shoots will appear in late spring.

BLACKBERRIES AND HYBRIDS

Gone are the days of small berries, carried on large, vicious plants – modern blackberries have been bred to have fewer thorns, often none, and to give generous harvests of plump, tasty fruit. They are also more disease resistant, which makes them easier to look after, and some new varieties fruit on new growth, making them easier to prune. If you also plant one of the blackberry hybrids, such as a loganberry or tayberry, you will have a wonderful range of fruit for jam-making.

	SPRING	SUMMER	AUTUMN	WINTER
PLANT				
HARVEST				

TIME TO HARVEST: 6–8 WEEKS

SUITABLE FOR: BEDS AND BORDERS

1-2 plants

3M (10FT) ROWS
Plant 1.5–3m (5–10ft) apart, according to variety

CONTAINERS
1 plant in each

1 GETTING STARTED

There are many blackberry varieties to choose from, with different qualities to suit your garden; these include thornless plants. Hybrid berries are more vigorous and result from cross-breeding blackberries with raspberries, or with other related hybrids. Mail order specialist fruit nurseries have the largest selection.

Blackberries fruit from mid- to late summer, and there are many varieties, some being thornless.

Loganberries are best cooked with plenty of sugar and taste like sharp raspberries.

Japanese Wineberries are orange–red to deep red and have a delicious sweet flavour.

Tayberries are a cross between a raspberry and a blackberry, and have delicious fruit.

Make a hole slightly wider than the root ball so you can firm the soil in after planting. Lower the plant in to check the depth.

Remove the plant and tease out the roots to help them establish. Spread out the roots of bare-root plants.

Pot-grown plants are planted level with the soil surface; bare-root plants to the depth of the soil mark on their stems.

2 PLANTING

Blackberries and hybrid berries are clambering shrubs, so plant them against a wall or trellis, or a system of posts and wires, where their stems can be trained. To help them establish quickly, they are best planted in autumn, while the soil is still warm and moist, although they can also be planted through winter into spring. Choose a sunny site, dig over the soil to remove weeds, and mix in organic matter and granular, general purpose fertilizer. Water well after planting.

> **TIP** New compact varieties of blackberries are ideal for planting in pots.

3 ROUTINE CARE

Keep plants well watered during summer and mulch them using well-rotted organic matter. If you use manure for this, no additional fertilizer is needed, otherwise apply a balanced granular fertilizer in spring. Net the fruits as they ripen, but keep nets taut to prevent birds getting snagged. Check regularly for gaps.

A fruit cage is ideal for protecting plants from birds, if you have space. If not, make a temporary structure of nets and canes until after harvest.

4 HARVESTING

Depending on the variety or hybrid, the fruit ripens from mid- to late summer. For maximum sweetness, wait until the berries are fully coloured when it should be easy to pull them from the plant. Unless the fruit is to be eaten straightaway, pick the fruit while it is still firm and only during dry weather.

Unlike raspberries, blackberries and the hybrid fruits pull off whole when picked, and don't leave behind a white core. The juice can stain fingers.

5 PRUNING

Most blackberries and hybrids fruit on canes in their second year. These should be cut to the base in autumn after fruiting, with new unfruited canes being tied in in their place. New "primocare" varieties that fruit on new summer growth can be cut completely to the ground in winter.

To help prune out fruited canes, untie them from their supports first. This will make the cut stems easier to untangle and remove.

6 TRAINING

Although these plants can be left to ramble, they are more manageable, and take up less space when trained against horizontal wires. In winter or early spring, train unfruited stems produced the previous summer to form a fan or spiral either side of the crown. This will encourage flower and fruit formation. Also tie in new season stems during summer to fruit next year.

Supporting horizontal wires can be attached to walls and fences, or stretched between upright posts. Train stems into a fan or spiral.

RED- AND WHITECURRANTS

If you have ever seen a well-cultivated red- or whitecurrant bush, you'll appreciate just how bountiful they are – they can literally drip with jewel-like fruit. They have the advantage that they are easy to grow, even in moderate shade, and can be planted against walls and in roomy containers if space is limited, which means they are ideal for smaller gardens. The fruits freeze well and have a high pectin content (making them excellent for jams and jellies).

	SPRING	SUMMER	AUTUMN	WINTER
PLANT				
HARVEST				

FLOWERING TO HARVEST: 10–12 WEEKS

SUITABLE FOR: BEDS AND CONTAINERS

3M (10FT) ROWS
Plant bushes 1m (39in) apart

CONTAINERS
1 plant in each

1 GETTING STARTED

Red- and whitecurrants grow best in a sheltered site on moist yet free-draining soil. Plants grown in pots are widely available throughout the year, or can be bought bare-root during autumn. If deciding between the two types, redcurrants generally have a sharper, more acidic flavour; whitecurrants are sweeter tasting.

'Jonkheer van Tets' is an early variety that produces a large crop of rich, bright red fruit.

'Red Lake' produces long "strigs" of berries from midsummer. It is a large, vigorous shrub.

'Junifer' is a compact, high-yielding, early-season, French variety with bright red fruit.

'Versailles Blanche' fruits in midsummer, giving a plentiful harvest of sweet-tasting berries.

Plant red- and whitecurrants so that all growth emerges from a short stem, or "leg", just above the soil surface.

Fill in between the roots of bare-root plants with soil; lightly tease out the roots of pot-grown bushes before planting them.

Firm the soil after planting to remove air pockets, ensuring the "leg" remains above the soil surface. Water in well.

2 PLANTING

Currants establish best when planted between autumn and spring, although container-raised plants can be planted at any time if kept moist. They can be planted in sun but don't mind a shady spot, and can be grown against north- or east-facing walls. Prepare the site by digging it over, space plants 80cm (32in) apart, then water well and mulch after planting. In smaller plots, plant into 50cm (20in) wide pots filled with soil-based compost.

TIP Plant pot-grown currants so the compost is level with the soil surface.

3 ROUTINE CARE

Plants will require regular watering in their first summer to encourage root establishment. After this time they become more drought-tolerant, but yields will be improved by regular watering in spring and summer. Mulch plants with rich, well-rotted organic matter, and apply a dressing of high-potash fertilizer every spring.

Organic mulch retains moisture, reducing the need for watering during summer. It also degrades, providing nutrients for your plants.

4 PROTECTING THE FRUIT

Birds will quickly strip plants of berries, so erect a cage of netting over your bushes as soon as the fruits begin to ripen. (Whitecurrants turn from green to translucent white as they near maturity). Ensure all netting is pulled taut to prevent birds becoming trapped. Remove the net after harvesting.

5 HARVESTING

The berries are carried on trailing stems or "strigs", which should be picked whole once all the berries along them have ripened. Pull the strig from the stem using your fingers, or carefully snip them with scissors. Check your bushes every three or four days to harvest the berries at their best.

Birds love berries and will repeatedly raid your plants. Net individual bushes or consider buying a fruit cage if you have several plants.

Harvest the fruit as whole strigs rather than as individual berries, as they are small and easily squashed. Eat the berries fresh or freeze them.

6 PRUNING

Currants fruit at the base of stems that are at least a year old. In early- to midsummer, prune the new stems back to 10–15cm (4–6in) to encourage more fruiting spurs, which will also help the fruit ripen and improve airflow. In winter, cut the pruned stems back to two buds above the cluster of buds at the base of the stem and remove any dead or diseased growth.

Pruning encourages fruiting spurs that develop in clusters at the base of cut stems.

BLACKCURRANTS

These robust bushes bear fruit in summer, producing long stems or "strigs" of intensely flavoured berries that are excellent eaten fresh, and even more delicious cooked and made into preserves, pies, and summer cordials. Blackcurrants are easy to grow and reliable croppers, even in colder areas, making them a good choice for beginner growers. They are easy to prune, and most available varieties are prone to few pests or diseases.

	SPRING	SUMMER	AUTUMN	WINTER
PLANT				
HARVEST				

FLOWERING TO HARVEST: 10–12 WEEKS

SUITABLE FOR: BEDS AND CONTAINERS

3M (10FT) ROWS
Plant bushes 1m (3ft) apart
3 plants

CONTAINERS
1 plant in each

1 GETTING STARTED

Blackcurrants growing in containers are readily available throughout the year, but they can also be bought and planted bare-root in autumn. Bare-root plants are cheaper than pot-grown, which is helpful if you want several on your plot. Look out for vigorous, disease-resistant varieties, which have 'Ben' in their names.

'Ben Sarek' is a free-fruiting variety, with a compact habit, and is ideal for smaller plots.

'Ben Connan' fruits from midsummer, and gives a good harvest of sweet, juicy berries.

'Ebony' is an early variety that crops from early summer. Its sweet fruit are especially large.

'Ben Lomond' crops freely from midsummer onwards, producing large, sweet berries.

Using a guide, plant slightly deeper than the soil mark on the stem, or deeper than the level of the compost if pot-grown.

Backfill the hole with soil, making sure that there are no large air pockets, and that the plant is upright.

Firm in gently and water in well. New blackcurrant bushes should be pruned immediately after planting.

2 PLANTING

The best time to plant is between autumn and spring, when the soil is warm and moist, although currants can also be planted in summer if watered well. Choose a sunny, sheltered site and weed it thoroughly. In smaller plots, plant into 50cm (20in) pots, filled with soil-based compost. Water plants in, mulch well, then cut back all the stems to soil level to promote sturdy new growth. If planting more than one bush, space them at least 1m (3ft) apart.

TIP Plant blackcurrants deeply, so all the stems emerge directly from the soil.

3 ROUTINE CARE

Keep young plants well watered throughout their first summer; established plants are more drought tolerant but will crop better if watered during dry spells. Mulch plants in spring with well-rotted organic matter, such as garden compost, and apply a granular high-nitrogen fertilizer. Use canes to support fruit-laden stems.

Mulch plants to help retain moisture in summer and to suppress weeds. As the mulch breaks down, it releases nutrients to your plants.

Support stems using a simple frame of string and canes to prevent them collapsing and snapping under the weight of the fruit.

4 PROTECTING THE FRUIT

Birds can strip plants of berries in a matter of days. As soon as fruit begins to ripen, protect your plants with netting, secured at the base to prevent birds sneaking in underneath. Check the nets regularly for gaps.

5 HARVESTING

Older blackcurrant varieties ripen as individual berries and can be picked one-by-one when ready. Modern types are only picked when the whole stem, or "strig", is ripe. The strigs should pull easily from the bush.

Use netting to prevent birds from targetting your berries. Keep it as taut as possible.

Ripe berries pull easily from the bush but handle them carefully as they are easily bruised.

6 PRUNING

Blackcurrants fruit mainly on one-year-old stems, and can be picked and pruned at the same time. Cut stems that have fruited to the base, leaving the new growth to crop next summer. Plants that are pruned this way must be fed well in spring with a high-nitrogen fertilizer. An alternative method is to allow the stems to fruit for three years, then prune them to the base in winter. This creates bigger plants, which may be better suited to larger gardens.

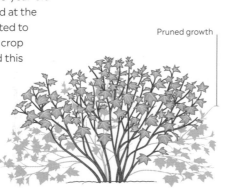

Pruned growth

GOOSEBERRIES

This easy-to-grow fruit gives its main crop in early summer, but you can enjoy an earlier harvest by using the tart fruitlets that are thinned out in late spring. Gooseberries are available as either culinary or dessert varieties; a few are dual-purpose, offering you the best of both worlds. Most gooseberries are reliable plants, and breeders are continually developing new varieties with improved disease resistance and yield, and thankfully, fewer thorns.

	SPRING	SUMMER	AUTUMN	WINTER
PLANT				
HARVEST				

FLOWERING TO HARVEST: 10 WEEKS

SUITABLE FOR: BEDS AND CONTAINERS

3M (10FT) ROWS
Plant bushes 1m (3ft) apart

3 plants

CONTAINERS
1 plant in each

1 GETTING STARTED

Young, pot-grown plants are widely sold throughout the year, and bare-root plants during autumn. There are many varieties to choose from, with fruit that varies in size, shape, taste, and colour. Some have sharp thorns, which you may want to avoid, especially in smaller gardens, or if you have young children.

'Careless' is suitable for eating fresh or cooking, and gives an early crop of tasty green fruits.

'Invicta' fruits from early- to midsummer, giving a heavy crop to cook or enjoy fresh.

'Early Sulphur' an early variety that produces medium-sized fruits with hairy, yellow skin.

'Hinnonmäki Röd' is easy to grow and ideal for beginners. Its sweet-tasting fruit mature red.

Dig a planting hole that is wide enough for the roots of bare-root plants to be spread out fully, or to fit the root ball of pot-grown bushes.

Plant bare-root bushes at the same depth as the soil mark on their stem; plant pot-grown plants so their compost is level with the soil surface.

2 PLANTING

Pot-grown gooseberries can be planted throughout the year if watered well, although they establish best between autumn and spring. Unlike many fruits they tolerate shade, so can be planted in north- or east-facing spots. Dig the soil over to remove all weeds, mix in some general purpose fertilizer, and water well after planting. Space plants 1m (3ft) apart. They can also be planted in 40cm (16in) wide containers, filled with loam-based compost.

TIP Keep plants in pots well watered, especially when in flower or fruit.

3 ROUTINE CARE

Water new plants well in their first year, and water established plants during dry spells. In spring, mulch plants with rich organic matter, and add granular balanced fertilizer on sandy or chalky soils. Protect the fruit from birds with fruit cages, or use netting held taut to stop birds becoming caught up. Check regularly for gaps.

Wire hoops and bent canes are ideal for supporting bird netting. The structure can be left in place all year or removed after fruiting.

Picked gooseberries keep in the fridge for about a week. They freeze well for longer-term storage, and can also be made into preserves.

4 HARVESTING

To encourage larger fruits, thin the developing gooseberries in late spring, and rather than waste them, use the sharp-tasting "thinnings" for cooking. Aim to take no more than half the berries and, if your bush has yet to establish a regular heavy cropping pattern, only take a quarter of them. Once the remaining berries are fully ripe they can be harvested. Hold the berry by the stalk when picking, not the fruit, to avoid bruising and subsequent decay. Pick over your bushes every few days as they ripen to enjoy the fruit at its best.

5 PRUNING

Gooseberries fruit at the base of stems that are at least one-year-old, and are pruned twice a year. In midsummer, cut back all of the growth produced this year to 15–20cm (6–8in) long. In winter, these pruned stems should be cut back further to leave only two or three buds on each, which will then bear fruit next year. While pruning, remove any dead, diseased, or damaged growth, as well as any thinner stems that look likely to droop to the ground once they are heavily laden with fruit.

Pruned growth

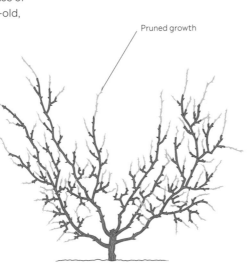

BLUEBERRIES

Incredibly popular with gardeners, blueberries were one of the first crops to be crowned with "superfruit" status, thanks to their naturally high levels of health-giving antioxidants and vitamins. Give blueberry plants an acid or "ericaceous" soil and plenty of water during the growing season, and they will yield abundantly. If you don't have acid soil, the plants will crop just as successfully in pots, making them an ideal choice for smaller gardens and patios.

	SPRING	SUMMER	AUTUMN	WINTER
PLANT				
HARVEST				

FLOWERING TO HARVEST: 8–10 WEEKS

SUITABLE FOR: BEDS AND CONTAINERS

4 plants

3M (10FT) ROWS
Plant bushes 75cm (30in) apart

CONTAINERS
1 plant in each

1 GETTING STARTED

Blueberries are usually sold growing in pots and can be bought throughout the year. The plants are self-fertile, so you only need one in order to produce a crop. However, they fruit more freely when cross-pollinated, so grow two or more varieties that flower at the same time if you have the space.

'Spartan' produces a generous crop of large, richly-flavoured berries in midsummer.

'Bluetta' is a compact variety, ideal for smaller gardens or for growing in containers.

'Jersey' is a tough variety for cooler areas. It must be grown near another variety to fruit.

'Herbert' fruits in late summer, giving a good crop of sweet, intensely flavoured berries.

Ease the plant from its pot and lightly tease the roots away from the root ball to encourage them to grow into the surrounding soil.

Plant the blueberry so the surface of the compost is level with the surrounding soil. Firm it in gently and water well.

Mulch with organic matter, such as ericaceous compost, which will help provide and maintain acid soil conditions.

2 PLANTING

Blueberries prefer boggy growing conditions, and are best planted between autumn and spring when the soil is moist. They also require acid soil with a pH below 6 (use a soil testing kit if you are unsure), so before planting, incorporate ericaceous compost into the soil and add sulphur chips to help maintain a low pH. Water plants in well and keep moist. If your soil is unsuitable, plant blueberries in containers filled with lime-free, ericaceous compost.

TIP Choose an open, sunny spot. Blueberries fruit more heavily in sunshine.

3 ROUTINE CARE

In spring, mulch plants in containers and borders with well-rotted organic matter, such as leaf mould or composted bark. Water plants well throughout the year, especially when in flower and fruit, especially plants in pots. Feed plants every fortnight from early- to midsummer with a liquid fertilizer suitable for ericaceous plants.

Use rainwater to water blueberries to help maintain the soil acidity. Tap water commonly contains lime, especially in hard-water areas.

Acid-loving plants require specific fertilizers, which are widely available as liquid or granular feeds. Don't use conventional fertilizers.

4 PROTECTING THE FRUIT

Blueberries flower in early spring and it's worth using garden fleece to protect them against frost damage in cold areas. The ripening fruit should also be protected from birds in summer using taut netting or a fruit cage.

5 HARVESTING

Check your plants every few days to ensure you pick the berries at their best. Ripe fruits pull easily from the plants but are also easy to squash, so take care. The berries are best enjoyed fresh, but a surplus can be frozen.

Handle bird nets carefully when picking, as the ripening fruit is easily knocked off.

Blueberries ripen over a long period, and each shrub can be in fruit for several weeks.

6 PRUNING

Blueberries are usually grown as freestanding bushes, whether in containers or beds, and are pruned just before they come into leaf in spring. Remove lower branches and weak growth, along with any dead, diseased, or damaged shoots. The fruit is predominantly produced on one-, two- and three-year-old wood. Using sharp loppers or a pruning saw, remove less productive, older stems completely at the base.

Pruned growth

APPLES

This most traditional of garden fruit is no longer the preserve of gardeners with large plots. The availability of dwarfing rootstocks has made it easy for gardeners with limited space to embrace apple growing too. There are hundreds of apple varieties to choose from with different flavours, uses, harvest times, cropping potential, and disease-resistance. Many can be grown in containers, or can be trained into neat, space-saving shapes, such as cordons.

	SPRING	SUMMER	AUTUMN	WINTER
PLANT				
HARVEST				

FLOWERING TO HARVEST: 14–20 WEEKS

SUITABLE FOR: BEDS AND CONTAINERS

1–4 plants

3M (10FT) ROWS
Plant trees 75cm (30in) apart, depending on rootstock

CONTAINERS
1 plant in each

1 GETTING STARTED

Container-grown apples are available all year, whereas bare-root trees can only be bought between autumn and early spring. In order to produce fruit, apple flowers must be pollinated. Unless your variety is self-fertile, you will need at least two compatible trees Seek advice before deciding what to buy.

'Cox's Orange Pippin' is a well-known dessert variety that bears richlyflavoured fruit.

'Greensleeves' fruits freely in early autumn, bearing sweet, sharp-tasting dessert apples.

'James Grieve' is a dessert apple that fruits in early autumn. It grows well in cool, dry areas.

'Bramley's Seedling' is a renowned culinary apple. It requires another variety for pollination.

Lay a guide across the hole and plant at the same depth as the soil mark on the tree, or the top of the compost if pot-grown.

Backfill the hole with soil, improved with organic matter, and firm it gently with your foot. Water the plant in well.

Stake the tree and attach it with an adjustable tree tie. Check the tie annually and loosen if need be.

2 PLANTING

Apple trees establish better if planted while dormant from autumn to spring, although pot-grown trees can be planted at any time if kept moist. Choose a sunny, sheltered site, dig over the area to remove weeds, and fork in organic matter if the soil is sandy or heavy clay. Pot-grown and bare-root trees are planted using the same technique (see left). Apples on dwarfing rootstocks can be planted into large containers of loam-based compost.

TIP Trees on dwarfing rootstock are best staked permanently.

3 ROUTINE CARE

Water trees well, especially in their first year, to help them establish. Trees in pots will always require regular watering; those in the ground will need less water once fully rooted. Mulch trees in spring with organic matter and apply a high-potash granular fertilizer. Apply liquid high-potash feed to pot-grown trees in spring and early summer.

Regular watering is vital for new apple trees while they are becoming established. Watering mature apples during dry periods will also help to prevent the disease bitter pit (see p.246).

A rich organic mulch helps to suppress weeds, while retaining moisture and keeping the roots cool. It also releases nutrients as it degrades, feeding the tree.

4 THINNING OUT

To encourage full-sized apples, thin the developing fruits in early summer, once they reach walnut-size. Thin dessert apples to one or two fruits per 15cm (6in); thin cooking apples to one every 15cm (6in). Always thin out the central fruit, which can grow abnormally.

To help new trees establish, remove any fruit that sets during its first year. Later crops can be allowed to develop once thinned.

5 HARVESTING

When fruits are ready to harvest, gently cup them in your hand, lift and twist. The fruit should come away without pulling, if it doesn't, try again in a day or two. Pick over the tree regularly as the fruit ripens, and handle the apples carefully to avoid bruising them.

Harvest apples regularly to enjoy them at their best. Early varieties are best eaten fresh, later varieties can be stored if you have a surplus.

6 PRUNING

Established freestanding apples are pruned in winter. Prune out congested growth from the centre to maintain an open shape, and remove dead, diseased, damaged, and weak growth. Cut back new stems by half to encourage fruit-bearing spurs at their base. Older fruit spurs should be thinned if they are congested.

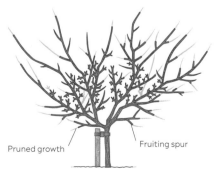

Pruned growth   Fruiting spur

PEARS

A perfectly ripe pear is a real indulgence, and something you're unlikely to appreciate until you grow your own. Shop-bought fruits are often rock hard and fail to ripen, or are soft and past their peak. As easy to grow as apples, pears come in culinary and dessert varieties, with a range of flavours and textures. The trees prefer a sheltered spot – where space is limited, they can be planted and trained against walls and fences. Pears on dwarf rootstocks can be grown in containers.

	SPRING	SUMMER	AUTUMN	WINTER
PLANT				
HARVEST				

FLOWERING TO HARVEST: 16–20 WEEKS

SUITABLE FOR: BEDS AND CONTAINERS

0   1m   2m   3m

1–4 plants

0   50cm

3M (10FT) ROWS
Plant trees 75cm (30in) apart, depending on rootstock

CONTAINERS
1 plant in each

1 GETTING STARTED

Pears are available in pots all year, or bare-root in autumn to early spring. You can also buy pre-trained trees to plant against walls. Most varieties must be pollinated before they will set fruit, so unless there are pear trees growing nearby, you will need to plant more than one. Seek advice for compatible varieties.

'Concorde' is easy to grow, has a good flavour, and stays compact. It is ideal for smaller plots.

'Doyenné du Comice' need a sunny spot but produces delicious fruit in mid-autumn.

'Beurré Superfin' crops in early autumn, bearing richly aromatic fruit. It is ideal for wall-training.

'Packham's Triumph' has richly flavoured fruit in mid-autumn. It grows best in a sheltered site.

To plant a pear tree in a pot, fill the bottom with loam-based compost and incorporate some slow-release fertilizer.

Tease out the roots of pot-grown trees and spread out those of bare-root plants. Fill around the roots with compost.

Make sure the tree is planted to the depth of the soil mark on the stem. Insert a stake for support and water it in well.

2 PLANTING

Pear trees flower in early spring and need plenty of sun to ripen the fruit, so choose a warm, sheltered site. Prepare the soil before planting by digging it over to remove weeds, and work in some granular general purpose fertilizer and organic matter. Once planted and staked, firm the soil gently, and water in well. Pears grown on dwarf rootstocks can also be planted in large containers, 50cm (20in) wide, filled with loam-based, John Innes No.3 compost.

TIP Protect the blossom with garden fleece on nights when frost is forecast.

3 ROUTINE CARE

Pears prefer to be kept moist, so water them well during their first year and during prolonged dry spells in the future. To help retain moisture and shade the roots, mulch around the trunk in spring with well-rotted organic matter, such as garden compost. Apply general purpose fertilizer in spring, followed by a high-potash feed in summer.

Water well in summer, especially container-grown trees. If trees become dry while in flower or fruit, the yield may be reduced.

High-potash feeds, such as tomato fertilizer, encourage plants to flower and produce more fruit. Apply it as a liquid as the fruit develops.

4 THINNING OUT

Trees can set a heavy crop, which should be thinned to promote full-size fruit. In midsummer, thin the fruitlets leaving one per cluster. As fruits swell, support heavily laden branches to stop them snapping.

Pears naturally shed some excess fruitlets in early summer, which is called "June drop". Wait until it has passed before thinning them further.

5 HARVESTING

Fruits will begin ripening from late summer, depending on variety. The best way to pick them is to cup a fruit in your hand, lift and twist. It should come away easily, without pulling, otherwise leave it a little longer.

Check early varieties regularly as they ripen quickly. Later varieties may need to be picked and ripened in storage.

6 PRUNING

Established freestanding pear trees are pruned in winter. Prune out congested stems in the middle of the tree to maintain an open shape. Also remove any dead, diseased, damaged, and crossing growth. Cut back stems produced in summer by half their length to encourage spurs to develop at their base – these will fruit next year.

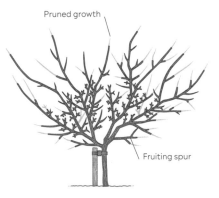

Pruned growth

Fruiting spur

PLUMS

Plums are deliciously sweet and juicy, and the trees fruit so freely that in most years you're almost certain of a glut, providing ample material for jams, bottling, and freezing. Plums, which include damsons, gages, and bullaces, are very easy to grow and need little pruning. If you choose a self-fertile variety you will only need one tree to produce a crop. Modern varieties grafted on dwarfing rootstocks are ideal for smaller gardens and can even be grown in containers.

	SPRING	SUMMER	AUTUMN	WINTER
PLANT				
HARVEST				

FLOWERING TO HARVEST: 14–16 WEEKS

SUITABLE FOR: BEDS AND CONTAINERS

0   1m   2m   3m

2 plants

0   50cm

3M (10FT) ROWS
Plant trees 1.5m (5ft) apart, depending on rootstock

CONTAINERS
1 plant in each

1 GETTING STARTED

Bare-root trees can be bought and planted from autumn to mid-spring; those sold in pots can be planted at any time. Some varieties need to be cross-pollinated to set fruit, so you will need two or more. Self-fertile varieties can be grown alone although may crop better when pollinated by a suitable variety.

'Victoria' is the classic plum and gives a heavy crop of tasty purple-red fruit in late summer.

'Shropshire Damson' is self-fertile, so you only need one tree. It crops in early autumn.

'Oullins Gage' bears sweet, golden fruits in late summer that are good eaten fresh or cooked.

'Marjorie's Seedling' is a reliable self-fertile variety that produces heavy crops of blue fruit.

Place a guide across the hole and plant at the same depth as the soil mark on the tree, or the top of the compost if pot-grown.

Backfill the hole working the soil in well between the roots of bare-root trees. Firm it gently as you go. Water the tree in well.

Attach the stake to the tree with an adjustable tie. Check all ties occasionally and remove the stake after two years.

2 PLANTING

Choose a sheltered, sunny site, dig it over to remove weeds, and work in well-rotted organic matter, such as garden compost, and some high-nitrogen granular fertilizer. When planting, stake the tree, firm it in gently, and water it well. Plums can also be planted in containers, although they must be kept well-watered as they are sensitive to drought. Fill a container at least 50cm (20in) wide with loam-based, John Innes No.3 compost.

TIP Plums and gages can be eaten raw; use bullaces and damsons for cooking.

3 ROUTINE CARE

Water trees well in the first year, and during dry spells in later years. Plums have relatively shallow roots and benefit from a thick mulch of organic matter in spring. They are especially hungry for nitrogen, which you can provide by mulching with well-rotted farmyard manure. Alternatively, apply a nitrogen-based granular fertilizer.

New plum trees need regular watering until well-rooted. Established trees can fend for themselves, except in dry spells or on sandy soils.

Mulch trees but leave the base of the trunk clear to prevent decay. Use well-rotted material that will release nutrients to the tree.

4 THINNING OUT

Plum crops vary because frost can kill the early flowers. After a mild spring when the crop is good, thin the fruit to 5–8cm (2–3in) apart. This will encourage full-size plums and prevent branches becoming overladen and snapping.

Leave the developing fruitlets into early summer, in case any drop from the tree naturally. Then thin them out to promote larger fruits.

5 HARVESTING

Leave plums and gages to ripen fully so they are as sweet as possible; bullaces and damsons can be picked while quite sour. Watch out for wasps when picking and hang up decoy nests if they become a problem.

Harvest the fruits regularly when they are ripe to enjoy them at their best. Underripe plums can be stored for a few days.

6 PRUNING

Plums are pruned as little as possible to protect the trees from the fungal disease, silver leaf (see p.246). As soon as fruit is harvested, use a clean saw or loppers to remove any dead, diseased, or damaged growth, along with spindly or crossing stems. Then thin out the remaining branches, if necessary, to reduce congested growth.

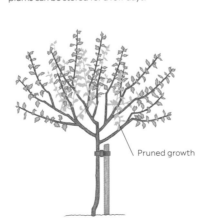

Pruned growth

CHERRIES

Sweet cherries are a real treat when eaten fresh in summer, whereas sharp-tasting acid varieties are excellent for pies and preserves. Whichever you prefer, progress with dwarfing rootstocks and self-fertile varieties means that these are rewarding times for cherry lovers. Modern compact trees are ideal for smaller gardens and can even be grown in pots. Their small size also makes it easier to protect them against the fruit's traditional enemy – birds.

	SPRING	SUMMER	AUTUMN	WINTER
PLANT				
HARVEST				

FLOWERING TO HARVEST: 10–14 WEEKS

SUITABLE FOR: BEDS

2 plants

3M (10FT) ROWS
Plant trees 1.5m (5ft) apart, depending on rootstock

CONTAINERS
1 plant in each

1 GETTING STARTED

Pot-grown cherries are sold all year and can be planted at any time; bare-root trees are available to plant between mid-autumn and mid-spring. Self-fertile varieties set fruit if grown alone, so you only need one tree. Some older varieties don't, and you'll need to plant two or more that flower at the same time for a crop.

'Lapins' is a self-fertile sweet cherry that bears large fruit in midsummer that ripen almost black.

'Morello' is an acid cherry that crops from late summer into early autumn. It is self-fertile.

'Sweetheart' is a sweet cherry with dark berries. It must be grown near a second variety to fruit.

'May Duke' is a sweet cherry with the sharper taste of an acid variety. It crops in midsummer.

Place a guide across the hole. Plant at the same depth as the soil mark on the tree, or the top of the compost if pot-grown.

Backfill the hole with soil, which should be improved with organic matter, firm it in gently with your foot, and water in well.

Attach the tree to a wooden stake using an adjustable tree tie. Check the tie annually and loosen it if need be.

2 PLANTING

Sweet cherries require a sunny, sheltered site to grow well; acid types are less demanding and will even tolerate shade. To prepare the site before planting, dig over the soil to remove weeds, and fork in sharp grit or composted bark to improve heavier soils. Insert a stake alongside your tree, then firm the soil gently and water in well while planting. There are dwarf rootstocks available, which will enable you to grow cherries in containers.

> **TIP** When choosing varieties, acid cherries are easier to grow in cooler regions.

3 ROUTINE CARE

Keep new trees well-watered during their first year, and water established trees in dry spells. Mulch in spring with well-rotted organic matter, ideally manure (if mulching with another material, provide additional feed by also applying general purpose fertilizer). To encourage a good harvest, feed the trees regularly in summer with a liquid, high-potash feed, such as tomato fertilizer.

Cherries flower in early spring when the blooms can be killed by frost. Cover with garden fleece but remove on mild days to allow pollination.

4 PROTECTING THE FRUIT

Cherries are notoriously favoured by birds and it is essential to net trees as soon as fruits show the first signs of colour – a cage of netting over individual trees is ideal. Keep nets taut and check them regularly for gaps.

Protect trees with netting, securing it at ground level to prevent birds sneaking in underneath. Wasps also like cherries so hang up deterrents.

5 HARVESTING

Once the first fruits begin to ripen fully, cover the tree with a waterproof sheet to stop rain getting to the cherries. Ripe fruits can absorb moisture through their skins which encourages splitting and decay.

Handle ripe fruits gently to avoid bruising them. Cherries can be stored for up to a week if kept in an open bag in the fridge.

6 PRUNING

To avoid the fungal disease silver leaf (see p.246), prune after fruiting, while the tree is still in leaf, but keep pruning to a minimum. To prune sweet cherries, only shorten over-long stems to keep the tree within bounds. To prune an acid cherry, cut one quarter of the fruited shoots back to the next branch, and remove any dead, weak, or damaged growth.

Pruned growth

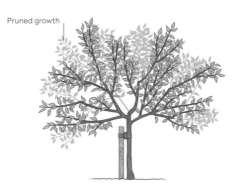

PEACHES, NECTARINES AND APRICOTS

Given a sunny, sheltered spot, these trees make delicious talking points in the garden. One tree can yield a sizeable harvest of juicy fruits, with a characteristically heady perfume when ripe. Many modern varieties are compact, which makes them easy to maintain and ideal for smaller gardens. They also grow well in containers, allowing you to move them to the best spot possible.

	SPRING	SUMMER	AUTUMN	WINTER
PLANT				
HARVEST				

FLOWERING TO HARVEST: 16–20 WEEKS

SUITABLE FOR: BEDS AND CONTAINERS

3M (10FT) ROW
Plant 75cm–3m (2½–10ft) apart, according to variety
1–4 plants

CONTAINERS
1 plant in each

1 GETTING STARTED

Trees are available bare-root to buy and plant between mid-autumn and mid-spring; pot-grown trees can be bought and planted at any time. Dwarf forms are frequently sold pot-grown, and are the only types suitable for growing on in containers. All trees are self-fertile, meaning you only need to grow one to set a crop.

Apricot 'Tomcot' produces many large fruits and is suited to a cool temperate climate.

Nectarine 'Lord Napier' is a good variety for cooler sites. It bears large, tasty fruit in midsummer.

Peach 'Garden Lady' is a dwarf variety, ideal for containers. It crops mid- to late summer.

Peach 'Peregrine' is a great variety for cooler areas and bears large fruit in midsummer.

2 PLANTING

If planting in the ground, choose a sunny, sheltered site, such as near a south-facing wall or fence. Dig over the soil to remove weeds and incorporate some well-rotted organic matter. To plant in a container, use a pot wth a minimum width of 50cm (20in), and plant into loam-based compost.

Use a cane to check the planting depth. Plant bare-root trees level with the soil mark on the stem.

Backfill the hole, holding the tree upright, and support it with a stake and adjustable tie. Water in well.

3 ROUTINE CARE

Water trees during dry spells, mulch well, and apply high-potash fertilizer in spring. To protect blossom from spring frosts, cover trees with garden fleece on cold nights, removing it on mild days so the blooms can be pollinated. To prevent peach leaf curl, use clear, plastic sheeting to shield nectarines and peaches from the rain until late spring. Bring container-grown trees under cover to protect them from frost damage and rainfall.

A frame supports a rain shield in winter and fleece during flowering. Both can be removed in spring.

4 THINNING OUT

Peaches and nectarines often set a very heavy crop, which is best thinned to encourage fewer, but larger, fruits. Thin conventional varieties to about 15–20cm (6–8 in) apart once the fruits are the size of walnuts; fruit on dwarf trees should be thinned to 10cm (4in) apart. As the fruit ripens it attracts wasps, so hang sugary traps.

A decoy wasp nest is designed to repel wasps by tricking them. They fear an attack from wasps in the rival fake nest and keep clear.

Thinning peaches and nectarines helps concentrate the tree's energy so that the remaining fruit are more likely to develop fully.

5 HARVESTING

Begin harvesting fruits as they ripen from midsummer onwards. Mature fruits will feel slightly soft to the touch and will release their characteristic scent. Ideally, leave the fruit on the tree to ripen as fully as possible, although you may find that wasp damage warrants picking earlier. To pick, cup the fruits in your hand and twist gently.

TIP Underripe fruits can be ripened indoors on a sunny windowsill.

Peaches and nectarines are the same species, and are grown and eaten the same way. The only difference is that peaches have fuzzy skins.

6 PRUNING

Peach, nectarine, and apricot trees mainly fruit along the length of stems produced during the previous summer; they should be pruned annually to promote new growth. Prune established trees immediately after harvesting the fruit in summer. Use sterilized tools to remove one third of the fruited stems to leave a framework of healthy, well-spaced, branches. To help avoid silver leaf disease (see p.246), refrain from pruning these fruit trees at any other time of year.

Pruned growth

FIGS

Figs are a true taste of the Mediterranean, and although they need a sunny spot and take a long season to ripen fully, they give a good crop in most gardens. Left to their own devices, figs are large trees but they can be kept to a more manageable size by restricting their roots, which also encourages them to fruit more freely. In colder areas, figs can be grown in containers and protected during winter. They can also be wall-trained where space is tight.

	SPRING	SUMMER	AUTUMN	WINTER
PLANT				
HARVEST				

FLOWERING TO HARVEST: 32–40 WEEKS

SUITABLE FOR: BEDS AND CONTAINERS

0   1m   2m   3m
1–2 plants

0   60cm

3M (10FT) ROWS
Plant trees 1.5–3m (5–10ft) apart

CONTAINERS
1 plant in each

1 GETTING STARTED

Figs are generally sold as container-grown plants, and establish best when planted in mid-spring. There are several varieties to grow although few are widely sold, so you may need to contact a specialist supplier. Fig flowers don't need to be pollinated in order to set fruit, so you only need to grow one tree.

'Brunswick' needs a mild site to crop well, and bears large, sweet figs in late summer.

'Panachee' produces unusual-looking striped fruit. It is best trained against a warm wall.

'Brown Turkey' is widely available and grows well in cool areas. It crops in late summer.

'Rouge de Bordeaux' produces delicious figs but needs a sheltered, warm spot to grow well.

Dig a hole and line the sides with stone slabs. To ensure good drainage, line the base with broken pots or stones to a depth of 20cm (8in).

Plant the tree at the same depth as it was in its pot, then backfill the hole with soil. Water the tree in well and hammer in a suitable tree stake.

2 PLANTING

If growing the tree directly in the soil, dig over the site to remove weeds, and incorporate sharp grit, composted bark, or manure for good drainage. To restrict the roots, create a planting pit, 60 x 60cm (24 x 24in), and plant the tree into it (see left). To plant into a container, choose one at least 60cm (24in) wide and deep, place stones or pieces of broken pot in the base for drainage, and fill it with good garden soil or loam-based compost.

TIP Fig trees become more drought-tolerant once they establish fully.

3 ROUTINE CARE

New figs should be watered in their first year but otherwise they thrive on neglect. Although the trees are fully hardy, the tiny fruitlets that overwinter from one year to the next (see below) can be damaged by frost. Cover free-standing and wall-trained trees with garden fleece if practical. The trees will benefit from annual pruning.

Fig trees grow well in pots and can be brought under cover during winter in colder regions to protect the developing fruitlets.

4 THINNING OUT

Our summers are too short for figs to ripen in one year. Instead, tiny fruitlets produced in late summer overwinter on the tree and mature the following summer. Any fruitlets larger than pea-size won't survive the winter however, and should be removed in late autumn by snapping them off.

Remove any larger fruitlets in autumn. Thinning them prevents the tree from wasting energy on fruits that won't reach maturity.

5 HARVESTING

It is important to let figs mature as fully as possible before picking them, as they won't ripen much further indoors. Ripe fruits hang downwards from the branch, sticky sap appears at their bases, and they soften and emit a slight scent; they will pull easily from the tree. Birds may target the soft, ripe fruits.

Ripe figs soon spoil, so eat them as quickly as possible to enjoy them at their best. Surplus fruit can be preserved or dried to eat later in the year.

6 PRUNING

Young trees only need pruning to keep them in shape. Older trees are pruned twice in spring to promote fruiting and a healthy shape. In early spring, cut out some of the older stems to encourage new growth. Then, in late spring, pinch out the tips of this new growth to promote the formation of new fruits.

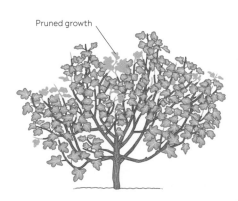

Pruned growth

TREE AND SOFT FRUITS

Fruits fall into two groups: sun-lovers and others that tolerate shade. Sweet, syrupy fruits, such as figs and peaches, thrive in full sun, where the warmth boosts their sugar levels. Tarter crops, such as currants and gooseberries, can take some shade. Regular moisture is important, especially when fruits are swelling and next year's flower buds are setting simultaneously.

Q Is it possible to grow fruit trees or bushes on a small patio garden?

There are many aids to growing fruit in a small space. Growing in pots will restrict roots and keep plants naturally compact. Also, many fruit trees are now available on dwarfing rootstocks (for example, apple M27, plum Pixy, and Gisela 5 for cherries). Training trees as cordons, espaliers, or fans also saves space, and many bush fruits, such as gooseberries and redcurrants, can be pruned in similar ways.

Q The yield of my strawberry bed has steadily declined over the years. It obviously needs an overhaul - what should I do?

This popular crop needs more care than other perennial fruits, with plants benefiting from a refresh every three to four years. Ideally, peg down runners from your plants in midsummer, then pot these up and transplant into newly prepared beds in autumn or early spring. Prepare the earth by digging in some well rotted farmyard manure, or similar, planting on a slight mound to boost drainage. Only propagate from healthy plants as strawberries suffer from viruses – otherwise buy in new certified virus-free stock.

Q We have an unnamed plum in our garden which sets fruits erratically - why is that?

Plum varieties are either self-fertile or require cross pollination. Self-fertile trees set a crop on their own, whereas those that need cross pollination must be close to a different, compatible variety that blooms at the same time. Because your plum is setting fruit irregularly, it may be that pollination is occurring but some other factor is at fault. Frost during flowering can damage blooms, whereas windy, stormy weather stops pollinating insects from visiting trees. In years when your plum sets a heavy crop, thin out small fruitlets in early summer to maintain a balance.

Q My cherry harvest was ruined by masses of tiny maggots within the ripening fruits. I could see fruit flies, too – were these to blame?

A relatively new pest to the UK, spotted wing drosophila causes symptoms such as these. The adult female drosophila fruit flies lay eggs around ripening fruits of a range of crops (grapes, plums, blueberries, currants, raspberries, blackberries, strawberries, and cherries). Cloak unripened fruits with fine insect-proof mesh. Limit infestations by spraying maturing fruits with a pyrethrum insecticide. Do not compost infected crops.

PEST AND DISEASE WATCH

Look out for the following pests and diseases within this large group of plants.

- Maggots tunnelling within mature apple or pear fruits implies codling moth (see p.240).
- Grey-white marks on raspberries and blackberries can be raspberry beetle attack (see p.240).
- If gooseberry foliage is steadily stripped within weeks, suspect sawfly (see p.242).
- Orange-pink maggots inside ripe plums and gages, and brown droppings signals plum moth (see p.242).
- If pear fruitlets turn black and fall prematurely, this indicates pear midge (see p.242).
- Apples and pears with corky black skin lesions have been infected by scab fungi (see p.244).
- Brown rot (see p.244) appears as brown rotten fruits smothered in creamy white pustules.
- If tree limbs die back, suspect canker damage (see p.246), confirmed by sunken, corky bark lesions.
- When whole plants die suddenly, honey fungus (see p.246) is a possible culprit among others.
- Silver leaf (see p.246) of stone fruits (especially plums and peaches) causes silvering, flecked foliage.

FRUIT CROP
PLANNER

Use this table to check when to plant, prune, and harvest your fruit crops. Timings will vary for different regions so adjust accordingly to suit your own site and conditions. When planting bare-root trees and shrubs, water them well afterwards, even during winter.

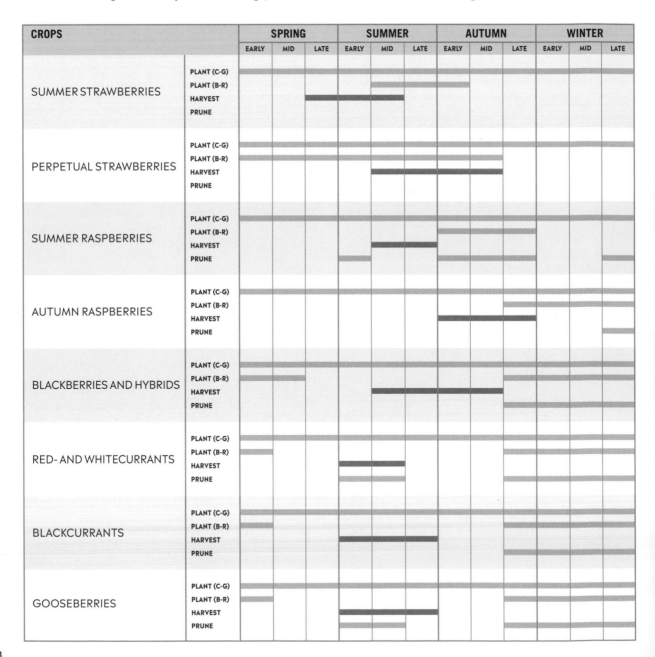

CROPS		SPRING			SUMMER			AUTUMN			WINTER		
		EARLY	MID	LATE	EARLY	MID	LATE	EARLY	MID	LATE	EARLY	MID	LATE
SUMMER STRAWBERRIES	PLANT (C-G)	▬	▬	▬	▬	▬	▬	▬	▬	▬	▬	▬	▬
	PLANT (B-R)					▬	▬	▬					
	HARVEST			▬	▬	▬							
	PRUNE												
PERPETUAL STRAWBERRIES	PLANT (C-G)	▬	▬	▬	▬	▬	▬	▬	▬	▬			
	PLANT (B-R)	▬	▬	▬	▬	▬	▬	▬	▬	▬			
	HARVEST					▬	▬	▬	▬				
	PRUNE												
SUMMER RASPBERRIES	PLANT (C-G)	▬	▬	▬	▬	▬	▬	▬	▬	▬	▬	▬	▬
	PLANT (B-R)							▬	▬	▬			
	HARVEST					▬	▬						
	PRUNE						▬						
AUTUMN RASPBERRIES	PLANT (C-G)	▬	▬	▬									
	PLANT (B-R)									▬			
	HARVEST							▬	▬				
	PRUNE												
BLACKBERRIES AND HYBRIDS	PLANT (C-G)	▬	▬	▬	▬	▬	▬	▬	▬	▬	▬	▬	▬
	PLANT (B-R)	▬	▬										
	HARVEST					▬	▬	▬	▬				
	PRUNE												
RED- AND WHITECURRANTS	PLANT (C-G)	▬	▬	▬	▬	▬	▬	▬	▬	▬	▬	▬	▬
	PLANT (B-R)	▬								▬	▬	▬	▬
	HARVEST				▬	▬							
	PRUNE				▬	▬							
BLACKCURRANTS	PLANT (C-G)	▬	▬	▬	▬	▬	▬	▬	▬	▬	▬	▬	▬
	PLANT (B-R)	▬	▬									▬	▬
	HARVEST				▬	▬							
	PRUNE										▬	▬	
GOOSEBERRIES	PLANT (C-G)	▬	▬	▬	▬	▬	▬	▬	▬	▬	▬	▬	▬
	PLANT (B-R)	▬											
	HARVEST				▬	▬							
	PRUNE				▬								

KEY

C-G: CONTAINER-GROWN PLANTS

B-R: BARE-ROOT PLANTS

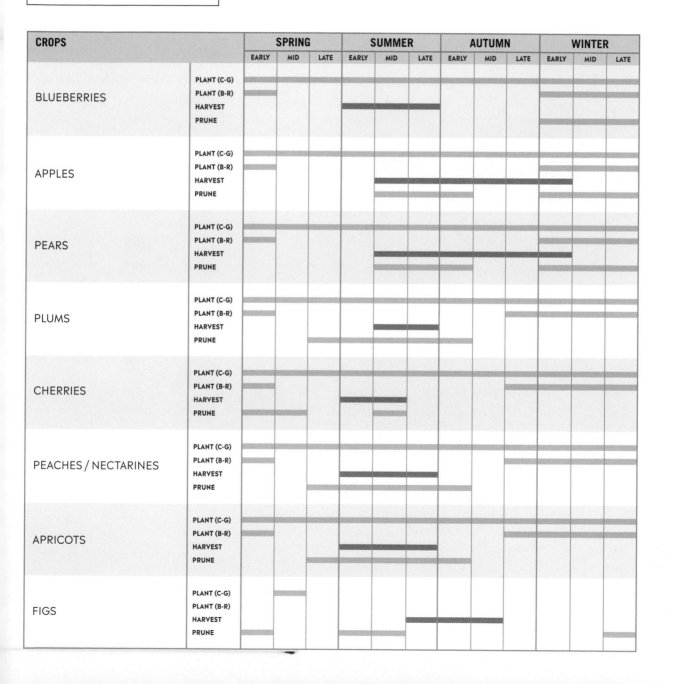

CROPS		SPRING			SUMMER			AUTUMN			WINTER		
		EARLY	MID	LATE	EARLY	MID	LATE	EARLY	MID	LATE	EARLY	MID	LATE
BLUEBERRIES	PLANT (C-G)												
	PLANT (B-R)												
	HARVEST												
	PRUNE												
APPLES	PLANT (C-G)												
	PLANT (B-R)												
	HARVEST												
	PRUNE												
PEARS	PLANT (C-G)												
	PLANT (B-R)												
	HARVEST												
	PRUNE												
PLUMS	PLANT (C-G)												
	PLANT (B-R)												
	HARVEST												
	PRUNE												
CHERRIES	PLANT (C-G)												
	PLANT (B-R)												
	HARVEST												
	PRUNE												
PEACHES / NECTARINES	PLANT (C-G)												
	PLANT (B-R)												
	HARVEST												
	PRUNE												
APRICOTS	PLANT (C-G)												
	PLANT (B-R)												
	HARVEST												
	PRUNE												
FIGS	PLANT (C-G)												
	PLANT (B-R)												
	HARVEST												
	PRUNE												

PROBLEM

SOLVER

THE
ORGANIC APPROACH

One of the best things about cultivating your own fruit and vegetables is that you can choose how you want to grow them. Organic produce is expensive to buy, yet achievable on your plot with careful planning, vigilance, and a range of natural products and strategies. Organic gardening uses every bit of waste in the garden and kitchen by recycling it into compost. Picking off pests such as slugs by hand, and hand weeding also protects visiting wildlife and beneficial pollinating insects.

DIFFERENT APPROACHES

While the non-organic approach to gardening uses man-made fertilizers and pesticides, organic gardening involves using natural, non-artificial methods to boost the soil and control pests and diseases. The essence of organic gardening is to harness nature for your benefit, creating a balance between predators and prey, and using natural resources sensibly and sustainably, with as little impact on the environment as possible.

FEEDING

There is a range of organic and non-organic fertilizers available, but you can't beat organic matter such as well-rotted manure or compost for mulching and improving the soil.

TACKLING PESTS AND DISEASES

Gardening without using chemical treatments for pests and diseases is rewarding but needs forward planning and a watchful eye on the plot.

Companion planting is a popular approach in potager gardens, which feature a mix of crops and flowers. It is based on the, largely unproven, theory that potential pests may be lured from crops onto nearby plants, or repelled by adjacent scent-emitting plants. You may have seen nasturtiums planted among beans in an attempt to lure blackfly away from them, cabbages interplanted with ferny-foliaged bulb fennel to confuse root flies, and scent-emitting French marigold among tomato plants to deter whitefly.

Planting sacrificial plants to draw slugs and snails away from valuable crops may be more effective. There are also organic sprays that target specific pests. Biological control using natural predators and parasites to prey on pests is useful for undercover crops.

WEED MANAGEMENT

If you are avoiding chemical weedkillers weeding manually is the best option. The saying that "one year's weed is seven years' seed" rings true, so try to remove weeds before they set seed.

(left) **Nasturtiums** can be planted as companion plants but are more useful as a crop – their edible leaves, flowers, and seeds have a peppery flavour.

(right) **Applying a mulch** of bark chippings between plants is a useful way to suppress weeds. Growing a mixture of crops helps to discourage attack from pests.

PROBLEMS

Whether you decide to go organic or not, your primary aim should be to encourage resilient, healthy plants, because these are best able to withstand competition from weeds. Making sure that your site and soil are suitable for your crops has benefits too, so improve any compacted areas by digging in plenty of bulky organic matter. Ensure that plants are well ventilated and not too crowded and enrich nutrient-deficient plots with an appropriate fertilizer.

COMMON PROBLEMS

The growth of plants is affected by several factors, including soil, nutrition, and climate. If plants look sickly, you may need to do some detective work. For example, if your soil is sandy, or very acidic or alkaline, it may be prone to nutrient deficiencies (see p.248), while an over-cropped site can be exhausted of a specific nutrient. Bear in mind that blindly applying fertilizers without the aid of a laboratory soil analysis (see p.26) is potentially wasteful and environmentally unsound.

Soils may also contain pockets of compaction that impede root growth, and inhibit drainage. Roots won't thrive where this occurs. "Rainshadows" against walls or fences can cause dry spots. Digging in organic matter to improve the soil structure will help. Weather-related damage, such as scorching of foliage by frost, sun, or wind, can look dramatic, but is often superficial and, because the root system is unharmed, plants will often re-sprout and recover.

PREVENTING WEEDS

Ideally, gardeners should prevent weeds appearing rather than controlling them once they are established. Fortunately, there are ways to tackle both situations.

Weed-suppressing mulches will help prevent growth around established plants and on bare soil. In summer, weeds will quickly exploit bare soil if you let them. You can prevent less troublesome winter weeds by covering bare soil with, ideally reusable or recycled, black plastic sheeting, or cardboard. Alternatively, sow smothering cover crops of ryegrass or vetches in late summer or early autumn.

A 5–8cm (2–3in) layer of garden compost or well-rotted manure, will suppress weeds, and release nutrients in spring as it decays but both are likely to contain weed seeds that will

Mature courgette plants and other trailing crops suppress weeds naturally. Other plants that are similarly effective include potatoes, squash, pumpkins, and vigorous leafy plants such as Swiss chard.

Preparation is key, so dig over the soil well at the beginning of the season, and remove any weeds that may have developed.

germinate in spring. Seedling crops are most vulnerable to weed competition when they are young, so try a nifty technique known as the "stale seedbed" to trick weed seeds into germinating before sowing. Simply prepare your bed, watering in dry spells. Two or three weeks later, weed seedlings will emerge. Remove them by shallow hoeing without disturbing the soil before you sow your chosen seeds.

DEALING WITH WEEDS

There are a number of organic tactics to try when removing weeds. Digging them out, or shallow hoeing, is often the best method, but be aware that shallow-rooted crops such as cherries and raspberries can sucker profusely if their roots are damaged.

Flame guns can be used to scorch annual weeds, and a weed-suppressing membrane is a useful organic control for perennial weeds. Highly effective non-organic weedkillers and others based on natural ingredients such as acetic acid are available. Always use as specified on the label.

WEEDING TIPS

It is vital to do all you can to prevent and remove weeds from your plot, as they will compete with your crops for water, nutrition, and space, and may also harbour pests and diseases. Try to do so before weeds have a chance to flower and produce seeds.

1 Hoeing and hand-weeding
Using a hoe to weed between rows of plants will help you to cover large areas with relative speed. If possible, weed on a dry day and leave the weeds on the soil surface to shrivel and die. If you are removing perennial weeds, do so with a garden or hand fork; try to ensure that you remove the entire root so the weeds do not regenerate.

2 Feeding Strong, healthy plants are best able to compete with weeds, so prepare the soil in advance with plenty of well-rotted manure or compost before you sow or plant. If is necessary to add fertilizer later on, weed your plot thoroughly before sprinkling the fertilizer beneath growing plants.

3 Mulching with straw Even vigorous, leafy plants like potatoes will benefit from a mulch of organic materials, such as woodchip or strulch (treated straw), to prevent competing weeds from germinating.

4 Reusable mats Mulch mats and collars prevent weeds and keep fruits such as strawberries clean by keeping them off the soil. About 40cm (16in) across, they come in a variety of materials and are easy to make at home from untreated natural fibre underlay or thick fabric.

COMMON WEEDS

1 Stinging nettle These tall-growing weeds can establish a spreading network of roots and their leaves deliver a painful sting. Dig them out completely to get rid of them.

2 Dock The broad, unattractive leaves of this perennial weed look unsightly in a vegetable patch. The plants have a long tap root, which should be entirely removed from the ground.

3 Creeping buttercup This common perennial weed is found in many gardens. It uses horizontal runners to creep across the ground – dig out its whole root system or it will regenerate.

4 Shepherd's purse This annual weed produces characteristic purple heart-shaped seed pods – to prevent it spreading, pull the plants up and compost them before seed pods form.

5 Groundsel This annual weed produces fluffy white seedheads from yellow, daisy-like flowers. Pull the plants out before the seeds have set.

6 Goosegrass Also known as "cleavers", this sticky, clinging weed is covered with tiny hooks and can rapidly spread throughout a vegetable patch. It can be pulled up by hand.

7 Dandelion A common perennial weed, dandelions must be dug out before the seeds are released. Remove the tap root completely as any pieces left behind will regenerate.

8 Hairy bittercress Target this fast-growing annual while young and easy to pull up. Once seed pods form, they split easily and will spread seed far and wide.

9 Creeping thistle This tough perennial is difficult to eradicate so you may need to consider using a chemical weedkiller.

10 Bindweed Remove the entire root before destroying this perennial weed. Consider applying a systemic weedkiller.

11 Annual meadow grass This common lawn grass is considered a weed in the vegetable patch. Hoe it regularly to prevent it flowering and setting seed.

12 Ragwort This rosette-forming annual weed has attractive yellow flowers but can produce a prolific amount of seeds; dig the plants out before these have a chance to form.

AVOIDING
PESTS AND DISEASES

No garden is immune to attack from pests and diseases, but there are measures you can take to reduce the risk, and methods you can use to deal with problems as they arise, both organic and non-organic. Maintaining good garden hygiene and encouraging strong crops, by keeping plants well fed, well watered, and well ventilated, is a good place to start. Keep in mind that it is better practice to prevent pests and diseases than to deal with their consequences.

Removal of infected crops is, in some cases, fundamental to the success of subsequent crops. Clearing diseased plants significantly reduces the risk of infection the following year.

Covering crops with insect-proof mesh or a tunnel cloche is the most effective organic method of prevention. Copper tape around containers is thought to deter slugs and snails, and companion planting (see p.234) is popular, though their effectiveness is unproven. Moving crops to a new location is useful for disrupting the lifecycle of soil-borne problems. And you can always remove larger pests, such as slugs and caterpillars by hand.

Of course, pesticides can be useful too – if the population of a pest is utterly out of control, they can offer a quick, effective solution. Choose from organic sprays based on fatty acid, natural pyrethrin, or insecticidal soap, or artificial pesticides with synthetic active ingredients. It is important to follow the instructions on the packaging carefully.

DEALING WITH DISEASES

The limited number of fungicides available to amateur gardeners means that avoiding or preventing plant diseases is a far better option than controlling them once they arrive. There is a range of organic and non-organic methods to try but one of the most fundamental goals should be good garden hygiene: keep

DEALING WITH PESTS

Building up a population of beneficial creatures is a useful method for keeping pests at bay. Encourage them by providing habitats, such as ponds and log piles for creatures that feed on slugs and other pests, and suitable flowers for pollinators such as hoverflies and bees. You may also decide to try biological controls, such as parasitic wasps to target whitefly, predatory mites to feed on red spider mite, and microscopic nematodes to infect slugs. Introducing the predators before the pests become too numerous is crucial to success.

pruning and digging tools sterilized. It also helps to keep plants well watered and well ventilated.

For non-organic gardeners, fungicides are also an option, but always follow the manufacturer's guidelines. If plants are severely affected, remove them from the garden, or burn them.

RESISTANT VARIETIES

Choosing resistant varieties and planting them in uncontaminated soil will also help to avoid infection. For some crops this can be important: 'Kilaxy' cabbage shows good resistance to clubroot, which is useful as there is no fungicidal cure for this root disease and its spores can survive in the soil for up to 20 years. There are resistant varieties available for many crops, so look out for them in seed catalogues. Remember though, that resistance is not the same thing as immunity, and plants may still succumb.

To prevent the risk of further contamination, do not compost any infected plant material. As a precaution, remove any diseased plants from your site or burn them.

SIMPLE MEASURES

Be pro-active in your garden and try to discourage pests from attacking. Daily walks among your crops will allow you to spot problems early, and once you have identified the symptoms of a specific problem, you'll be well armed with the tools to make an informed plan of attack. For more specific pests and diseases information, see pages 238–247.

1 Pollinating Planting nectar-rich flowering annuals and perennials will attract hoverflies, many of whose larvae have a voracious appetite for aphids. As well as looking beautiful, these flowers will also attract other pollinating insects to the garden. Provide overwintering sites for them.

2 Beneficial wildlife A wildlife pond, log pile, or shady, damp corner will entice frogs, toads, ground beetles, centipedes, and many other predators that love to eat many garden pests. A log pile will provide habitat and shelter for a wide range of predators

3 Insect-proof mesh Fine mesh is good for protecting crops against a range of pests. On brassicas, it will deter their common pest: cabbage white butterflies. Support the mesh on sticks and bury it in the soil, all the way around the plants, to stop the pests getting underneath.

4 Companion planting Rows of nasturtiums look beautiful on your plot and may draw pests such as blackfly from your crops, although their effectiveness is debatable.

COMMON PESTS

1 Brassica flea beetles These tiny beetles pepper brassica seedlings with holes. Transplant seedlings when large and water well. Prevent with insect-proof mesh; spray colonies with insecticide.

2 Cabbage caterpillars These pests nibble leaves and bore into the heart of the cabbages. Pick them off, use insect-proof nets, or apply an appropriate insecticide.

3 Onion fly These maggots attack the roots of onions and leeks and the base of the vegetables, causing them to rot. Destroy infested plants. Rotate crops and cover with netting.

4 Leek moth There is no insecticide for these caterpillars, which mine the leaves and flesh of leeks and onions. Kill any that you find, and cover crops with insect-proof netting.

5 Colorado beetle Not established in the UK; report sightings to your local Defra inspector. The yellow and black beetles and their red larvae eat potato and tomato foliage.

6 Pea moth Eggs are laid in summer; the caterpillars hatch and burrow into the pods. Sow early or late types to avoid the egg-laying period, or protect plants with netting.

7 Carrot fly The maggots tunnel into carrots and parsnips. Use insect-proof mesh or grow resistant varieties.

8 Codling moth The caterpillars of this pest tunnel into apples and pears and feed around the cores. Use pheromone traps and spray with an appropriate insecticide in summer.

9 Wireworms These larvae of the click beetle kill seedlings and feed on potatoes and onions. They are usually only a problem on vegetable plots recently converted from grass.

10 Mealy cabbage aphids Massed under brassica leaves, they turn outer leaves yellowish-white (but can also affect the rest of the plant). Control using an appropriate insecticide.

11 Cabbage whitefly The pest sucks sap from the underside of leaves, excreting honeydew that encourages sooty mould. Tolerate or use an appropriate insecticide.

12 Raspberry beetle This pest causes grey-brown patches on various berries. Avoid pesticides when the plants are in flower; a spray can be used when the first fruits turn pink.

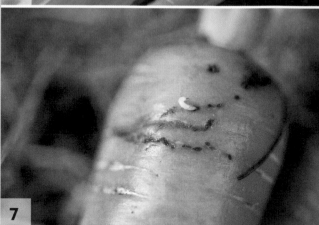

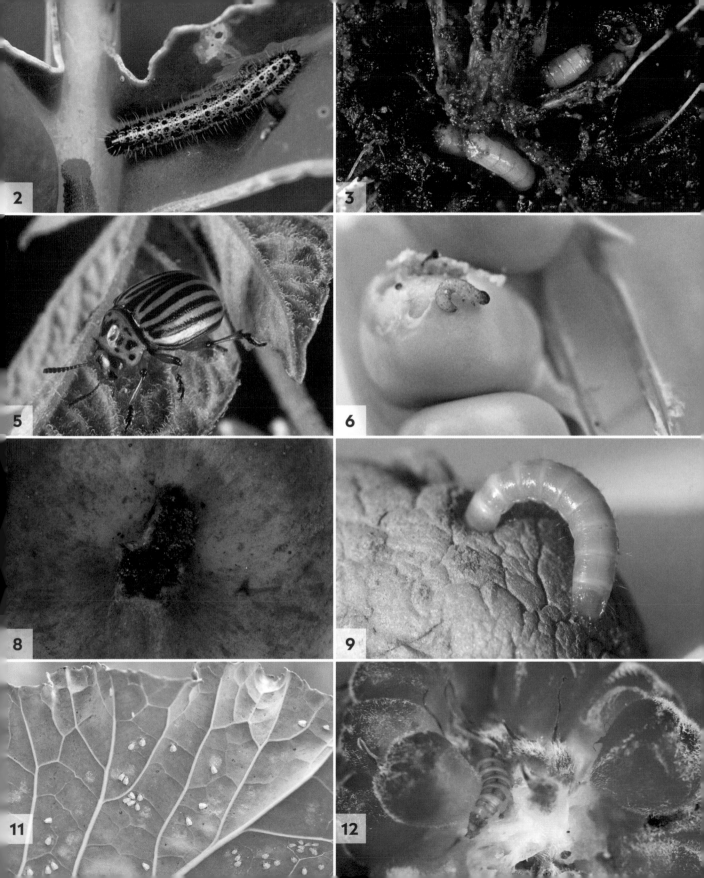

13 Pea and bean weevil This pest targets the leaves of peas and beans, eating neat "U" shapes out of the margins. Plants usually tolerate the damage, so control may be unnecessary.

14 Gooseberry sawfly Causing severe damage to gooseberries and redcurrants, this pest can strip plants of their leaves. Pick insects off or use a biological pesticide.

15 Plum fruit moth The pale pink caterpillars feed on the flesh of plums, damsons, and greengages. Hang pheromone traps in early summer to catch adult males – this can reduce damage.

16 Pear midge This pest lays its eggs in pear blossom; the maggots hatch and then feed inside the fruits, causing them to turn black and shrivel. Remove infested fruits as you spot them.

17 Apple capsid Sucking the sap from apples, this pest creates corky, brown patches on the skin of fruits. Pesticide controls are available, but affected fruit is still edible.

18 Cabbage root fly The white larvae of this common brassica pest feed on roots and severely damages young plants. There is no insecticide: insect-proof netting is the best defence.

19 Aphids Greenfly or blackfly are small, sap-sucking insects common on many plants that can distort new growth. Attract natural predators or use an appropriate insecticide.

20 Red spider mite Common during summer and in greenhouses, this mite causes plant leaves to turn yellow and drop. Use biological controls or fatty acid sprays.

21 Cutworms These brownish white caterpillars target the roots of seedlings and eat holes in root vegetables. There is no effective cure, so remove the pest by hand if you spot it.

22 Slugs and snails These common pests will target leafy crops, seedlings, and potato tubers, causing rapid damage. Remove them by hand, set up beer traps, use organic pellets. Nematode biological control is effective against slugs.

23 Root aphids Carrots and lettuces are vulnerable to these insects, which suck sap from roots, which may cause the plants to wilt. There is no cure, so practise crop rotation and keep plants well watered.

24 Asparagus beetle The adults and their larvae target asparagus plants and can rapidly defoliate them, killing the stems. Pick off any you find, or apply an insecticide.

COMMON DISEASES

1 Scab Causes brown patches on apple and pear skins and can spread to leaves and branches. Dispose of infected fruit, leaves, and stems, as it can overwinter.

2 American gooseberry mildew Look for powdery fungal patches and browning on leaves, fruits, and stems. Improve air circulation, prune out infected shoots, and keep well watered.

3 Rusts These fungi cause disease on many plants – bright orange pustules form on leaves or stems. Remove infected material, improve air circulation, and rotate crops.

4 Bacterial leaf spot Yellow-ringed dead patches form on the leaves of crops such as peas and beans. Remove and destroy affected leaves and rotate crops in future years.

5 Clubroot Affects brassica crops, causing roots to swell and the foliage to wilt, which can prove fatal. Reduce soil acidity with lime and improve drainage. Grow resistant varieties.

6 Downy mildew Causes brown patches on the leaves of various crops, with mouldy growth beneath. Destroy infected leaves, keep plants well ventilated, and rotate crops.

7 Tomato blight Affecting mainly outdoor types, stems, leaves, and fruits to discolour and rot: remove and destroy them. Rotate crops and grow under cover if possible.

8 Cucumber mosaic virus (CMV) Creates mottled, distorted leaves and stunted fruit growth – destroy infected plants.

9 Onion neck rot Onions, shallots, and garlic bulbs become soft and coated with a fluffy grey mould and black seed-like structures (sclerotia). Rotate crops and water well in dry spells.

10 Onion white rot Can survive in soil for many years. Causes bulbs to rot and foliage to become yellow and wilt. Destroy infected plants carefully to avoid contamination.

11 Brown rot Affecting a range of tree fruits including pears and apples, the fungus rots the flesh and causes cream pustules to appear on the skin. Remove infected fruits promptly.

12 Fungal leaf spot This disease causes discoloured leaves on a range of crops such as celery, lettuce, peas, and strawberries. Remove and destroy infected leaves.

13 Sclerotinia Causes crops to turn yellow and wilt, with white, fluffy growth. Stems can contain black structures. Persists in soil so it is vital to remove and destroy infected plants promptly.

14 Strawberry viruses These cause a number of problems, such as yellowing leaves and stunted growth. Remove and destroy infected plants, and rotate crops.

15 Bacterial canker Enters existing wounds or scars to grow or distort, often causing resin to ooze from the bark. Prune the infected growth during summer and paint with wound paint.

16 Blossom end rot Caused by a calcium deficiency, this disorder results in dark circular patches at the base of tomatoes and peppers. Remove affected fruits and water well.

17 Bitter pit Black spots or indentations appear on apple skins, causing bitter flesh. Keep affected trees mulched and well watered as it is caused by drought.

18 Potato common scab Common in dry soils that lack organic matter, this disease causes unattractive corky, brown patches on the skin. Choose a resistant variety and water plants well.

19 Scorch Caused by either hot sun or cold, dry winds; both can strip the plant of its moisture and cause it to become brown and crisp. Shelter plants and water in the cool of the evening.

20 Raspberry cane blight Results in split, brittle canes and withered foliage. Cut diseased wood out to below soil level and destroy it. Encourage good ventilation by spacing canes.

21 Powdery mildew Affecting a range of crops, from courgettes to currants, this host-specific disease causes a white coating on leaves and fruits; remove these and water plants well. Decrease humidity around crops by spacing plants correctly and improving ventilation.

22 Honey fungus This root disease can be fatal to trees; its honey-coloured toadstools may appear in the autumn. Any plant with white fungal growth under the bark at soil level and/or on larger roots should be dug up and destroyed.

23 Silver leaf Various fruit trees are at risk, developing a silvery hue on the leaves; branches may die back. Look for a stain in the centre of the wood. Prune in summer to reduce the risk of infection.

24 Botrytis A fluffy, grey mould that causes rot and die-back on leaves, buds, and fruit of a wide range of crops. Remove infected material promptly.

13

16

19

22

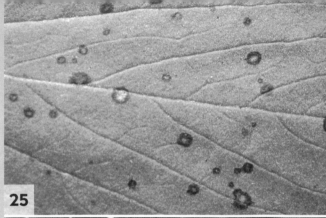

25 Chocolate spot Affects broad beans, resulting in dark brown or greyish spots on the foliage, stem, and pods. Improve air circulation and destroy any infected material.

26 Potato black leg Leaves become yellow and stems rot and become black at the base; remove and destroy any infected plants. Rotate potato crops in future seasons.

27 Tomato ghost spot Fruits do not become inedible, but develop faint yellow or green rings on the skin.

28 Damping off This disorder causes greenhouse seedlings to collapse and affects their roots and stems. It is deterred by using clean pots and watering with mains water.

29 Parsnip canker Orange-brown rot develops on roots, or spots on leaves. Caused by damage, drought, or rich soil. Rotate crops, improve drainage, grow resistant varieties.

30 Potato blight Causes patchy, rotten foliage and later spreads to the tubers – destroy infected foliage. Rotate crops and choose more resistant, 'Sarpo' range cultivars.

NUTRIENT DEFICIENCY

1 Iron Leaves yellowing between the veins and later browning at the edges can indicate a lack of iron. Add chelated iron to the soil.

2 Calcium Drought or acidic soil can inhibit a plant's uptake of calcium, resulting in disorders such as blossom end rot (pictured). Keep plants well watered and lime the soil.

3 Magnesium Plants develop yellowing foliage that turns brown between the veins. Symptoms affect the oldest leaves first. Spray a solution of epsom salts on the leaves.

4 Boron Affects a variety of crops, causing roots to split and prevents sweetcorn from developing properly. Apply borax to the soil or use as a foliar spray for fruit trees.

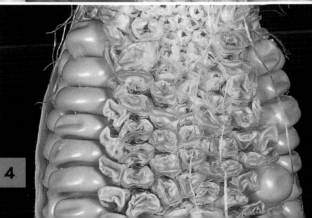

5 Potassium Causes leaf browning or scorching and plants flower and set fruit poorly. Potassium leaches from the soil easily, so apply sulphate of potash or tomato feed to plants.

6 Nitrogen Plant foliage becomes yellow and growth is weak. Dig in well-rotted manure or apply balanced fertilizers.

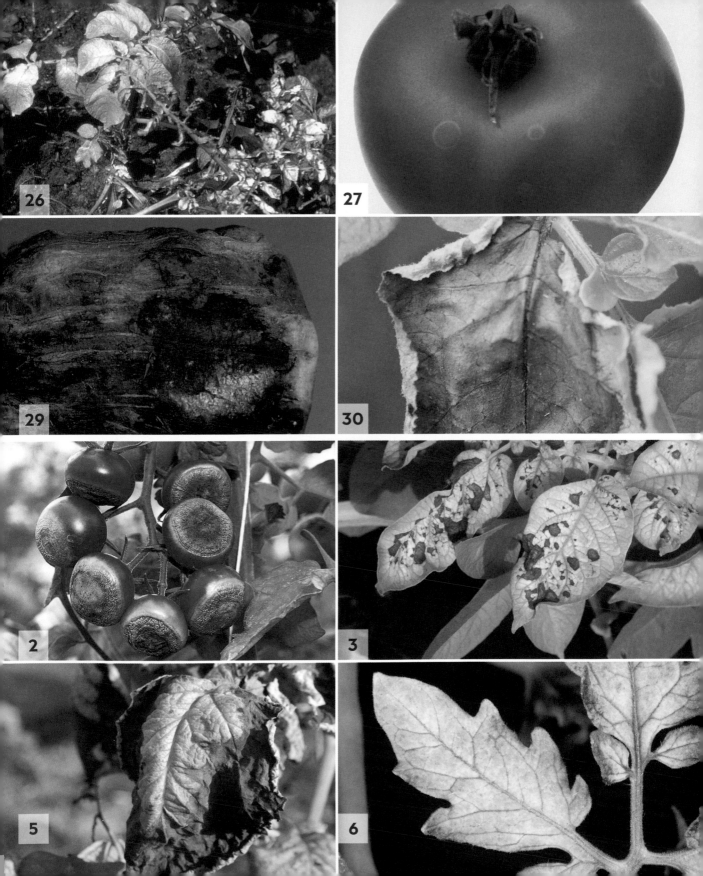

INDEX

Main entries are indicated by **bold** page numbers. Main entries for crops include full details for sowing, growing, feeding, watering, cultivation, and harvesting. These details are not indexed separately.

INDEX